THEISM

CLEMENT DORE

Department of Philosophy, Vanderbilt University, Nashville

THEISM

D. REIDEL PUBLISHING COMPANY

A MEMBER OF THE KLUWER  ACADEMIC PUBLISHERS GROUP

DORDRECHT / BOSTON / LANCASTER

Library of Congress Cataloging in Publication Data

Dore, Clement, 1930–
   Theism.

   (Philosophical studies series in philosophy; v. 30)
   Bibliography: p.
   Includes index.
   1. God—Proof. I. Title. II. Series.
BT102.D67 1984   231'.042   84-1948
ISBN 90–277–1683–8

Published by D. Reidel Publishing Company,
P.O. Box 17, 3300 AA Dordrecht, Holland.

Sold and distributed in the U.S.A. and Canada
by Kluwer Academic Publishers,
190 Old Derby Street, Hingham, MA 02043, U.S.A.

In all other countries, sold and distributed
by Kluwer Academic Publishers Group,
P.O. Box 322, 3300 AH Dordrecht, Holland.

Printed in The Netherlands

to
Mary, Florence,
Joe and Katherine

CONTENTS

PREFACE

In this book, I discuss the question whether God exists, not as a Tillichian religious symbol, but as an actual person, albeit a person who is very different from you and me. My procedure is to examine arguments both for and against God's existence *qua* person and to assess their relative merits. I shall try to show that there is more evidence that God exists than that he does not. This position is, of course, rejected nowadays, even by most religious thinkers, who hold, for one reason or another, that evidence has nothing to do with religious belief, properly understood. My reply to these thinkers is simply to ask them to examine what follows.

A useful companion to Chapters 4, 5, 6, 7, and the Appendix of this book would be Alvin Plantinga's *The Nature of Necessity*.[1] Though I avoid technical terminology wherever possible, those chapters presuppose an elementary understanding of 'possible worlds' discourse; and a clear and concise explanation of that terminology can be found in Chapter IV of Plantinga's book. Also, I use 'logical' throughout to mean what Plantinga means by 'broadly logical' on page 2 of *The Nature of Necessity*.

Plantinga has recently been arguing that the proposition that God exists is properly basic, in the sense that it is logically implied by such propositions as "God is speaking to me", which are such that the religious believer is warranted in holding them even though he does not have evidence that they are true.[2] (Belief in the proposition that God is speaking to me is *occasioned* by such events as my reading the Bible, though what the Bible says is not literally *evidence* that I am in contact with God.)

I have my doubts about this. First, apart from "God is speaking to me", "God forgives me", etc. (religious propositions which Plantinga claims to be properly basic), credible candidates for properly basic propositions are such that there is a set of circumstances, C, such that any rational person who is in C believes those propositions. Thus, whenever any rational person seems to see a tree he believes the properly basic proposition that he seems to see a tree. (The reason for this, I think, is not just that one's seeming to see a tree *causes* him to believe that he does so, but that the former is overwhelmingly good *evidence* for that belief.) However, it is certainly not the case that a rational person's reading the Bible always gives rise to the belief that God is speaking to him (that God is good, etc.). And I think that Plantinga owes us an explanation of why that should be so. Also, we need to be told whether Plantinga thinks that, say, "Jesus is God" is properly basic for religious believers (so that attempts to discern the nature of the historical Jesus are, from their point of view, beside the point), and if not, why not.

But it is not my purpose to refute the envisaged thesis. Rather, I want to stress (what Plantinga would surely agree to) that the proposition that God exists is plainly not basic, relative to *all* rational people, or even relative to *all* rational religious believers, and, hence, an attempt to provide evidence for that proposition is not *ipso facto* epistemically redundant.

I am grateful to the following journals for permission to reprint parts of articles of mine which have appeared, or are to appear, in those journals: *American Philosophical Quarterly* ('Seeming to See'), *Religious Studies* ('Agnosticism'), *International Journal for the Philosophy of Religion* ('Rowe on the Cosmological Argument'), and *Philosophy and Phenomenological Research* ('Does Suffering Serve Valuable Ends?'). I am also grateful to the Notre Dame Press for permission to reprint part of 'Descartes's Meditation V Proof of God's Existence' (in *The Existence and Nature of God*, ed. Alfred Freddoso). Part of this book was written while I held a Vanderbilt University Summer Research Grant (in 1982), for which I am also grateful.

The book has benefited from conversations with many friends and colleagues, among others, John Arthur, Paul Hamilton, Alvin Plantinga, and William L. Rowe. I am especially indebted to William P. Alston, Alasdair MacIntyre and William H. Shaw, all of whom read a shorter version of the book and offered some useful criticisms.

CHAPTER 1

DOES SUFFERING SERVE VALUABLE ENDS?

1.1. The concept of God which I shall be discussing in this book is the Anselmian concept of a maximally great being, i.e., a being than which no greater being is logically possible. This is, I think, the concept of God which is held by at least most orthodox members of the Judeo-Christian tradition. Now a maximally great being would be maximally good, knowledgeable and powerful, i.e., so good, knowledgeable and powerful that it is logically impossible that he be exceeded in those respects. And atheists have typically argued that since a being of that sort would not, if he existed, allow the instances of intense and prolonged suffering which we find in the world, it must be false that such a being exists. I shall call this atheistic argument "the argument from suffering". Theists have often responded to it by advancing the thesis that it may well be that God allows suffering to exist because its consequences are such that their positive value outweighs the negative value of the suffering. In this chapter I want to discuss the question whether this thesis, which I shall call '*T*', is plausible.

 1.2. In view of the fact that if God exists, then he is maximally powerful, it is not enough for the proponent of *T merely* to claim that instances of intense and prolonged suffering serve valuable ends. He must add that this suffering is a logically necessary condition of the existence of those ends. Otherwise, it is logically possible that the ends exist even in the absence of the suffering; and, hence, a being who could not bring those ends about without the suffering would be such that it is logically possible to have more power than he does. (Or, at any rate, even if that is not true, there is an onus on *T*'s defender to explain why it is not true. I shall discuss this onus in more detail in Chapter 5.) The atheist must concede that in fact we *do* sometimes observe good ends which are served by suffering and with respect to which suffering is a logically necessary condition. I have in mind virtuous responses to suffering, such as charity and heroism.[1] However, it is, I think, very dubious that, e.g., a charitable response to the terrible suffering of a badly burned person is sufficiently positively valuable to outweigh the negative value of his suffering. Moreover, it is plainly not the case that all suffering serves those ends. The widespread suffering of lower animals in parts of the world to which human beings rarely go is an example of suffering which obviously does not serve them. Nor are there any other observable good ends which are served by that suffering and of which that suffering is a logically necessary condition. (E.g., a predator getting a nourishing meal from another animal which he has painfully killed does not count as such an end, since the suffering is not a logically necessary condition of the nourishment.) It follows that the proponent of *T* must claim that at least a great deal of suffering serves good ends which are not observed by us. And it is this contention (call it '*T'*') which I now want to discuss.

An obvious criticism of *T'* is that if the very numerous instances of apparently useless suffering which occur in the world served numerous valuable ends, then it is unlikely that no one would ever be in a position to determine by observation that any of those ends were achieved. The proponent of *T'* can, perhaps, diminish the force of this objection by maintaining that there is only one, enormously valuable end which is served by the sum of instances of apparently useless suffering (which I shall henceforth call simply 'suffering'), and of which the latter is a logically necessary condition, rather than a separate valuable end which is separately served by each instance of suffering. But, even thus construed, *T'* can be seen to be a very implausible thesis. Consider the analogous thesis that, e.g., *whistling* serves, and is a logically necessary condition of, a single, enormously valuable end, which is such that we have been unable to determine by observation that it exists. Surely this claim is incredible on its face. And it appears to be sufficiently similar to T' so that rejecting the former claim epistemically obliges us to reject the latter one as well. Moreover, there is a very plausible explanation of what is wrong with both theses. Suppose that someone claims that, e.g., heating water to the boiling point causes tornadoes, though the causal connexion is too subtle to be detected by ordinary empirical means. The proper reply is that we know by observation the kind of effects that heating water to the boiling point normally has in various circumstances, and that, since none of those effects is at all like a tornado, it is highly unlikely that causing water to boil brings about tornadoes. Analogously, we know by observation the kind of effects that suffering (and whistling) have under various circumstances; and, since none of those effects is at all like an enormously valuable state of affairs which is such that suffering (and whistling) are logically necessary for it, it is highly unlikely that suffering (and whistling) do have that effect.

Another objection to T' is as follows: "One proof that T' is implausible is that not even its proponent believes it, except in moments of theological bemusement. For if the proponent of T' had an opportunity easily to put an end to an instance of apparently useless suffering, he would think that he was morally obliged to do so. And he would *not* believe this, if he really thought that the suffering was logically necessary for a divinely intended, good end."

Evidently, the way to meet this criticism is to produce a plausible explanation of how human beings could sometimes be morally obliged to relieve suffering even though T' is true. But what could such an explanation be? The claim that our obligations with respect to suffering are *anti-utilitarian* (since they abolish an enormously valuable end) is incredible on its face, and, moreover, it entails that, since some people have in fact relieved some suffering, that end is no longer achievable, i.e., it entails that T' is false. Another explanation is that charitable responses to suffering are themselves valuable ends which the suffering serves and which have enough positive value to outweigh the negative value of the suffering. But, as I have said, it is very doubtful that the positive value of charitable responses to intense and prolonged suffering outweighs the negative value of that suffering. Moreover, if, in abolishing an instance of suffering, a person would be doing away with an enormously valuable end (call it 'E') for which all instances of suffering are logically necessary, then (a) that person would be frustrating God's intentions and (b) surely the positive value of his charitable response would be (unlike the positive value of E) not great enough to compensate for the negative value of *all* the suffering which God intended to contribute to E (whatever may be thought of the claim that the charitable response would have enough positive value to compensate for the negative value of just the suffering which it relieves). The claim that the charitable response would serve an *undiscernible* good end which is at least as valuable as E gets around the criticism which is expressed by (b), but not the criticism which is expressed by (a): surely it is incredible that we would be thwarting God's will by abolishing suffering-cum-E.

Another explanation is that whenever a human being relieves an instance of suffering at a given moment, M, that suffering would not have served E beyond M. (Hence, if the suffering were not relieved by a human being, then God would have relieved it.) But this explanation is subject to the following criticism: it is incredible that it happens, *just by chance*, that every time a human being relieves an instance of suffering at M, that suffering would not have served E after M. Hence, the advocate of the present explanation needs to add that, whenever a human being relieves an instance of suffering at M, God *causes* him to do so, having in view the fact that the suffering would have been pointless had it continued beyond M. But it is normally irrational to believe that God intervenes in this way. Suppose that a coin yields 90% heads over a long series of tosses. Surely it would be irrational to claim that the coin is a normal one and that it is God's intervention which accounts for the statistical deviation. And the analogous claim that God is the cause of our relieving suffering whenever we do so is just as implausible.

Still another explanation is this: Instances of suffering *simpliciter* are not what is logically necessary, and causally sufficient, for E, but rather the following disjunctive state of affairs: *either* a given instance of suffering being relieved by a human being at a given time, t, *or* its lasting beyond t and finally being dissipated by natural causes other than human actions. But the proponent of this explanation must obviously add that God is unlike human beings in that *his* abolishing suffering would not *also* serve E; and it might well be thought that he owes us an explanation of why this should be so. And, even if we set that aside, there is another objection which is analogous to the original objection to T' : we know enough about the effects which the envisaged disjunctive state of affairs normally has in various circumstances to know that it is highly implausible that E is one of those effects.

1.3. But now consider the claim (call it 'T''') that the following, complex state of affairs (which I shall call 'S') serves E: the unimpeded operation of scientific laws on the matter which the universe contains. If T'' is true, then, though suffering does not serve E, it is an *effect* of something (namely, S), which does serve E. T'' is not open to the objection that we know that none of the effects which S normally has under various circumstances is at all like E; for there are obviously a very large number of effects of S which we have not observed and are not at present in a position to infer with epistemic warrant.

It is of note that the proponent of T'' can adopt one of two interpretations of that thesis: (1) S is logically necessary, as well as causally sufficient, for E; (2) though S *per se* is not logically necessary for E, it is a necessary truth (which even a maximally powerful being cannot falsify) that any state of affairs (including any alternative set of scientific laws and any different kind of matter) which is causally sufficient for E would also be causally sufficient for at least as much suffering as S produces, i.e., *some* pain-producing state of affairs or other is logically necessary for E. (2) is, I think, just as plausible as (1); but I shall, for simplicity, omit reference to it in what follows.

We have seen that the advocate of T' would find it very difficult to give an adequate answer to the question, "Why do human beings have moral obligations with respect to apparently useless suffering?" However, the proponent of T'' does not have that problem. The claim that S serves E is perfectly compatible with human beings having, in some circumstances, moral obligations to relieve suffering, since in relieving suffering we are not interfering with the operation of scientific laws, i.e., we are not falsifying any predictions which could be made on the basis of a knowledge of scientific laws plus boundary conditions.

But another question arises here, viz., "Why is it true that *God* has no moral obligations with respect to suffering? What could be a relevant difference between God and man which would account for the fact that, though human beings have those obligations, God does not?" The following is a plausible theistic reply: Any effect in nature which God directly causes is a miracle. (Thus, if God directly caused the big bang, then that was a miracle, though it is reasonable to understand by 'miracle' something such that it does not follow from the fact that X is a miracle that the *effects* of X are also miracles.) So if God were to abolish an instance of suffering, then he *would* be interfering with the operation of scientific laws. The present thesis (call it 'ϕ') is rendered not implausible by the consideration that God may be essentially disembodied and, hence, that what he directly causes is *eo ipso* brought about by something like telekenesis, which appears likely to be at odds with at least one scientific law. I shall demonstrate in Chapter 6 that God is essentially disembodied. But even if that demonstration fails, the present (weak) defense of ϕ is all that the theist requires. For if ϕ is not implausible on its face, then since the atheist has taken on the onus of proving that God does not exist, it is up to him to provide evidence that ϕ is false, not up to the theist to demonstrate its truth.

But here the atheist may raise the following objection: "If it is really true that if God brings anything to pass in the world, then he *ipso facto* interferes with at least one scientific law, and that his *not* doing the latter is logically necessary for E, then nothing that happens in the world has God as a cause – not even as an ultimate cause. And this conclusion is a far cry from what theists have traditionally believed." This objection can be met[2] if T'' can be modified in such a way as to render it compatible with God's occasionally acting in the world. And this can be accomplished by changing S as follows: "The *for the most part* unimpeded operation of scientific laws on the matter which the universe contains". The claim that it is S, thus modified, which serves E is plainly compatible with God's occasionally bringing about miraculous effects in nature.

But are miracles logically possible? Isn't a necessary condition of something being a miracle that it shows that a given scientific law-statement is false? And isn't it also a necessary condition of something being a miracle that it is *not* just a falsifier of a scientific law-statement (as, e.g., the orbit of Mercury falsifies Newton's law of gravity)? One answer is that a miraculous event is not an *ordinary* falsifier of a scientific law-statement, i.e., though it is contrary to at least one event which is predicted by a scientific law-statement, L, plus a true description of boundary conditions, so that it falsifies L, it is also such that it could only be brought about by a maximally powerful being, so that it is an *extraordinary* falsifier of L. An alternative answer is to formulate L as follows: "*Barring the* (*very infrequent*) *intervention of a maximally powerful being*, any A would be a B in circumstances C". Given that formulation, God does not *ipso facto* falsify L when he brings it about that there is an A which is not a B in circumstances C, though there being an A which is not a B in C does falsify L in case something other than a maximally powerful being brings it about. The reason for the qualifier, 'very infrequent', in the contemplated formulation is that if God *frequently* intervened with respect to the claim that any A would be a B in circumstances

C, then L would become useless as an instrument for prediction, and, in that case, it would be best thought of as false. However, a single miraculous falsification of the claim that any A would be a B in C (or, at any rate, extremely infrequent falsifications of that claim) would not render L unfit for prediction and, hence, best taken to be false.

The last consideration gives rise to the following question. Can E be specified as our having serviceable scientific laws, which are necessary for our knowing anything about the future, and, hence, necessary for our survival? (Hume discusses this question in Part XI of *Dialogues Concerning Natural Religion.*) It appears unlikely that the answer is "Yes" for at least two reasons: (1) it certainly looks as though God could intervene a good deal more than he does without interfering with our common sense knowledge of the future (whatever may be thought of the much more specific predictions which science can make); (2) it looks on its face to be logically possible for us to know as much about the future through clairvoyance as we now know through predictions which are based on observed relative frequencies; and, hence, there would be an onus on anyone who claimed that a maximally powerful being could not make us thus clairvoyant to show why this should be so.[3] (It would be inappropriate to claim here that God's making us clairvoyant would substantially interfere with the operation of scientific laws. For we are contemplating an attempt at explaining precisely what would be lost were God thus to interfere; and the claim that what would be lost is the unimpeded operation of scientific laws is, in this context, merely a pseudo-explanation.)

1.4. But does the advocate of T'' need to specify E any further than he has already specified it? What is wrong with the claim that the atheist is not able to show that E, specified just as an enormously valuable end which is served by S, and of which S (or some S-like state of affairs) is a logically necessary condition, is in fact unlikely to be served by S? Here the atheist may raise the following objection: "By 'trans-empirical' let us mean 'neither empirically observable nor soundly inferable from empirical observations (at least at present) and, hence, not affirmed by any well-founded scientific theory'. Now it is *normally* true that it is irrational to affirm the existence of trans-empirical things. Suppose, for example, that someone claimed that we cannot get evidence that bringing water to the boiling point does not cause tornadoes, because it cannot be shown that it does not cause trans-empirical tornadoes. Or suppose that someone argued that we cannot know that all emeralds are green, since we cannot prove that there are no trans-empirical blue ones. Surely these contentions would be profoundly irrational. And what is wrong with them is evidently that they take seriously the claim that there may be trans-empirical things. But E is trans-empirical; so it is also irrational to believe that E exists."

However, this argument is less than compelling. The claim that there may (well) be trans-empirical blue emeralds is, in the envisaged context, really just a way of saying that the fact that all *observed* emeralds have been green is not evidence that all emeralds *simpliciter* are green. And the claim that there may (well) be trans-empirical tornadoes which are caused by bringing water to the boiling point, is, in the contemplated context, simply a denial of the fact that having observed the effects of causing water to boil under a wide variety of circumstances, and never having observed, or had reason to infer, a tornado under those circumstances, is evidence that boiling water does not cause tornadoes. However, the claim that E (exists and) is trans-empirical is *not* an expression of inductive skepticism. For it is false that we have observed lots of S's under various circumstances and have never, in any of those circumstances, observed, or had reason to infer, an E. S is not the sort of thing which (like emeralds and boiling water) can be observed; and, moreover, the nature of S is such that there can only be one S. It follows that there is no question of our rejecting inductive evidence that no S's are E-producing. And it follows in turn that the alleged analogy between trans-empirical E and trans-empirical emeralds and tornadoes is a false one.

Still, suppose that somebody affirms that there are, e.g., trans-empirical angels. This would not be an expression of inductive skepticism, but wouldn't it nonetheless be irrational? And isn't it in general irrational to affirm the existence of trans-empirical things, regardless of whether in doing so, we are expressing inductive skepticism? Chapters 4, 5, 6, 7 and the Appendix will provide support for a negative answer to this question. But a reply is also presently available: Call the principle that it is irrational to affirm the existence of trans-empirical things 'P'. And suppose that God is trans-empirical. (If there were empirical evidence for God's existence, then this would *eo ipso* be evidence for E's existence, and, hence, E would not after all be trans-empirical.) Now we have seen that what the argument from suffering actually establishes is, not that God does not exist, but rather the disjunctive proposition (call it 'D') that either God does not exist or that E exists. And the addition of principle P here rules out the second disjunct and thereby entails the first. But since P *directly* entails that God does not exist (in case there is no empirical evidence for his existence), the envisaged disjunctive syllogism is superfluous and, hence, so is the argument from suffering.

Here the atheist may wish to argue as follows: "We can view the argument from suffering as establishing that the theist (who denies the first disjunct of D) is commited to the claim that E exists (i.e., to D's second disjunct). So the argument shows that the theist is committed to *two* trans-empirical entities, God *and* E, rather than just to one (namely, God). Moreover, the more trans-empirical things which one affirms, the more irrational he becomes. Hence, the argument from suffering is not after all superfluous."

But this reply is unimpressive. If it really is (as my critic affirms) significantly irrational to believe that a given trans-empirical thing exists, it is dubious that one's degree of irrationality is a function of the number of such beliefs which he holds. Suppose that I believe that there are three angels, one red, one blue and one green. Would I really be compounding my irrationality if I came to believe in a fourth, orange one? Moreover, it is part of the concept of the God of orthodox theism that he brings good out of evil. And this characteristic can, at this point, be more perspicuously specified as follows: God *collaborates* with S in bringing about E, i.e., S alone is not causally sufficient for E, but, rather, S-cum-God is. Hence, the claim that the theist is committed, not just to the existence of (a trans-empirical) God, but to the existence of (a trans-empirical) E, is an instance of the more general claim that the theist is committed, not only to God's existence, but to everything that God's existence entails. But this latter claim is a truism, and the theist can hardly be expected to be either surprised or upset by it.

1.5. Before bringing this chapter to a close, I want to say something about what my refutation of the argument from suffering entails about God's power. Consider the following objection: "Dore's refutation commits him to the thesis that the sentence (call it 'Q'), 'God frequently intervenes in nature without preventing E from coming about', expresses a necessary falsehood. But it does not express a proposition which is self-evidently false; nor does it express the denial of a Kripkean *a posteriori* necessary truth. Moreover, it is surely unlikely that it expresses a proposition which is demonstrably necessarily false as does, e.g., 'There is a barber who (a) is a Bostonian and (b) shaves all and only those Bostonians who do not shave themselves'.[4] (If this barber shaves himself, then he does not shave himself, and if he does not shave himself, then he does shave himself. But either he does not shave himself or he does shave himself. Hence, the concept of this barber is demonstrably logically incoherent.) It follows that it is very unlikely that Q *does* express a necessary falsehood. Indeed, it is no more likely to express a necessary falsehood than is, say, 'God frequently intervenes in nature (*simpliciter*)'. So Dore's 'refutation' of the argument from suffering is (1) very implausible and (2) unnecessarily complex, since the simpler claim that it is necessarily false that God frequently intervenes in nature is just as plausible as the claim that Q expresses a necessary falsehood."

But it is easy to see that this argument is amiss. Since we do not know the precise nature of E, we are not in position to *intuit* that it is necessarily false that God frequently intervenes in nature without preventing E. But if we are justified in believing that God exists, then we know that if E were *fully and precisely described* by the expression 'Ex', then "God frequently intervenes in nature without preventing Ex" would be strongly analogous to, e.g., "God both intervenes in nature and does not intervene in nature", i.e., "God frequently intervenes in nature without preventing Ex" would express a self-evidently false proposition or, at any rate, a demonstrably necessary falsehood. However, the fact that sentences like "God both intervenes in nature and does not intervene in nature" express necessary falsehoods is perfectly compatible with God's being a maximally powerful being, since no logically possible being can both intervene in nature and not intervene in nature. And, by parity of reasoning, $Q's$ expressing a necessary falsehood does not entail that God is not maximally powerful. However, "God frequently intervenes in nature *simpliciter*" is intuitively *not* a candidate for expressing a necessary falsehood. For it contains no term which is such that if we replace it with a full and precise description of what it refers to, we would turn that sentence into one which expresses a necessary falsehood. (If things were otherwise, then, of course, the theist would have reason to feel very uncomfortable about the extent of God's power. If even "God frequently intervenes in nature *simpliciter*" might express a necessary falsehood, then why shouldn't the same be true of, e.g., "God creates something" or "God punishes the wicked"?)

1.6. I have said that empirical evidence for God's existence would be *eo ipso* evidence for E's existence. And, of course, the same holds true of non-empirical evidence for God's existence, if in fact there is any. The rest of the book will be devoted to a discussion of the question whether in fact there *is* any evidence, empirical or non-empirical, for God's existence. What I hope to have shown in this chapter is that such evidence, since it is evidence against the first disjunct of D ("Either God does not exist or E exists") is *eo ipso* evidence for *D*'s second disjunct. It should be stressed that this conclusion is significantly different from the conclusion that, whether or not there is evidence for God's existence, there is strong countervailing evidence (i.e., suffering) that God does not exist.

CHAPTER 2

THE COSMOLOGICAL ARGUMENT

2.1. Almost everyone who has reflected on theism is aware of the following argument: "The universe must have had a beginning, since an infinite series, or a set of infinite series, of causes and effects stretching back into the past *ad infinitum* is impossible". I shall discuss that argument briefly at the end of this chapter. But before doing so, I shall consider a somewhat similar argument which originated with the 18th century English philosopher, Samuel Clarke. The latter argument does not deny the possibility of an infinite regress into the past; and, for that reason, a number of theists have found it more compelling than the anti-infinite regress argument. Now I think that in fact the anti-infinite regress argument has more merit than does Clarke's argument. But, in order to facilitate an accurate assessment of the latter, I shall, for the time being, proceed on the assumption that an infinite causal regress into the past cannot be known to be impossible.

By far the most extensive, careful and interesting treatment of Clarke's argument has been given by William L. Rowe. The two most severe and plausible criticisms of Clarke's argument were set out in Hume's *Dialogues Concerning Natural Religion*, Part IX; and Rowe's defense of the argument against these criticisms cannot, I think, be improved upon. If I am right, then a rebuttal of Rowe's defense makes it highly unlikely that Clarke's argument is sound. Hence, I shall be discussing Rowe's defense of the argument throughout most of this chapter. I shall follow Rowe in calling it 'the cosmological argument'.

On pages 120-121 of his book, *The Cosmological Argument*,[1] Rowe quotes Clarke's argument against the claim that reality consists only of an infinite succession of beings, each one of which is caused by another:

If we consider such an infinite progression, as one entire endless series of dependent beings; 'tis plain this whole series of beings can have no cause from without, of its existence; because in it are supposed to be included all things that are or ever were in the universe: And 'tis plain it can have no reason within itself, of its existence; because no one being in this infinite succession is supposed to be self-existent or necessary ...[2] but every one dependent on the foregoing. ... An infinite succession therefore of merely dependent beings, without any original independent cause; is a series of beings, that has neither necessity, nor cause, nor any reason or ground at all of its existence, either within itself or from without: That is, 'tis an ... impossibility.

It is of note that, even if this argument is sound, it does not establish the existence of (a full-fledged) God (though Clarke subsequently argues, unsuccessfully, I think, that the 'original, independent cause' of the contemplated succession – the existence of which the above argument does, if sound, establish – must in fact be God).[3] Still, if the cosmological argument is sound, it *does* establish the existence of a being having one characteristic, which is prominently part of the concept of God, namely, being creator of the natural universe. So the argument, if sound, provides *some* (weak) evidence for God's existence.

In maintaining that the infinite succession "can have no reason within itself, of its existence; because no one being in this infinite succession is supposed to be self-existent or necessary", Clarke appears to be claiming that an infinite succession of nonnecessary (contingent) beings must itself be contingent. On page 135 Rowe in effect rejects this claim on the ground that Clarke's 'infinite succession' is in fact a set, and, hence, is likely to be, unlike its members, a logically necessary being. (This is an up-to-date formulation of Hume's argument, in *Dialogues* IX, that the cosmological arguer cannot show that it is false that the natural universe itself is a necessarily existent being.) But now logically necessary beings are not causally dependent and, hence, given (what seems likely) that Rowe is right, it looks as if Clarke's argument for an external cause of the natural universe collapses.

However, Rowe thinks that Clarke's argument is subject to an interpretation which makes it plausible, even given that Clarke's 'collection' of contingent things is a necessarily existent set. On page 136 Rowe writes

Let A be the set consisting of [contingent and, hence, causally dependent [4]] beings... I suggest that the question "Why does A exist?" be taken to mean "Why does A have ... members ... rather than none at all?"

Rowe thinks that it is plausible that this question can be truly answered by referring to something external to A (i.e., to a logically necessary being), if it is not the case that it is a necessary truth that A has members. Rowe sees that it does not follow merely from the fact that each member of A is non-necessary that A's having any members at all is non-necessary. (Analogously, it does not follow, e.g., from the fact that it is possible that something, X, is square at time t and also possible that X is circular at time t that it is possible that X is both square and circular at time t.) But on pages 163–166 Rowe tentatively advances a defense of the claim that A's having members is non-necessary. This defense essentially involves the unproven assumption that God's existence is logically possible and, as we shall see in Chapter 6, this assumption needs to be discussed at length.

2.2. But I do not want to dwell on that criticism. Rather, I want to discuss here a certain principle, the so-called 'Principle of Sufficient Reason', which is central to Rowe's interpretation of Clarke's argument. (I shall follow Rowe in calling it 'PSR'.) At this point, it looks as if Rowe requires PSR to be formulated as follows: "For any set, W, the members of which are concrete individuals [5] and which is such that it is not a necessary truth that W has members, there is a cause of W's having members which does not reduce to the immediate causes of the individual members of W". This latter qualification is necessary to rule out the claim that the cause of A's having members reduces to those causes of A's members which are their immediate contingent predecessors.

However, the contemplated interpretation of PSR is, as Rowe sees, unacceptable. On page 129, Rowe quotes another of Hume's criticisms of the cosmological argument (which occurs, once again, in *Dialogues* IX):

Did I show you the particular causes of each individual in a collection of twenty particles of matter, I should think it very unreasonable, should you afterwards ask me what was the cause of the whole twenty. This is sufficiently explained in explaining the cause of the parts.

Claiming that there is a cause of the whole twenty which does not reduce to the individual causes of the individual members of the envisaged collection appears to be very much like claiming that, even though each item in the infinite set of contingent things can be causally explained in terms of its immediate predecessor (so that no item must go unexplained), it is nonetheless true that, since that set's having any members is non-necessary, its having any members has a causal explanation which does not reduce to an explanation in terms of the immediate causes of the individual members of the set. Moreover, it certainly looks as if Hume is right about the twenty particles of matter and similar collections. It is not a necessary truth that my philosophy of religion class has members, but it would be preposterous to maintain that my class has an explanation which does not reduce to the individual explanations of its individual members. So if PSR requires this to be the case, then it can be dismissed out of hand.

However, on pages 154–155 Rowe presents what he thinks is an answer to Hume:

The principle underlying [Hume's] criticism seems plausible enough when restricted to finite sets, i.e., sets with a finite number of members. But the principle is false ... when extended to infinite sets in which the explanation of each member's existence is found in the causal efficacy of some other member. Consider M, the set of men. Suppose *M* consists of an infinite number of members, each member owing its existence to another member which generated it. ... We do not have an explanation of the existence of *M* until we have an explanation of why *M* has the members it has rather than none at all. But clearly if *all* we know is that there always have been men and that every man's existence is explained by the causal efficacy of some other man, we do not know why there always have been men rather than none at all.

The application of this argument to the infinite set of contingent things is obvious. Rowe thinks that, in explaining why each member of the set exists by referring to an immediately prior cause which is another member of the set, we fail to answer the question "Why are there any contingent things at all?".

It follows that, in order to support the cosmological argument, PSR must be interpreted this way: "For any *infinite* set, *W*, which is such that its having any members is non-necessary and each of whose (concrete individual[6]) members can be explained by another member, the question 'Why are there any members of *W*?' can (only) be truly answered by referring to a cause which is not itself a member of *W*." In his recent book, *Philosophy of Religion, An Introduction*, Rowe writes as follows about the cosmological argument and PSR:

The Cosmological Argument ... is not a proof of its conclusion because it rests on a principle (PSR) which we don't *know* and can't prove to be true. But PSR, nonetheless, may be a plausible principle, a principle which someone might reasonably judge to be worthy of belief. Insofar as this is so, the Cosmological Argument may lend weight to theistic belief, while still falling short of proving it.[7]

But I think that reflection will show that PSR, on its present interpretation, is in fact totally unworthy of belief.

Consider the question, "Why are there any things which are at least as large as a quark?". Rowe's claim that PSR (as presently interpreted) may be plausible appears to commit him to the thesis that the following may be plausible: "If there is a finite number of members of the set of things which are at least as large as a quark (call it '*W'*'), then *W'* is like Dore's philosophy of religion class, in that we do not need to infer an irreducibly distinct cause of its having members. However, if W' has an infinite number of members, then it is subject to a causal explanation which does not reduce to the individual explanations of the individual members, namely, the following one: the individual members of W' exist because there is something smaller than a quark which is their ultimate cause."

However, it is surely incredible that if we knew that W' is an infinite set, then we would have good reason to believe this explanation.[8] I do not mean to suggest that present physical theory entails that in fact there *are* no things which are smaller than a quark. Leptons, photons and gluons are candidates for bearing that description. But (I am told by an authority) physicists do not *know* that they are smaller than quarks. And my point is that it is incredible that, given that it was known that W' is an infinite set, then philosophers could settle the matter by employing the present version of PSR.

Here the cosmological arguer may wish to respond as follows: "(1) The present version of PSR entails that if W' is infinite, then the ultimate cause of things which are at least as large as a quark is *either* something which is smaller than a quark *or* something which has no size at all. And since the God of orthodox theism is a purely spiritual being and, hence, has no size, the present version of PSR licenses no inference which can be expected to make the cosmological arguer uncomfortable. (2) PSR can be plausibly supplemented as follows: If a given set, S_1, contains all and only the members of another set, S_2, then if we are warranted in inferring that the cause of S_1's members is C, we are *ipso facto* warranted in inferring that C is also the cause of S_2's members. Moreover, since it may well be that the set of things which are at least as large as a quark is coextensional with the set of contingent things, there would be no reason for the cosmological arguer to be embarrassed by finding himself obliged to infer that the ultimate cause of things which are at least as large as a quark is (like the ultimate cause of contingent things) a purely spiritual (and, hence, sizeless) being."

But these responses are unimpressive. The trouble with (1) is simply that, regardless of whether the cosmological arguer is contented with the *conclusion* that the ultimate cause of things which are at least as large as a quark is a purely spiritual being, it is surely incredible that the nature of things which are at least as large as a quark could give us the basis for a *warranted inference* to that conclusion. Moreover, as we have seen, what the present version of PSR really licenses here is the conclusion that if W' is infinite, then *either* the envisaged cause is sizeless *or* it is smaller than a quark, i.e., on the present version of PSR, if we knew that W' is infinite, then (what is surely incredible) we would have *some* evidence for this second disjunct. (PSR does more than *truth-functionally* entail the envisaged disjunction. Rather it entails that there is evidence for the claim that if W' is infinite, then the ultimate cause of things which are at least as large as a quark has no size and also evidence (namely, the *same* evidence) that if W' is infinite, then the envisaged cause is smaller than a quark. There are, of course, numerous cases in which the same evidence supports conflicting hypotheses.) (2) suffers from three defects. The first, a relatively minor one, is that to the extent that Cartesian dualism is plausible, it is implausible that the set of contingent things is coextensional with a class, all of the members of which are at least as large as a quark and, hence, extended. The second defect is that Clarke's argument-cum-Rowe's defense appears to give us no reason to infer that the alleged necessarily existent cause of contingent things is a purely spiritual (and, hence, sizeless) being.[9] And even if we set those criticisms aside, the proponent of (2) must agree that if we knew that W' is infinite and that Cartesian dualism is false, then the answer to the question of whether the inference to a spiritual (sizeless) cause of things which are at least as large as a quark is legitimate would depend on whether high energy physics will eventually disclose contingent things which can be known to be smaller than a quark and, hence, show that the set of contingent things and the set of things which are at least as large as a quark are not after all coextensional.

And it is, I should think, highly unlikely that the cosmological arguer would wish, upon reflection, to agree that his argument can be undermined by what goes on in particle accelerators. (Analogously, it is unlikely that the cosmological arguer will wish to maintain that if and only if science discovers that the infinite expansion-contraction hypothesis is true, so that it is likely that W' is infinite, we will have reason to believe that the members of W' are caused either by something which is smaller than a quark or by something which has no size at all.)

2.3. It is unclear why Rowe should think that the version of PSR which we are presently contemplating is at all plausible, but the following (on page 137 of *The Cosmological Argument*) gives us a clue:

> The theory of evolution might be a part of the explanation of why M [the set of men] is not included in the null set. [And] if the question "Why does M exist?" makes sense, why should not the question, "Why does A [the putatively infinite set of causally dependent beings] exist?", also make sense?

Presumably, Rowe is here taking M to have a finite number of members, since if there were a series of generations of men stretching back into the past without end, then there could be no true theory of the origins of the human race and, hence, evolutionary theory would be incorrect. So Rowe is suggesting that, since the finite set of men is explicable by reference to something outside the set, it is reasonable to believe that the infinite set of contingent, and, hence, causally dependent, things must also have such an explanation.

In more detail, Rowe appears to have the following argument in mind: "When we explain the fact that a given set, W, has a *finite* number of members, the explanation must refer to at least one item which is not a member of W. Otherwise, at least one member of W will be left unexplained. Consider a set which has three members, A_1, A_2, and A_3. If we explain A_1 by reference to A_2 and A_2 by reference to A_3, then either we can go beyond the set to explain A_3, or A_3 has no adequate explanation at all, since, given that A_3 explains A_2 and

A_2 explains A_1, it is impossible that either A_2 or A_1 adequately explains A_3. And it is reasonable to infer that infinite sets are like finite sets in this respect, i.e., that in giving an adequate explanation of why an infinite set has any members, we must also refer to something *beyond* the set."

This argument presupposes, but does not prove, that causal explanation must be asymmetrical. Moreover, the argument does not really establish that the explanation of why an infinite set has members does not reduce to the individual causal explanations of the individual members of the set. It shows at most that at least *one* of its members is caused by something outside the set. But there is a still more serious objection. Surely it does not follow from the fact that we cannot adequately explain why a *finite* set has any members without going beyond the set, that we cannot explain why an *infinite* set has any members without going beyond it. The argument that A_3 would be unexplained unless we explained it in terms of an item outside the envisaged set does not apply in the case of an infinite set. For even granting that causal explanation is asymmetrical, we can explain any given item, I, in an *infinite* succession of items by referring to a prior item, I', which is not explained by I or by any item which I explains (but is explained by a prior item, which is not explained by I' or by any item which I' explains, and so on *ad infinitum*).

It follows that, *pace* Rowe, if there were an infinite series of generations of men, we could give an entirely appropriate answer to the question, "Why are there any men at all?" by saying "Because there is an infinite series of generations of men, each one of which is caused by a prior generation, so that the series is causally self-sustaining". The alternative is that we cannot explain, e.g., why there are any things which are at least as large as a quark by referring only to items which bear that description, even if there is an infinite number of such things. (Moreover, if the kind of explanation which we are contemplating here is inadequate, then it is reasonable to believe that there *is* no adequate explanation, since it is, as we have seen, very implausible that the nature of things which are at least as large as a quark would, if we knew that W' is infinite, warrant an inference to the conclusion that the ultimate cause of those things is either smaller than a quark or has no size at all.)

Finally, we can, of course, ask the question "Why is a given set, W, a causally self-sustaining set?", i.e., "Why is it the case that W's members are such that each member can be causally explained by referring to at least one other member of W" But surely this looks very much like a question which neither has, nor needs, a true answer. And if PSR says otherwise, then, in the absence of a proof that the question can be truly answered, PSR is a very dubious principle indeed.

2.4. I shall conclude this chapter with a few words about the denial of the possibility of an infinite regress into the past. I think that there is a simple and plausible argument that such a series is in fact impossible,[10] namely, that, just as it is impossible for the natural number series to terminate in a largest possible number, so, too, it is impossible for an infinite series of moments and/or events, which moves from the past to the future, to culminate in a moment and/or event which exists or happens now, i.e., no such infinite series could be gone through. It is, of course, true that there are series which are infinite only in one direction, i.e., series which, like the natural number series, have a beginning. But, since the direction of any temporal series is from past to future, it is dubious that the present moment, like the number 0, is only the beginning, rather than the end, of a series.

There is, however, a question as to whether the contemplated argument establishes that theism is true – that the first, uncaused cause which comes at the beginning of the envisaged series is God or, at any rate, a being which is essentially different from any natural causes. The answer traditionally given by theists who favor the present argument is that the first cause differs radically from natural causes in that it must be a *non-contingent* being. Theists who subscribe to this view are relying on the principle that every uncaused thing is a logically necessary being. However, this principle needs qualification, since there are demonstrably quantum mechanical events which are both contingent and uncaused, and we need an explanation of why the envisaged first cause should be thought to differ in this respect. No doubt there is a strong *prima facie* case, with respect to any *ordinary* event in nature, on behalf of its having a causal explanation. But, needless to say, a first cause, even if it were not supernatural, would be far from being ordinary.

CHAPTER 3

THE DESIGN ARGUMENT

3.1. One version of the design argument affirms that the natural universe, or some things within the natural universe, which are known not to be the products of human design, are sufficiently similar to things which *are* the products of human design so that we are warranted in inferring that the former things have been brought about by a nonhuman designer. It seems much less likely that the universe as a whole bears a sufficient resemblance to the products of human design so that it is probable that it, too, is designed, than that this is true of certain things *within* the universe, such as the human body and its parts. Since the human body is a highly complex system of parts which cooperate in such a way as to produce desirable ends (prolonged life, consciousness, vision, etc.), it resembles sophisticated man-made machines, which are also systems of functionally inter-related parts, which work together to produce desirable ends. In what follows, I shall, for simplicity, discuss just the claim that the human *eye* is sufficiently similar to a *camera* so that we can soundly infer that it is the product of (nonhuman) design. I should point out before proceeding that the design argument does not prove that the non-human designer has all of God's characteristics. However, the argument does, if sound, show that there is a being who has at least *one* characteristic, which is prominently part of the concept of God, namely, being the ultimate, intelligent cause of such enormously desirable things as the human body and its parts.

The version of the design argument which I have in mind can be precisely formulated as follows:

(1)   The eye resembles a camera.
(2)   Cameras are the products of design.

(3)   Similar effects have similar causes.

So

(4)   the eye is the product of design.

But how plausible is this argument? Consider the following parody:

(1′)   Large, flat rocks resemble chairs, in that both can be sat upon.

(2′)   Chairs are the products of design.

(3′)   Similar effects have similar causes.

So

(4′)   large, flat rocks are the products of design.

What this parody shows is that (3) needs to be reformulated as follows: "*Strongly* similar effects have similar causes". Given that reformulation, the design arguer can maintain that the contemplated parody is defective, since large, flat rocks do not *sufficiently* resemble chairs to warrant the conclusion that both are designed. But now, given the reformulation of (3), premiss (1) (of the original design argument) also needs reformulation, viz., "The eye *strongly* resembles a camera". And it is, I think, doubtful that this proposition is true.

Here the design arguer may claim that (1), thus reformulated, is something about which reasonable people can disagree and, hence, that reasonable people can disagree about the cogency of the present version of the design argument. But, even if we accept the former claim, the latter one does not follow, since the reformulation of (3) (call it (3′)) can itself be questioned. The motion of an automobile and the motion of a greyhound are strongly resembling (in any straightforward sense of those words), but the cause of the former is very different from the cause of the latter. Of course, those causes are resembling in some respects, but then so, too, are any two entities. (Even, e.g., the number 3 and Napoleon have in common that they are sometimes thought about.) But we are here envisaging only a weak resemblance; and the design arguer hopes to prove that the cause of the eye *strongly* resembles the cause of the camera, in that both the former and the latter are intelligent design.

Counter-examples to (3'), construed as affirming a significantly strong resemblance between the causes of strongly resembling effects, can be multiplied indefinitely. The smoke which is caused by a smoke bomb strongly resembles the smoke which is caused by a fire; the sound of a speeding car, which is caused by a phonograph record, strongly resembles the sound of a speeding car, which is caused by a car in one's vicinity; and so on. I do not wish to deny that (3'), construed as non-trivial, holds true for a wide range of cases. But these are all cases in which there is a *nomological* connexion between a given kind of thing, X, and a given kind of cause, C, i.e., they are cases in which *causal necessity* is involved. So before we can know that (non-trivial) (3') holds true for the eye and the camera, we must first know that there is a nomological connexion between camera-like things, including eyes, and intelligent design. But that is the *conclusion* which the present version of the design argument seeks to establish. Hence, the argument is entirely uncompelling.

3.2. At this point, I want to turn to what looks to be a more respectable version of the design argument – a version which is similar to one which Alvin Plantinga tentatively endorses in *God And Other Minds*.[1] I have the following argument in mind:

(a)   Every camera-like thing which is such that we know whether or not it is the product of design, is in fact the product of design.

(b)   The eye is a camera-like thing.

So

(c)   the eye is probably the product of design.

Call the earlier version of the design argument 'A_1' and the present version 'A_2'. A_2 has the same form as arguments of the following sort (which I shall call 'Type-T arguments'):

(a)   Every instance of heating water to $100°C$ at the pressure which obtains near the surface of the earth, which is such that we know whether or not water boils at that temperature and pressure, is a case of water boiling at that temperature and pressure.

(b)   This is an instance of heating water to the envisaged temperature at the contemplated pressure.
So
(c)   this will probably be an instance of water's boiling.
And, since this argument is respectable (if *any* non-deductive arguments are), it may well appear that A_2, which has a similar form, is respectable as well.

3.3. But consider the following criticism of A_2 which is (based on a criticism in Hume's *Dialogues Concerning Natural Religion*[2]):

(a)   All the intelligent designers about whom we know whether or not they have human bodies, do, indeed have human bodies.

(b)   If a designer of the eye exists, then he is an intelligent designer.

So

(c)   if a designer of the eye exists, then probably the designer of the eye has a human body.

But

(d)   it is highly unlikely that a *human being* designed the eye (one reason being that if that were so, then *another* human being must have designed *his* eyes, and so on *ad infinitum*).

Hence

(e)   there is no designer of the eye.

What makes this criticism (call it 'H_1') appear to be especially effective vis-à-vis the proponent of A_2 is that (a) through (c), like A_2 itself, is a Type-T argument, and, hence, it may well look as though the design arguer cannot consistently reject H_1 and continue to accept A_2.

But in fact this may be mere appearance. The design arguer can reply as follows: "(a) through (c) does, indeed, constitute a sound Type-T argument. But, like all Type-T arguments, it establishes only a likelihood – in this case the likelihood that the designer of the eye has a human body. And the *prima facie* case for this conclusion (established by (a) and (b)) is overthrown by step (d) (which is a highly credible claim). The point is that instead of inferring (e) from (c) and (d), we should infer the *falsity* of (c) from (d). However, there is no analogous refutation of A_2. So one can accept A_2 and reject H_1 in perfect consistency. Of course, in view of (d), we must agree that A_2 cannot establish that it is likely that the designer of the eye is a human being. But A_2 can, when supplemented by the following principle (call it 'R'), establish that the eye has a nonhuman designer: If all the X's about which we know whether or not they are Y's are, indeed, known to be Y's, but Y's of type-W, and we know that there is an X which is *not* a Y of type-W, then we are warranted in inferring that, though the latter X is not a Y of type-W, it is nonetheless a Y."

It is of note that if R is a plausible principle, then it will enable the proponent of A_2 to cope with yet another Humean objection (call it 'H_2'), viz., "The thoughts of *human* designers are machine-like. Hence, it is likely that the thoughts of *any* designer are machine-like. So, if all machine-like things are designed, then since the thoughts of the eye's designer are machine-like, they are designed by another designer, and so on *ad infinitum*."[3] Given R, the proponent of A_2 can claim that, even if (what is surely doubtful) Hume's theory of *human* thought is correct, we are nonetheless warranted in inferring that the eye's designer's thought is *not* machine-like (in order to avoid multiplying explanatory entities way beyond necessity.)

Now I suspect that there are counter-examples to R and, perhaps, corresponding suitable refinements which would enable the design arguer to cope with H_1 and H_2. But I do not want to dwell further on this topic, since, as we shall see, there is another, much more compelling objection to A_2.

3.4. One fact about A_2, which makes it appear to be an improvement over A_1, is that it does not contain the principle that strongly resembling effects have significantly resembling causes, so that it looks as if A_2 cannot be faulted either by rejecting that principle (as I have done) or by denying that the eye and the camera are sufficiently alike to make the argument work. But Plantinga has argued that even Type-T arguments depend for their cogency on whether the things to which they refer are strongly or weakly resembling. Plantinga asks us to consider the following argument:

(1)   Every contingent object such that we know whether or not it was the product of intelligent design, was the product of intelligent design.

(2)   The universe is a contingent object.

So

(3)   probably the universe is designed.[4]

Call this argument 'A_3'. The trouble with A_3, according to Plantinga, is that the classes to which it refers can be divided into classes, the members of which are very dissimilar.[5] If Plantinga is right, then the question whether A_2 is a sound argument does after all depend on the extent to which eyes and cameras are similar.

But is Plantinga right? It is certainly not a *sufficient* condition of a Type-T argument being sound that it refer to a class with very similar members. For consider the class of New Yorkers of Irish descent, who wear glasses and weigh over 175 pounds. And add to this class Joe O'Reilly, about whom we know that he is a New Yorker of Irish descent who wears glasses, but about whom we do not know that he weighs over 175 pounds. The members of *this* class (call it 'K') resemble one another to a greater extent than do the members of many classes which can be cited in perfectly respectable Type-T arguments. But plainly the following argument is unacceptable:

(1)   Whenever we have been in a position to observe whether or not the members of K have weighed over 175 pounds, they have.

(2)   Joe O'Reilly is a member of K.

So

(3)   probably Joe O'Reilly weighs over 175 pounds.

What is wrong with this argument? Before his discussion of A_3, Plantinga asks his readers to consider the following argument: Let class K' be the class which is constructed by annexing Julius Caesar to the class of snub-nosed persons.

Then

(1)   every member of K', who is such that we know whether or not he is snub-nosed, is snub-nosed.

(2)   Julius Caesar is a member of K'.

So

(3)   probably Julius Caesar is snub-nosed.[6]

Obviously, this argument is totally amiss. But what, precisely, is wrong with it? Plantinga points out that we can 'prove', with exactly the same degree of plausibility, that Julius Caesar is *not* snub-nosed by cooking up another class, K'', consisting of non-snub-nosed members plus Julius Caesar and substituting K'' for K' in the envisaged argument. And he suggests that arguments of this sort can be ruled out on the grounds that counterpart arguments, yielding opposite conclusions, can always be constructed. If Plantinga is right, then what is wrong with the argument about Joe O'Reilly is that there are equally persuasive counterpart arguments which 'prove' that Joe O'Reilly weighs more than 175 pounds and also less than 175 pounds.

But it looks as though Plantinga's diagnosis does not get to the heart of the matter. It is easy to imagine scientifically respectable arguments for a given hypothesis, H, and also for not-H, both of which arguments are based on our total knowledge of the world. (Indeed, this looks very much to be the case at present with the hypothesis that there is intelligent, extraterrestrial life.) So it will not do to propose a *general* rule to the effect that, whenever an argument establishes a given proposition, p, and there is an equally persuasive argument for not-p, then both arguments are (like the Julius Caesar and Joe O'Reilly arguments) wildly fallacious.

Plantinga may well want to say at this point that a pair of arguments which establish contradictory conclusions are seriously amiss when they refer to a class which is constructed of members about whom we know that they have a given property, P, plus a member,

M, about whom we do not know this and about whom we conclude that he has *P*. But surely we need an *explanation* of why just members of *this* species of argument-pairs, which establish contradictory conclusions, should never be taken seriously.

Well, then, what precisely is wrong with arguments of the contemplated kind? It will not do to rule them out simply on the grounds that the classes to which they refer are composed of radically disparate items. For, as we have seen, this is not true of the members of class *K*. (Indeed, they are much more similar than the members of the class which is referred to by the version of the design argument which Plantinga tentatively endorses, viz., the class of things in which means are curiously adapted to ends.) Rather, what is wrong with the envisaged arguments is this: When Type-*T* arguments are plausible, they are plausible for the following reason: We have been in a position to observe whether or not some *Q*'s (e.g., water heated to 100°C at pressure *X*) are *P*'s (e.g., have the property of boiling at that pressure and temperature); and we have failed to observe any *Q*'s which are not *P*'s. Moreover, we have observed *Q*'s being *P*'s under a wide variety of circumstances. Now there are two possible explanations of our observations here: (1) It is a mere coincidence that all the *Q*'s that we have observed have been *P*'s. (2) Probably there is a *nomic connexion* between being a *Q* and being a *P*, and, hence, probably *all* *Q*'s are *P*'s. And plainly (2) is the superior explanation.

However, we know that there *can* be no nomic connexion between being a bespectacled New Yorker of Irish descent and the property of weighing over 175 pounds, since we know, e.g., that there are bespectacled New York children of Irish descent who weigh less than 175 pounds. Moreover, a similar criticism applies to Plantinga's pseudo-arguments about Julius Caesar: there is no question of there being a nomic connexion between being snub-nosed, or non-snub-nosed, and being Julius Caesar (or Julius Caesar-like).

But what is wrong with Plantinga's pseudo-argument that, since the universe belongs to the class of *contingent things*, it is probable that the universe is designed? Is it just *palpably false* that there is a nomic connexion between being a contingent thing and being designed (as it is palpably false that there is a nomic connexion between being, e.g., Julius Caesar and being snub-nosed or being non-snub-nosed)? But how can that be so, if it really is the case, as the present argument asserts, that every contingent object such that we know whether or not it was the product of intelligent design *was* the product of intelligent design? (The argument about Joe O'Reilly fails because it is false that every bespectacled New Yorker of Irish descent, who is such that we know whether he weighs over 175 pounds, does so. And the arguments about Julius Caesar fail because the claim that every Julius Caesar-like person about whom we know whether or not he is, e.g., snub-nosed *is* indeed snub-nosed presupposes both (a) that we are acquainted with people who are very like Julius Caesar and (b) that all of those people are snub-nosed. And if (a) is not false, then surely (b) is.)

The answer is that it is flatly *false* that there are no contingent objects which are known *not* to be the products of design. We know that, e.g., the configuration of the specks of dust under my living room rug is not the product of design. And, if I close my eyes and throw some paint at a canvas, I can know that the result of *that* act is not the product of design. Another counter-instance are the random noises which are produced by John Cage's randomizers. (No doubt, the randomizers themselves are the products of design, but not the random noises which they produce.) Now all of these non-designed configurations are contingent things. So it is false that there are no contingent things about which we know that they are not the products of design. And it follows that we know that there is no nomic connexion between being a contingent thing and being a product of design.[7]

3.5 Let us return at last to A_2. It follows from what I have been saying that A_2 cannot be faulted on the ground that eyes and cameras are not sufficiently strongly resembling to warrant the conclusion that they have significantly resembling causes, at least if the following argument is sound: "All the camera-like things about which we know whether or not they are the products of design are, indeed, the products of design. Moreover, either this is a mere coincidence or there is a *nomic connexion* between being a camera-like thing and being designed – so that *all* camera-like things, including the eye, are the products of design. And surely the latter explanation is preferable to the former one." But is this in fact a persuasive argument?

One obvious criticism of the argument is that, in view of evolutionary theory, it is simply false that we do not know that the eye is not the product of design, and, hence, false that all the camera-like things about which we know whether or not they are the products of design are, indeed, the products of design. But I think that the design arguer can plausibly circumvent this criticism by claiming that evolutionary theory is compatible with the design hypothesis. There are two ways in which a supernatural designer (call him 'G') could be ultimately causally responsible for the human eye, given evolutionary theory: (1) G was the direct cause of (at least some of) the genetic mutations and recombinations which, with natural selection, led to the eye. (2) G caused the kind of matter which the universe contains and the scientific laws which operate on that matter, having in view the fact that the natural mechanisms which are involved in evolution would eventually bring about the eye. On this second view, G is something like human beings who make steel and plastic, knowing that those materials are in turn suitable for making various kinds of artifacts.

(1) is less plausible than (2), since it is irrational to believe that God has directly intervened in nature, in the absence of very strong evidence to the contrary; and since G is, at least, a God-like being, it looks as if the same holds true for G. (But *could* G be God? Couldn't a maximally great being have brought about living organisms with much more efficiency and much less pain? If I am right in Chapter 1, then God could have done a better job than the evolutionary

mechanisms, which have in fact been operative, only at the cost of losing E.)

Still, in the end we must concede that A_2 is not a compelling argument. For, even if we grant that all the camera-like things, about which we know whether or not they are the products of design, are, indeed, the products of design, there is a perfectly adequate explanation of that fact which makes no reference to a nomic connexion between camera-like things and intelligent design. The explanation is just that it is much *easier* for us to get information about the causes of the camera than it is for us to get information about the origins of the eye, so that, though we know that the camera is the product of intelligent design, we do not have sufficient evidence with respect to the origins of the eye so that we can know enough about the latter to know that intelligent design was not its (ultimate) cause. However, A_2's form is such that it is a cogent argument only if the best explanation of its first premiss is that there is a nomic connexion between camera-like things and intelligent design. Since this is false, argument A_2 is a failure. Of course, the argument which shows that it is a failure contains as a premiss the claim that we do not *know* that the ultimate cause of the eye is *not* an intelligent designer. But the design arguer has traditionally thought that he could establish the much stronger conclusion that we *do* know that it is likely that an intelligent designer caused the eye. And, if I am right about A_1 and A_2, then *this* conclusion is not warranted by them.

CHAPTER 4

A MORAL ARGUMENT

4.1. It is an obvious truth about a person's moral obligations (his over-all obligations, not his *prima facie* ones) that his fulfilling them is of overriding importance to him, not in the sense that he believes that it is of overriding importance, but in the sense that his well-being will in fact be significantly affected by his fulfilling or not fulfilling those obligations, whether or not he believes this to be so. Plato tried to account for this by claiming that the nature of the human soul is such that a person's wrongdoing inexorably harms him, regardless of whether he is punished by others. I shall return to Plato's theory later in the chapter. Much more recently, Kurt Baier has offered us this explanation of the overriding importance of our avoiding wrongdoing:

The very *raison d'être* of a morality is to yield reasons which over-rule the reasons of self-interest in those cases when everyone's following self-interest would be harmful to everyone. Hence moral reasons are superior to all others. ...[1] Moral rules are not designed to serve the agent's interest directly. Hence it would be quite inappropriate for him to break them whenever he discovers that they do not serve his interest. They are designed to adjudicate primarily in cases where there is a conflict of interest, so from their very nature they are bound to be contrary to the interest of one of the persons affected. However, they are also bound to serve the interest of the other person, hence his interest in the other's observing them. It is on the assumption of the likelihood of a reversal of roles that the universal observation of the rule will serve everyone's interest. ... It is better for everyone that there should be a morality generally observed than that the principle of self-interest should be acknowledged as supreme.[2]

Baier is here advancing the familiar Hobbesian view that moral rules have the function of adjudicating conflicts which arise from self-interest, and that everyone is better off when moral rules obtain, since failure to adjudicate such conflicts leads to the use of force in order to get one's way when one's interests conflict with those of another person; and this leads in turn to a short and unhappy life for all involved.

But this is an inadequate explanation of the overriding importance of morality. It is certainly true that each of us is better off if everyone follows moral rules than if no one does, or most people do not. But it does not follow that *I* am better off if everyone, including me, does what is morally right, rather than everyone *but me* doing so. There are, in the lives of many of us, at least a few occasions on which our short-range interests will be best served by breaking a moral rule (perhaps because we will not be found out), and which are such that, since this violation will not lead to the breakdown of civilized society, the Hobbesian cannot explain why our long-range interests will be harmed by our wrongdoing. No doubt there are some people who could never do something significantly wrong without suffering such pangs of conscience that they are worse off for their wrongdoing, no matter how it may benefit them. But surely whether one has a moral obligation, e.g., to refrain from cruelty, does not depend on whether or not one has a sensitive conscience.

4.2. My fulfilling my (stringent, over-all) obligations is, *on every occasion of my doing so*, of overriding importance, not just to others, but to *me*. And that entails that my wrongdoing will result in my being harmed, regardless of the circumstances in which it occurs. It is this fact that Plato tried to explain and that is a stumbling block for Hobbes. But what *kind* of harm are we contemplating here? One very simple answer is that the harm which anyone suffers as a result of his wrongdoing is just his being a morally bad person. However, this is very doubtful, for the following reason: The meaning of 'harm' is roughly[3] such that "Z suffers harm for doing X" analytically entails that, because of his doing X, either (1) Z loses something which he strongly desires to have as an end-in-itself, or (2) Z acquires something which he strongly desires the absence of as an end-in-itself.[4]

(The qualifier, 'end-in-itself', is important here. Suppose that Z desires to be of good moral character, not as an end-in-itself, but because he thinks that it is a means to a good reputation and that the latter is necessary for a successful career. Then Z is not harmed by becoming a wrongdoer, so long as this does not in fact adversely affect his career.) Now there are some people who do not strongly desire to be morally good people as an end-in-itself and, hence, who do not strongly desire the absence of a bad moral character as an end-in-itself. And these people would not be harmed just by their bringing on themselves a bad moral character. But since it is of overriding importance to Z that he fulfill his obligations, no matter what kind of person he may be, it cannot be true, at least as a general rule, that the harm which we are examining is simply the loss of moral innocence.

Let us pursue this matter further. It looks as though some people (especially in extremely acquisitive societies like our own) desire only their own pleasure and the avoidance of their own pain as ends-in-themselves. Moreover, it is frequently the case that their doing wrong does not cause them to suffer the pangs of a guilty conscience. I shall call these people 'hedonists'. Now, since it is of overriding importance for *any* person, Z, that he avoid significant wrongdoing, Z will be harmed for doing wrong even if Z is a hedonist. Moreover, just as it is the case that Z will be harmed for doing wrong, regardless of what he values as ends-in-themselves, so, too, Z will be harmed for doing wrong, no matter how powerful and shrewd he may be. (Recall Plato's story about Gyge's ring.) The alternative is that, given a certain high degree of shrewdness and power on Z's part, then either he does not *have* stringent obligations and, hence, is not capable of significant wrongdoing, or, though he has stringent obligations (as do ordinary men and women), it is not of overriding importance to Z that he fulfill them. But surely it is a necessary truth that, given that Z has a stringent obligation to do a given thing, X, then it is of overriding importance to Z that he do X, regardless of how powerful and shrewd

Z may be. And it is surely also true that whether or not Z has that obligation does not depend on how powerful and shrewd he is (as it does depend, e.g., on Z's being *able* to fulfill it).

We need an explanation, then, of the following facts: (1) Even if Z had vastly greater power and knowledge than any actual human being, Z would be doing what is seriously wrong in failing to do X and, hence, would be significantly harmed for not doing it. (2) This latter would hold true even if Z were a hedonist. But if Z were a hedonist, then Z would be significantly harmed if and only if Z was deprived of pleasure or afflicted with pain, i.e., one or both would befall him. Now it is, I think, clear that the best explanation of (1) and (2) is that there is a being (a) who has what I shall call 'God-like power', i.e., power so great that it is not logically possible for any wrongdoer to surpass, or even rival, it, and (b) who has what I shall call 'God-like knowledge', i.e., knowledge so great that it is not logically possible for any wrongdoer to outwit him. The reason for (a) is that the contemplated God-like being must be able successfully to deprive any logically possible hedonistic wrongdoer of pleasure and/or able successfully to inflict pain on him. And the reason for (b) is that this God-like being must be able to *detect* the wrongs of any logically possible hedonistic wrongdoer. (Actually, (a) entails (b): if the God-like being could be outwitted by a wrongdoer, then (a) would not be true of him. However, I want to make it explicit that the contemplated punisher resembles God, not only with respect to power but also with respect to knowledge.) Finally, a being who is able to detect any logically possible act of wrongdoing and to act on that knowledge is, at least to that extent, a person.

It should be noticed that my argument does not require that there actually *are* hedonists (though in fact I think there are), only that hedonists, like wrongdoers with super-human power and knowledge, are logically possible. It is also of note that if such beings were *not* logically possible, then the counterfactual proposition (call it 'C') that, if such beings (existed and) did what is significantly wrong, then they would be punished, would be trivially true,[5] and, hence, the explanation of its truth which I have just offered would be otiose.

4.3 Once again, we are contemplating a counterfactual state of affairs – one in which a hedonistic wrongdoer, who is much more powerful and shrewd than any wrongdoers who in fact exist in our world, does wrong and is, as a consequence, punished. This is because I am giving a reason for believing that a *God-like* punisher exists, and we do not require a God-like punisher in order to deal with any actual wrongdoers. But now why should we believe that this God-like being exists, even in the absence of the envisaged, super-human wrongdoers? Why not say instead that the God-like being *would* come into existence (only) *if* those wrongdoers in fact existed?

This latter claim can be interpreted in two ways: (1) The God-like being would just happen to come into existence (uncaused) were the wrongdoers to exist. (2) The God-like being would be *caused* to come into existence by the fact that the wrongdoers existed. But (1) is surely incredible on its face; and (2) is also plainly false, since the causal laws in the actual world do not countenance the existence of wrongdoers being the cause of the existence of a God-like being, and it is unlikely that the closest possible worlds in which there are super-human, hedonistic wrongdoers[6] differ from the actual world in this respect.

4.4. But why should we think that *C* has an explanation? Why shouldn't we be satisfied with the claim that it is simply a brute fact that any hedonistic wrongdoers there might be, no matter how powerful and shrewd they are, would suffer pain or a significant loss of pleasure because of their wrongdoing? The answer is simply that, whether or not it is plausible that *some* facts (e.g., the existence of an infinite succession of contingent beings) are brute facts, in the sense that there is no true explanation of them, it looks on its face to be very unlikely that the fact that any wrongdoers do, or would, come to grief because of their wrongdoing is also a brute fact. Claiming that it has that status is strongly analogous to claiming of a particular wrongdoer at a particular time, say, Adolph Hitler in 1933, that he will come to grief, though there is no true explanation, which is available even in principle, of why that will come to pass. A slightly more plausible move for my critic to make at this point would be to claim that, though the fact that any hedonistic wrongdoers do, or would, suffer pain or a loss of pleasure very probably has a true explanation, we are not in a position to specify what that explanation is. But the answer to this objection is simply that I have given a plausible explanation of why any hedonistic wrongdoers would be punished and that there is an onus on my critic to prove that it is not the best explanation available – and, hence, one which we are rationally constrained to accept – by advancing another, superior one. (It goes without saying that the best explanation of a given state of affairs at time t does not always remain the best explanation after t. But, given that it is both not implausible and the best explanation at t, it is irrational to reject it until a better one comes along.)

It is of note that Plato evidently agreed with the claim that the fact that C is true is not a brute fact, since part of *The Republic* is devoted to an attempt to show that the soul is divided into three parts, which inexorably come into painful conflict with one another as a result of wrongdoing. But this attempt to explain the truth of C rivals my own only if the psychology of *The Republic* is not mere misleading metaphor. And it is, I think, highly unlikely that it is not.

4.5. The foregoing considerations indicate that some accounts of the meaning of moral language are superior to others. In particular, a definition of 'morally obliged', from which it follows that "Z is morally obliged to do X" analytically entails that it is, at least, of considerable importance to Z that he does X, is superior to any analysis of moral language which does not have this consequence, so long as there are no cogent criticisms of that definition. Now *The Webster's Third New International Dictionary* (1976) gives, as a sense of 'oblige' (and as the only plausible candidate for the sense of '*morally* oblige'), "to constrain ... by ... moral force " and "to bind as subject to a penalty" (p. 1556). And other major dictionaries do not significantly differ.[7] On this definition, Z's being morally obliged to do X is equivalent to Z's having a certain property, namely, being constrained by moral force to do X and being bound in this regard as subject to a penalty; and this entails that it is of considerable importance to Z that he does X.[8] However, I know of no other analyses of "Z is morally obliged to do X," e.g., prescriptivism, which have this consequence.[9] So, given that there is no good reason to *reject* the dictionary definition, we should accept it, at least until we have an analysis of moral language which has the same advantage.

But isn't there reason to reject the contemplated definition? R. M. Hare, the leading opponent of descriptivism (i.e., of analyses of moral language from which it follows that moral discourse is essentially descriptive) argues that "naturalism and most other kinds of descriptivism" cannot account for the fact that the moral reformer uses 'obliged' in the same sense in which his more conventional opponent uses it:

The meanings of the moral words cannot tie them to the fixed properties of actions, etc., if they are not to tie us, their users, to the moral views fixed by received opinion. ... You and I can be using the world 'wrong' in the same sense but disagree fundamentally on what properties of actions make them wrong. This is possible because 'wrong', unlike descriptive words, does not have its meaning fixed for it by descriptive criteria. ...[10]

But, though it is descriptivistic to claim that "Z is morally obliged to do X" ascribes to Z the property of being bound to do X as subject to a penalty, *this* kind of descriptivism, at least, is totally immune to Hare's criticism. For surely we can easily understand how people who are using 'morally obliged' in the same sense could disagree about whether Z is in fact thus bound to do X.

Another related criticism which Hare advances is this:

Descriptivism of any sort ... will lead to the adoption ... of a 'So what?' morality; [people] will be able to say "Yes; I know it would be wrong: so what?"[11]

What Hare has in mind here, presumably, is that merely ascribing properties to an action gives no one any reason to perform it. But surely this depends on what properties are being ascribed. In particular, ascribing to X the property of being such that Z is bound to perform it as subject to a penalty is plainly a motivating description relative to Z. (Another such property is, e.g., being a necessary condition of saving Z's life.) In short, the contemplated dictionary definition looks to be invulnerable to Hare's criticisms. And, as for the possibility of further criticisms, there is an onus on my critic to produce them.

4.6. We have seen that the being who is central to my explanation of C's truth is God-like in power and knowledge. It is also possible to show that this being may have a further characteristic which has traditionally been ascribed to God, namely, necessary existence. It looks very much as if some moral sentences, e.g., "Z is morally obliged to avoid promoting himself at the considerable expense of another person by telling a falsehood", express necessary truths, since, given that they are not essentially prescriptive, they certainly express *truths*; and, since we cannot conceive of any counter-examples to them, they have what is an identifying feature of a necessary truth. Call Z's promoting himself at the considerable expense of another person by telling a falsehood, 'A'. It may be thought that, in fact, we can conceive of a counter-example to the proposition that Z is morally obliged to refrain from doing A, namely, a case in which, e.g., Z knows that the world will be destroyed by an evil scientist unless he does A. But we can easily accommodate this counter-example by redefining 'A' as "the action of promoting one's self at the considerable expense of another person by telling a falsehood, solely in order to satisfy one's desire for luxuries".[12] Given this redefinition of 'A', "Z is morally obliged to refrain from doing A" would not express a false proposition, even if Z knew that the world would be destroyed unless he promoted himself at the considerable expense of another person by telling a falsehood. But now imagine the following situation:

At time *t*, *Z* knows that the world will be destroyed unless he takes a pill which will make him greedy and, as a result of his greed, promote himself at the considerable expense of another person by telling a falsehood. But we can deal with *this* counter-example by redefining '*A*' as "the action of promoting one's self at the considerable expense of another person by telling a falsehood, solely in order to satisfy one's greed at *t*, *when the latter motive is not the result of a prior action which is morally justified by a worthy motive*". And if that does not satisfy my objector, let us take the following moral obligation sentence as our example of a necessary-truth-expressing sentence: "*Z* is morally obliged to refrain from inflicting intense and prolonged pain on someone when *Z* knows that doing so is not connected with any useful purpose". It appears very unlikely that there are counter-examples to *that* claim and very likely that if (*mirabile dictu*) there are, then it can easily be modified to accommodate them.

We are justified, then, in thinking that some moral obligation claims express necessary truths. Let us continue to use '*A*' to refer to an action which one of those claims prohibits. Since it is a necessary truth that any person is morally obliged not to do *A*, this proposition is true in every possible world. So it is true in every possible world that if a hedonist with super-human power and knowledge does *A* there, then he will be punished. Hence a person with God-like power and knowledge exists in every possible world. And if the God-like being in one possible world is identical with the God-like being in every other possible world, then he possesses a property which philosophers such as Anselm, Hartshorne, Malcolm, and Plantinga have (plausibly) ascribed to God, namely, necessary existence.

Or, at any rate, this is true if this being exists even in possible worlds which have causal laws which are very different from our own and in which there are *in fact* no hedonistic wrongdoers who are sufficiently powerful and shrewd to require a God-like punisher. I have in mind the objection that, though it is true in such worlds that a God-like punisher *would* be caused to come into existence by a wrongdoer of the contemplated kind, *in fact* no God-like punisher exists in those worlds, since no such wrongdoer exists there. But it is, I think, plausible that (*pace* Hume) it is not even *logically possible* for the existence of wrongdoers to cause the existence of a God-like punisher, and *a fortiori* it is plausible that there are no possible worlds in which there are causal laws which countenance the envisaged causal transaction.

The above argument presupposes that the following argument is cogent: Since hedonistic wrongdoers are logically possible (and, indeed, may well exist) in the actual world, such wrongdoers are logically possible in every possible world. For if there were some possible worlds in which those wrongdoers were *not* logically possible, then C ("If the envisaged wrongdoers existed, then they would be punished") would be trivially true in those worlds,[13] and, hence, an explanation of its truth which referred to a supernatural punisher would be otiose. Moreover, the claim that, since the envisaged wrongdoers are logically possible in the actual world, they are logically possible in *all* possible worlds presupposes the more general (familiar) thesis that if any given thing, t, is logically possible in a given possible world, W, then it is logically possible in all possible worlds. I shall have more to say about the latter thesis in the Appendix.

4.7. Still, though the argument of this chapter takes us a considerable way toward proving the existence of God, it does not take us all the way. For one thing, I have not proved that it is the *same* God-like punisher who exists in each possible world, or, for that matter, that there is only *one* God-like punisher in any given possible world. Moreover, my argument does not establish that the God-like punisher is perfectly good, nor does it show that the God-like punisher is omnipotent and omniscient. What it does show is that he is more powerful and knowledgeable than any wrongdoer could possibly be. But, in order to deduce omnipotence and omniscience from that, we need to know that it is logically possible for a wrongdoer to have power so great that anyone who had more power would be omnipotent and for a wrongdoer to have knowledge so great that anyone who had more knowledge would be omniscient. And I do not think that we do know that. (The reason will emerge in 7.4.)

4.8. However, though the considerations set forth in this chapter do not conclusively prove the existence of the full-fledged God of orthodox theism, they do imply that another doctrine, which is normally associated with theism, is true, namely, that human beings survive earthly death. Maintaining that Z's fulfilling his obligation to do X is of overriding importance to him, even though he may well not suffer more as a result of his not doing X than do morally superior people who do fulfill their obligation to do X, is in effect claiming that it will be strongly against Z's self-interest for him to fail to do X, even though he may well be just as badly off if he does X as he will be if he does not do it. Hence, serious wrongdoers will suffer *more* than people who are relatively morally innocent. But now we know from observation that the morally innocent (e.g., children and lower animals) are just as apt to suffer in this world as are moral reprobates. And since this is (alas!) a well-substantiated inductive generalization, it would be irrational to claim that all wrongdoers are worse off in this life than they *would* have been if they had remained relatively morally innocent. Given our observations of the widespread misery of, e.g., starving children, maintaining that all serious wrongdoers would have been significantly better off in this world if they had refrained from doing wrong, is like maintaining that, e.g., all native Bostonians would have been significantly better off if they had been natives of London, despite widespread observations which support the thesis that life in London, like life in Boston, is no bed of roses. So, given the truth of C, it follows that there is an afterlife in which those wrongdoers who flourish in this world are punished. But all of us are wrongdoers to some degree, an most of us sometimes do what is significantly wrong without suffering (here and now) for it. It follows that there is reason to believe that many of us survive our earthly death.

An alternative argument is that (1) the overriding importance of morality entails not only that the wicked are *worse* off in the long run than the relatively righteous, but that the latter are *better* off in the long run than are the wicked (indeed, the former entails the latter) and, hence, that (2) those among the relatively righteous who suffer greatly in this world will be compensated in an afterlife. But this argument, like the former one, establishes that *some* people, at least, survive earthly death. And that conclusion renders it much more likely than it would otherwise be that *all* people live on after they leave this world.

In Chapter 1, I raised the question "Why are human beings sometimes morally obliged to relieve suffering, given that suffering serves *E*?" And a similar question is raised by the argument for survival of earthly death that I have just presented, viz., "Why are human beings morally obliged to refrain from killing a person about whom they have reason to believe (a) that he will survive his earthly death, (b) that he will not be sorely missed by someone after he dies, and (c) because of his moral stature, that he will be happier in the afterlife than he is in this world? Could we really have an *anti-utilitarian* obligation not to kill this person?" The answer, I think, is that, though we have an anti-*act*-utilitarian obligation not to kill him, this obligation is compatible with, and, indeed, conforms to, rule-utilitarianism. Given human ignorance, greed, malice and self-deception, a moral prohibition against killing, which made an exception of killing the righteous, would inevitably lead to unjustified killings in borderline cases and, hence, make all but the most stupid of us excessively fearful.

God, on the other hand, is not, if he exists, constrained by the rule-utilitarian's prohibition against killing, since, unlike human beings, he is neither ignorant, nor greedy, nor malicious, nor self-deceiving, and, hence, not apt to abuse a merely act-utilitarian prohibition. I do not mean to imply, however, that if God exists, then human death is always, or for the most part, the result of God's deliberations about the moral stature of the individual who is to die. Rather, if God exists, then if I am right in Chapter 1, human death is, for the most part, the result of the unimpeded operation of scientific laws, which is logically necessary for *E*. However, this conclusion is compatible with the claim that human death is *sometimes* the result of miraculous, divine intervention.

CHAPTER 5

A MODAL ARGUMENT

5.1. The following is a version of a familiar type of modal argument for God's existence:

(a)   Since the concept of God is the concept of a being than which no greater being is logically possible, the concept of God is such that it is true in each possible world that if God exists in that world, then it is logically impossible for him to fail to exist there, i.e., his existence in that world is logically necessary.

(b)   There is a possible world, *W*, in which God exists.

Hence

(c)   in *W*, God's existence is logically necessary. (From (a) and (b) by *modus ponens*.)

But

(d)   what is logically necessary in one possible world is logically necessary in all possible worlds.

So

(e)   God's existence is logically necessary in the actual world, i.e., God, a maximally great being, exists.

The next chapter will be devoted to a discussion of premiss (b); I shall, for the most part, be discussing premiss (a) in this chapter. But first I shall present a brief defense of premiss (d). To say that God's existence is logically necessary in *W* is to say that in *W*, the proposition that God does not exist is necessarily false. For simplicity, let us look just at (what is entailed by (d)) the claim that if there is a possible world, *W*, in which a given proposition, *p*, is necessarily false, then *p* is necessarily false in the actual world. Suppose that someone claims that there are propositions such that, though they are necessarily false in W, it may well be that they are not necessarily false in the actual world (call it 'W''). Then it would be reasonable to ask him for *examples* of such propositions. But what would they look like? E.g., the proposition expressed by '2 + 2 = 5' is not an illustration, since *that* proposition *is* necessarily false in W'. Well, then, what about, say, the proposition expressed by "There are no trees in Wisconsin"? This has the advantage of not being necessarily false in W', but the distinct disadvantage of looking very much as though it is not even *possibly* necessarily false, i.e., not necessarily false *in W*. In short, it appears unlikely that the opponent of (d) can shoulder the burden of producing a plausible candidate for being necessarily false in W, though not necessarily false in W'.[1] It follows that it is rational to hold that if the proposition that God does not exist is a necessary falsehood in one possible world, then it is a necessary falsehood *simpliciter*, i.e., that God exists with logical necessity in the actual world.

5.2. Premiss (a) is an explication of the proposition that it is a necessary truth that if God exists, then it is logically impossible for him to fail to exist. The following arguments will show that premiss (a) is true:

I. Since the concept of God is the concept of a maximally great being, the concept of God is, as St. Anselm saw, such that it is a necessary truth that if God exists, then his non-existence is impossible. Now there are two kinds of impossibility: (a) physical impossibility – the kind of impossibility that we have in mind when we say, e.g., that it is impossible for a piece of lead to float unsupported a few feet above the earth; and (b) logical impossibility – the kind of impossibility that we have in mind when we say, e.g., that it is impossible that 2 + 2 equals 5 and that the number 9 is even. And we need a reason for thinking that if God exists, then the impossibility of his nonexistence is of the latter, rather than the former, variety. But such a reason is available: Since the concept of God is the concept of a maximally great being, the concept of God is clearly such that it is a necessary truth that if he exists, then he is not causally dependent on anything which is distinct from him, i.e., there is no explanation, in terms of external things, of why he exists. But nothing can be the cause of its own existence. Hence, if God exists, then it is not (even in principle) possible to provide a causal explanation of that fact. But if something, X, is such that it is physically impossible that a given predicate, P, is true of it, then it is possible (at least in principle) to provide a causal explanation of not-P's being true of X. Thus, it is physically impossible that when pure water is heated to 100 °C at the pressure which obtains near the surface of the earth, it fails to boil. And this can be explained in terms of the increase in the motion of water molecules under those circumstances. However, there are lots of questions of the form "Why is it impossible that X has P?" which cannot be answered thusly, e.g., "Why is it impossible that Socrates is a number?" and "Why is it impossible that the number 9 is even?" Clearly a causal explanation of the fact that Socrates has the property of being a non-number and that the number 9 has the property of being non-even is neither possible nor appropriate. But it is *logically* impossible that Socrates is a number and that the number 9 is even; and, in general, when and only when it is *logically* impossible that X possesses P, there is no question of providing a causal explanation of the fact that X possesses not-P. But, again, when X is God and P is God's nonexistence, it is a necessary truth that if God exists, then it is not possible (even in principle) to provide a true causal explanation of the fact that he exists. So it follows from the fact that it is a necessary truth that if God exists, then his nonexistence is impossible that it is a necessary truth that if God exists, then his nonexistence stands to him as being a number stands to Socrates and being even stands to the number 9, i.e., God's nonexistence is *logically* impossible.

The reader will recall that I argued at the end of Chapter 2 that there might be a *contingent*, though uncaused, first cause, i.e., an uncaused cause whose nonexistence is logically possible. But I have not denied that here. What I have claimed, rather, is that if something's non-existence is *impossible*, then, if it is uncaused, it is non-contingent. And it is surely very unlikely that, given that the first cause is both contingent and uncaused, its non-existence is impossible. Its non-existence is not *physically* impossible. For *ex hypothesi* no prior conditions constrain it to exist, i.e., there are no antecedent conditions such that, in conjunction with a scientific law, they entail that the first cause exists. And since it is contingent, its non-existence is not logically impossible. But physical and logical impossibility are the only kinds of impossibility there are (given that we construe logical impossibility as broadly logical impossibility, in Plantinga's sense). So if there was in fact a contingent and uncaused first event, its non-existence was *not* impossible.

II. A simpler argument for the claim that it is a necessary truth that if God exists, then his non-existence is logically impossible is as follows:

(1) The concept of God is such that the sentence "If God exists, then his non-existence is impossible" expresses a (necessary) truth.

Moreover,

(2) the concept of God is such that there is no accepted sense of 'impossible' in which that sentence expresses a falsehood. (Medieval philosophers, who did not draw an explicit distinction between physical and logical impossibility, were nonetheless rightly not hesitant to affirm that the concept of God is such that if God exists, then his non-existence is impossible.)

But

(3) one accepted sense of 'impossible' is (nowadays) 'logically impossible'.

So

(4) the concept of God is such that it is a necessary truth that if God exists, then his non-existence is logically impossible.

5.3. There are two interpretations of sentences of the form, "It is logically impossible for X to be not-P": (1) "X is P in every possible world in which X exists"; (2) "X is P in every possible world *simpliciter*." Call (1) 'the weak sense ' and (2) 'the strong sense'; and let us say that when it is logically impossible in the strong sense for X to be not-P, it is 'SS logically impossible' for X to be not-P and 'SS logically necessary' for X to be P.

Now the defender of the modal argument (call it 'M'), with which this chapter begins, needs to maintain that it is a necessary truth that if God exists, then his non-existence is SS logically impossible. For suppose that if God exists, then his non-existence is only weakly logically impossible. Then premiss (c) of M should be taken to mean that in W any possible world in which God exists is a world in which God exists. And *this* proposition is clearly not strong enough to entail, in conjunction with (d), that God exists in the actual world.

But in fact there is an argument for the conclusion that it is a necessary truth that if God exists, then his non-existence is SS logically impossible:

(1)   The concept of God is such that the sentence, "If God exists, then his non-existence is logically impossible", expresses a (necessary) truth. (This was demonstrated in 5.2.)

Moreover,

(2)   the concept of God is such that there is no kind, K, of logical impossibility which is such that, if we interpret that sentence as referring to K, then it expresses a falsehood.

But

(3)   one kind of logical impossibility is SS impossibility.

So

(4)   the concept of God is such that it is a necessary truth that if God exists, then his non-existence is SS logically impossible, i.e., his existence is SS necessary.

The proof of (2) is as follows: It is plainly partly because of the concept of God, a maximally great being, that "If God exists, then his non-existence is logically impossible" expresses a (necessary) truth. But suppose that the envisaged sentence (call it 'Q') were false, when construed as referring to SS logical impossibility, and true only when taken to refer to 'weak sense' logical impossibility, i.e., only when taken to mean "If God exists, then any possible world in which he exists is a world in which he exists". Call this latter sentence, 'Q''. Q' expresses only a vacuous truth, i.e., it would continue to express a true proposition, no matter what name, noun or definite description we might substitute for 'God'. Hence, it is not because of the concept of (precisely) *God* that Q' expresses a truth. But, again, part of the explanation of the fact that Q expresses a truth is that it is about (precisely) God. Hence, Q does not mean the same as Q'. So Q is true when the logical impossibility of which it speaks is SS logical impossibility. (I shall discuss a very similar argument at greater length in Chapter 7.)

5.4. Thus far, I have established that if God exists, then he exists with SS logical necessity and, hence, that, given that he exists in one possible world, then he exists in the actual world. But here the following questions arise: Even granting that we know that God is possible and, hence, that he exists in every possible world, how do we know that God is omnipotent, omniscient and perfectly good in every possible world and, hence, in the actual world? How do we know that God is not only SS necessarily existent, but that he is SS necessarily existent *qua* God, i.e., that he is SS necessarily omnipotent, omniscient and perfectly good? In what follows, I shall answer this question.

We have seen that it is a necessary truth that if God (i.e., the person who can truly be called 'God' when he is omnipotent, omniscient and perfectly good[2]) exists, then his non-existence is SS logically impossible. And arguments which are similar to the ones which established that proposition will also establish that it is a necessary truth that if God exists, then it is logically impossible for him to fail to be omnipotent:

I.′ The concept of God (a maximally great being) is such that it is a necessary truth that if God exists, then it is impossible in *some* sense for him to fail to be omnipotent. But there can be no true causal explanation of how God came to be omnipotent, since (a) the concept of God is such that it is a necessary truth that if God exists, then he is not causally dependent on any other being with respect to such properties as omnipotence, and (b) no non-omnipotent being could cause himself to be omnipotent. For having the power to *become* omnipotent is *eo ipso* having the power to do everything which an omnipotent being can do, and, hence, it is equivalent to being omnipotent. It follows that it is a necessary truth that if God exists, then it is *logically* (rather than physically) impossible for him not to be omnipotent. (Again if it is impossible for X not to have P, and no causal explanation of that fact is even in principle possible, then it is *logically* impossible for X not to have P.)

But now that argument, in conjunction with my argument that if God exists, then he exists in all possible worlds, shows that if God exists, then he is omnipotent in the actual world. For the present argument establishes that if God exists, then he is omnipotent in every possible world in which he exists, and, in conjunction with the proposition that if God exists, then he exists in every possible world, the former proposition entails that if God exists, then he is omnipotent in every possible world, including the actual one. (It is of note that we cannot directly justify this conclusion on the ground that "If God exists, then he is omnipotent in every possible world in which he exists" is, like "If God exists, then he exists in every possible world in which he exists", trivially true. For almost everything is such that it is *false* that any possible world in which it exists is a world in which it is omnipotent.)

II.′ A simpler argument for the same conclusion is as follows:

(1)   The concept of God is such that the sentence "If God exists, then it is impossible for him to be non-omnipotent" expresses a (necessary) truth.

Moreover,

(2)   the concept of God is such that there is no accepted sense of 'impossible' in which that sentence expresses a falsehood.

But

(3)   one accepted sense of 'impossible' is 'logically impossible'.

So

(4)   the concept of God is such that if God exists, then it is logically impossible for him to be non-omnipotent, i.e., if God exists, then any possible world in which he exists is a world in which he is omnipotent.

But

(5)   if God exists, then he exists in every possible world, including the actual one. (This was established in 5.2 and 5.3.)

Hence

(6)   if God exists, then he is omnipotent in every possible world, including the actual one.

5.5. I′ and II′ establish in effect that if God exists, then he possesses his omnipotence with SS logical necessity, i.e., in every possible world, including the actual one. It follows that, given God's existence, it is true, not only that God cannot diminish his power and continue to be truly called 'God' (so long as 'God' does not change its meaning), but that God cannot diminish his power *simpliciter*, as the following will demonstrate: Suppose that there is an individual, I, of whom a certain name, 'N', is true, and that 'N' analytically entails the possession of a certain property, P. And suppose further that I exists in possible worlds in which he does not have P. Then, even though 'N' is not true of him in those worlds, I does exist there, and, hence, in possible worlds in which 'N' *is* true of I, the fact that this is so does not entail that it is not logically possible for I to bring it about that he does *not* have P and, hence, that 'N' is not true of him. However, if I has P in *every* possible world, then it is *not* possible for I to bring it about that he does not have P and, in that way, bring it about that 'N' is not true of him.

The relevance of this to God's SS necessary omnipotence is obvious: If the individual, who is truly named by 'God' in some possible worlds, exists in possible worlds in which he is non-omnipotent and, hence, *not* truly named by 'God' (since 'God' analytically entails 'omnipotence'), then the mere fact that he is omnipotent and truly named by 'God' in some possible worlds does not entail that it is not logically possible for him to divest himself of his omnipotence. Rather, all that follows is that he cannot do the latter while continuing to be truly named by 'God'. However, if there is no possible world in which God is not omnipotent, then there is no possible world in which it is logically possible for God to divest himself of his omnipotence. But even an omnipotent being does not have the power to do what is not logically possible. It follows that God does not have the power to diminish his power *simpliciter*.[3]

Now I shall subsequently argue that if God exists, then he is omniscient and perfectly morally good in all possible worlds, i.e., that God is SS necessarily omniscient and morally good. And the latter entails that if God exists, then he cannot restrict his knowledge or engage in wrongdoing, not just in the sense that, were he to do those things, then 'God' would no longer truly apply to him, but *simpliciter*. (For simplicity, I shall henceforth omit this qualifier.) Moreover, since it is true that if God exists, then he is SS necessarily existent, it follows that if God exists, then he cannot make himself non-existent. Hence, if God exists, his power is restricted in ways other than the obvious ones (his not being able to make a square circle and the like). And this consideration gives rise to the following questions: What does God's omnipotence really amount to? Isn't it compatible with God's being as puny as Satan might desire?

But a theistic response to these questions is available. Since the concept of God is the concept of a maximally great being, it is a necessary truth that if God exists, then his power is such that, for any statement to the effect that God performs a certain action, A, which is not self-evidently false, there is a *prima facie* case for the thesis that God has the power to make it true, i.e., it is up to the critic of this latter claim to prove that it is false. And I think that reflection will show that this onus can only be very rarely shouldered. We can know that there are at least the following things which God cannot do: (1) diminish his power; (2) restrict his knowledge; (3) make himself non-existent; (4) engage in moral wrongdoing; (5) perform logically impossible actions like making a square circle, the impossibility of which does not arise from God's possessing some property with SS necessity. Moreover, Chapter 1, plus my subsequent demonstration in Chapter 6 that God is essentially disembodied, give us reason to believe that God cannot directly cause non-miraculous events in nature. However, there is no reason to believe that if God exists, then there are further limitations on his power. In particular, the merely *speculative* claim that God cannot perform some action, A, because he *may* possess some property, P, with SS necessity is an unacceptable refusal to shoulder the burden of *proving* that God has P with SS necessity.

5.6. Argument I of 5.2 affirms that God could not have caused himself to exist. And argument I' of 5.4 asserts that God could not have caused himself to be omnipotent. However, an analogous argument that if God exists, then he possesses his moral goodness with logical necessity is not available. For it is far from clear why God, if he exists, could not be the cause of his own moral goodness. But if there is no reason to think that if God exists, then he possesses his moral goodness with logical necessity, then even if God exists, there may well be possible worlds in which God (or, rather, the person who is truly called 'God' if he is good, omnipotent and omniscient) is evil. And, if that is so, then we have no way of knowing that if God exists, then he is good in the actual world.

However, though no analogue of I and I' is available here, there is an analogue of II and II':

II.''

(1)   The concept of God is such that the sentence "If God exists, then it is impossible for him not to be morally good" expresses a (necessary) truth.

Moreover,

(2)   the concept of God is such that there is no accepted sense of 'impossible' in which that sentence expresses a falsehood.

But

(3)   one accepted sense of 'impossible' is 'logically impossible'.

Hence

(4)   the concept of God is such that it is a necessary truth that if God exists, then it is logically impossible for him not to be morally good, i.e., if God exists, then any possible world in which he exists is a world in which he is morally good.

But

(5)   if God exists, then he exists in every possible world, including the actual one. (This was demonstrated in 5.2 and 5.3.)

So

(6)   if God exists, then he is morally good in every possible world, including the actual one.

The conclusion of this argument is that if God exists, then he is SS necessarily morally good. And, as I pointed out in the preceding section, if it really is the case that if God exists, then he is SS necessarily morally good, then if he exists, he is not able to do other than what is morally right – *simpliciter*, rather than in the sense that he is not able to do other than what is morally right, while retaining all his defining characteristics. Now, since a person *freely* performs a morally right action only if he is able to do otherwise, if it really is true that if God exists, then he is SS necessarily morally good, then God is not a free moral agent. And it may look as though being a free moral agent is a perfection and, hence, a property which a maximally great being would possess. But this, I think, is mere appearance.

Being a free moral agent entails having a capacity for wrongdoing. So the former is a perfection only if being able to do wrong is a perfection; and that is extremely doubtful.[4]

It is very plausible that no one is able to perform a given action, X, unless he has *some inclination* to do X. Thus, since I have no inclination at all, e.g., to strangle my youngest daughter (and would not have any inclination to do it unless, perhaps, there were some highly unusual, overriding *prima facie* obligation), it is very unlikely that I am (mentally as well as physically) able to strangle her. Now my having the envisaged inclination would surely be a grave defect in me. And, since a necessary condition of my being able to strangle my youngest daughter is my having that inclination, it is surely very unlikely that my being able to strangle her would be a perfection of mine. Moreover, there appears to be no reason why we should not generalize here and conclude that having a capacity for wrongdoing of *any* kind is never a perfection. My example is of a capacity for extremely *grave* wrongdoing. But the fact that *it* is very plainly *not* a perfection makes it seem doubtful enough that a capacity for *any* kind of wrongdoing is a perfection so that II′′ is a plausible argument.

I do not want to deny that *human beings* are free moral agents. If the central argument of the preceding chapter is correct, then a supernatural being guarantees that malicious people who cause great harm will be punished. And that would be an injustice if wrongdoers (or, rather, people who are wrongdoers if they are able to do otherwise) were unable to do other than what they do. But it does not follow from the fact that it is better than not that people who exercise their capacity for wrongdoing have a capacity for refraining from doing so, that it is better than not that beings who exercise their capacity for virtuous conduct have a capacity for vicious conduct as well.

But why, then, did God give us the ability to do wrong? The most plausible answer, in view of Chapter 1, is that this ability is the product of evolutionary processes which God could change only at the cost of preventing E from coming about.

5.7. Finally, an argument which is similar to II, II′, and II′′ will show that if God exists, then he is omniscient in the actual world:

II.′′′

(1)   The concept of God is such that the sentence "If God exists, then it is impossible for him not to be omniscient" expresses a (necessary) truth.

Moreover

(2)   the concept of God is such that there is no accepted sense of 'impossible' in which that sentence expresses a falsehood.

But

(3)   one accepted sense of 'impossible' is 'logically impossible'.

Hence

(4)   the concept of God is such that if God exists, then it is logically impossible for him to fail to be omniscient, i.e., if God exists, then any possible world in which God exists is a world in which he is omniscient.

But

(5)   if God exists, then he exists in every possible world and, hence, in the actual world. (This was demonstrated in 5.2 and 5.3.)

So

(6)   if God exists, then he is omniscient in every possible world, including the actual one.

CHAPTER 6

IS GOD'S EXISTENCE LOGICALLY POSSIBLE?

6.1. Let us turn now to a discussion of *M*'s premiss (b), which asserts in effect that God's existence is logically possible. Norman Malcolm has maintained that, though it is legitimate to expect proponents of *M*-like arguments to *defend* the claim that God is logically possible (call it 'GLP') against plausible criticisms, there is no onus of proof on the modal arguer to give a positive demonstration of GLP.[1] And it looks, at least to the casual observer,[2] as if Malcolm is right. It looks as if, given that something, *X*, does not appear on its face to be logically impossible, then there is an onus on anyone who affirms that *X* is logically impossible to prove his claim. Suppose that I maintain that, e.g., Ronald Reagan's going to Jupiter in a space ship is logically possible. Then it is clearly not up to me to prove that I am right. Rather, it is up to anyone who denies my claim to show that I am wrong. The claim that *X exists* (occurs or obtains) is not, of course, similar in this respect to logical possibility claims. If I assert, not that it is logically possible for Ronald Reagan to go to Jupiter, but that in fact he has gone there, then it is up to me to provide evidence for my claim. (First person reports on states of consciousness are an exception.) It follows that if Malcolm is right about GLP, then, in inferring God's existence from that proposition and the other premisses of *M*, we pass from the more certain to (what would be, in the absence of *M*-like arguments) the less certain, i.e., since GLP is, like the other premisses of *M*, epistemically prior to the proposition that God exists, *M* is not redundant.[3]

6.2. But now it may well look as though the critic of GLP *can* shoulder the burden of showing that it is false. Consider, for example, the following parody:

Let 'super-centaur' = Df "a centaur which is SS necessarily existent". It follows that:

(1)   it is true in every possible world that if a super-centaur exists there, then it is SS necessarily existent there.

And

(2)   there is a possible world in which a super-centaur exists.

Hence

(3)   it is true in that world that a super-centaur is SS necessarily existent there.

But

(4)   what is necessarily existent in one possible world is necessarily existent in the actual world. (See my 5.1 argument that what is logically impossible in one possible world is logically impossible in the actual world.)

So

(5)   a super-centaur exists in the actual world.

Needless to say, this 'proof' can be converted into a 'proof' of the existence of a mind-boggling myriad of super-centaurs (e.g., four-legged ones, five-legged ones, etc.) and of the existence of their next of kin, super-unicorns, super-dragons, etc. Hence, in the interest of an acceptably modest ontology, it behooves us to reject the envisaged arguments. And the only reasonable way of doing that is to reject the claim that super-centaurs and the like are logically possible. But now God, like super-centaurs (etc.), is necessarily such that if he exists, then he is SS necessarily existent. And it may well look as if it follows that, in the absence of a proof of God's logical possibility, it would be irrationally arbitrary to deny that super-centaurs (etc.) are logically possible, while refusing to deny that God is.

But this is mere appearance. There is a relevant distinction between God, on the one hand, and super-centaurs (etc.) on the other, namely, that (a) the concept of God is the concept of a maximally great being and (b) it is demonstrable that only one such being is possible and, hence, existent, while, as we have seen, the contemplated Gaunilo-type entities have no such desirable limitation. The point is that we cannot avoid commitment to a bloated ontology except by denying the possibility of super-centaurs and the like, while, as I shall now show, it is false that ontological modesty also dictates denying the possibility of God.

We saw in the last chapter that it is a necessary truth that if God exists, then he possesses omnipotence with SS necessity. Now omnipotence is (as befits a maximally great being) maximal power, i.e., power so great that it is logically impossible for anyone to have more power. But not only does the concept of maximal greatness entail maximal power in that sense; it also entails absolutely preeminent power, i.e., power so great that is is logically impossible for any other individual to possess *as much* power. The reason for this is as follows: A maximally great being must be an absolutely preeminently great being, i.e., a being so great that it is logically impossible for any other individual to have *as much* greatness. Otherwise, a still greater being would be possible, namely, one who *is* absolutely preeminently great. (Or, at any rate, this is true, given – what I hope to render plausible – that a maximally great, and, hence, absolutely preeminently great, being is logically possible.) But what holds true for maximal greatness *per se* holds true for maximal-greatness-making properties. It follows that any maximally great being would be maximally powerful in the strongest sense, i.e., he would be absolutely preeminently powerful.[4] And, since he would be maximally powerful in every possible world (this was demonstrated in the last chapter), he would be absolutely preeminently powerful in every possible world.

Now no more than one such being is logically possible. For there is no possible world in which there are two or more absolutely preeminently powerful beings. It follows that, given that *any* maximally great being is logically possible, then only *one* maximally great being is logically possible (namely, God, the logically possible one), and that, as a consequence, *M* establishes the existence of only one maximally great being, namely, God. Very similar arguments can be based on the fact that a maximally great being would be absolutely preeminently knowledgeable and absolutely preeminently good. However, similar considerations do *not* apply to super-centaurs (etc.) for there is no reason to think that being a super-centaur entails being absolutely preeminently anything. Hence, it is not irrationally arbitrary to deny (in the interests of a modest ontology) that super-centaurs are logically possible, while continuing to maintain that God is logically possible.

It may be objected at this point that, even though we have *more* reason to reject the logical possibility of super-centaurs and the like than to reject the logical possibility of God, the fact that the former beings are (best thought of as) logically impossible gives us *some* grounds for denying that *any* being, which is like them in being necessarily such that if it exists, then it exists with SS necessity, is logically possible. But this is very doubtful. For it is plausible that, e.g, the property of being three in number is such that it is SS necessarily existent, and, hence, is both logically possible and necessarily such that *if* it exists, then it is SS necessarily existent. And it would surely be unacceptable to deny this on the ground that super-centaurs and the like are not logically possible. So, *pace Gaunilo*, it will not do to maintain that just anything, which is necessarily such that if it exists, then it exists with SS necessity, must be logically impossible.

But now what about the concept of, say, a maximally great centaur? Doesn't being a maximally great centaur entail being SS necessarily absolutely preeminently powerful?[5] And, if so, how can *this* kind of Gaunilo-type entity, which is not subject to Ockam's razor, be discredited? One answer is that even if I cannot prove that such a being is not logically possible, I *have* demonstrated that only *one* maximally great (and, hence, absolutely preeminently powerful) being (namely God) is logically possible and, hence, existent; so what follows from the envisaged parody is not that the universe is crowded with Gaunilo-type entities, but just that it *might* be that the logically possible and, hence, existent maximally, great being is a maximally great centaur, who is God.

But, even if we can accept that possibility, Gaunilo remains troublesome. For consider the following argument: "Let 'Extra-super-Gaunilo-type entity' = Df 'an SS necessarily existent and SS necessarily *absolutely preeminently powerful* Gaunilo-type entity, who is, in other respects, quite unexceptional and, hence, is distinct from God'. Then it is a necessary truth that if such a being exists in any possible world, then it exists in *every* possible world, including the actual one, i.e, if it is possible, then it exists. Now, given its definition, we cannot claim that, if it is possible, and, hence, existent, then it is God. And if we wish (as we should) to deny the logical possibility of this being, we cannot do so on the ground that otherwise a myriad of such beings must exist. For, as we have seen, only one SS absolutely preeminently powerful being is logically possible. Hence, it would be irrationally arbitrary to deny the logical possibility of this being while continuing to affirm God's logical possibility. Similar considerations apply to 'Super-special-Gaunilo-type entity', defined as '*the one and only* Gaunilo-type entity who exists with SS necessity but is unexceptional in other respects'."

One obvious reply to this criticism is that there remains a relevant distinction between God and these latest monstrosities, namely that the latter beings are sufficiently *similar* to *ordinary* super-centaurs and the like so that the fact that we have good reason to deny the logical possibility of ordinary super-centaurs (etc.) casts doubt on the claim that the former beings are logically possible; while God (like the property of being three in number) is *not* sufficiently similar to super-centaurs and the like so that *his* logical possibility is, for the same reason, also in doubt.

But there is another reply to the contemplated criticism, namely, that it is demonstrable that Gaunilo-type entities, which are such that if they exist, then they are SS necessarily existent, do not *in fact* exist and (since if they are logically possible, then they do exist) are also not logically possible. For Gaunilo-type entities (with an exception to be presently noted) are beings which have physical bodies of certain kinds (e.g., the body of a centaur). And it can be demonstrated that physical bodies are contingent beings.

In St. Anselm's *Reply to Gaunilo*, Chapter 1, Anselm sets out the following argument:

Whatever at any place ... does not exist – even if it does exist some place ... can be conceived to exist nowhere. For ... what is not here, and is elsewhere, can be conceived to be nowhere just as it is not here ...[6].

Anselm goes on to draw the conclusion that God, whose non-existence he claims to be inconceivable, "exists as a whole everywhere"[7], i.e., that every place is a place in which God exists in his entirety. (Apparently Anselm thinks that if God had parts, (only) one of which occupied place P_1, another of which occupied place P_2, etc., then each part would be conceivably non-existent, since there are places which it does not occupy, and, hence, the whole which they compose would also be conceivably non-existent.) Actually, all that Anselm's argument warrants is the conclusion that if God's non-existence is, indeed, inconceivable, then, given that he exists, *either* he exists as a whole everywhere *or* he does not exist in space. For it follows from the fact that a being "can be conceived to exist nowhere" *either* that it can be conceived to be non-existent *or* that it can be conceived to be a non-spatial being. But, at any rate, the quote from Anselm provides the basis for the following proof (in which I shall substitute 'possible' for 'conceivable') that physical bodies are not SS necessarily existent:

(1)   If X does not exist at a given place, P, then it is possible that X does not exist at P.

But

(2)   if there is a place, P, such that it is possible that X does not exist at *that* place, then *every* place is such that it is possible

that X does not exist there, i.e., it is possible that X does not exist in space.

Hence

(3)   if it is necessarily true that if X exists, then it exists in space – i.e., if it is not possible that X exists and does *not* exist in space – then it is possible that X does not exist (*simpliciter*).

Now

(4)   it is necessarily true of physical bodies that if they exist, then they exist in space.

And

(5)   no physical body occupies all of space, i.e., any physical body is such that there are some places which it does not occupy.

So

(6)   no physical body exists with logical necessity.

Hence

(7)   Gaunilo-type entities do not exist.

But

(8)   if Gaunilo-type entities are logically possible, then they exist.

So

(9)   Gaunilo-type entities are not logically possible.

I said in Chapter 1 that it is demonstrable that God is essentially disembodied. The demonstration is simply this: since God is essentially a non-contingent being, and since all physical bodies are contingent, having a physical body is not a part of God's essence. (Hence, God *per se* cannot be a centaur or the like.)

However, the above argument does not lay Gaunilo *completely* to rest. For consider the following definition: Let 'Super-Demon' = Df "the one and only disembodied and SS necessarily existent person and one who hates everyone but himself". We cannot rule out the logical possibility of *this* being either on the ground that accepting his logical possibility entails multiplying entities beyond necessity or on the ground that it is demonstrable that all embodied beings are contingent. Moreover, Super-Demon is defined in such a way that if he is possible and, hence, existent, then God (who is also such that if he exists, then *he* is a disembodied and SS necessarily existent person) is *not* possible and, hence, not existent. Well, then, can we plausibly claim that Super-Demon is more like the other, *embodied* Gaunilo-type entities which we have considered than is God and, on that ground, maintain that it is less likely that Super-Demon is possible than that God is? One obvious similarity between Super-Demon and the other Gaunilo-type entities which I have discussed lies in the fact that their concepts are 'cooked up'. And, of course, the concept of God is not also artificial. (Norman Malcolm points out that "it has a place in the thinking and the lives of human beings"[8].) Still, a rational person could, I think, deny that this similarity is strong enough to warrant a high degree of confidence in the claim that God is more apt to be possible than Super-Demon.

6.3. A further criticism of GLP can be based on the fact (a) that a maximally great being would be SS necessarily good and (b) that such a being would be maximally powerful: "It was argued in effect in the preceding section that if a putatively maximally powerful being, Z_1, were not absolutely preeminently powerful, then another, more powerful being, Z_2, would be possible, namely, one that has as much power as Z_1, plus further power, in virtue of which Z_2, unlike Z_1, is absolutely preeminently powerful. But now an analogous argument shows that no being who is SS necessarily good and, hence, unable, e.g., wrongfully to harm a given individual, I, can be maximally powerful: 'If a putatively maximally powerful being, Z_1, cannot wrongfully harm I, then another being, Z_2, who has as much power as Z_1 plus the power wrongfully to harm I, is possible, and, hence, Z_1 is not in fact maximally powerful.' It follows that, since maximal greatness entails both SS necessary goodness and maximal power, the concept of a maximally great being is logically incoherent."

So goes the criticism. Very similar criticisms can be based on the fact that a maximally great being would be both maximally powerful and (1) SS necessarily powerful and, hence, unable to diminish his power, (2) SS necessarily omniscient and, therefore, unable to diminish his knowledge, and (3) SS necessarily existent and, hence, unable to destroy himself. But, for simplicity, let us examine just the argument from SS necessary goodness. Similar considerations apply in an obvious way to the other criticisms. The essence of the former criticism is that we have as much reason to think that a being who cannot wrongfully harm I is not maximally powerful as we have to hold that a being who is not absolutely preeminently powerful is not maximally powerful. But the proponent of M need not accept that conclusion. He can hold instead that, though there is a *prima facie* case on behalf of the thesis that any maximally powerful being can wrongfully harm I, this can be overthrown by the consideration that any maximally great, and, hence, maximally powerful, being would be SS necessarily good and, hence, unable wrongfully to harm I. And he can add the further claim that we *cannot* thus overthrow the *prima facie* case for the thesis that maximal greatness, and, hence, power, entail absolutely preeminent greatness and, hence, power.

My central point here can be put this way: the fact that a maximally great being would be both SS necessarily good and maximally powerful can be construed in two mutually exclusive ways, namely, (a) it entails that the concept of maximal greatness is logically incoherent or (b) it entails that the *prima facie* case on behalf of the thesis that a maximally great, and, hence, powerful, being would have the power wrongfully to harm I can be overthrown by the consideration that a maximally great, and, hence, powerful, being would be SS necessarily good, and, hence, unable wrongfully to harm I. Now I think that there is nothing epistemically *wrong* with accepting alternative (b) rather than (a). But, on the other hand, I think it is clear that (a) is equally acceptable, in the absence of a plausible argument that (1) God (a maximally great being) is logically possible and, hence, (2) the concept of maximal greatness is not logically incoherent.

6.4. There are two more criticisms of GLP which we need to consider. The first one is as follows: "We have seen that if God exists, then he is SS necessarily omnipotent, good and omniscient. But it follows from that characterization of God, in conjunction with the claim that God is logically possible, and, hence, exists, that some propositions, which appear to be possibly true, are in fact necessarily false, viz., (a) some facts are unknown; (b) every person is morally imperfect; (c) no one has any significant power. If God is logically possible and, hence, exists, then, since God exists in every possible world, and is omniscient, omnipotent and perfectly morally good in every world in which he exists, then (1) an omniscient being exists in every possible world, and, hence, (a) is necessarily false; (2) a perfectly good person exists in every possible world, and, hence, (b) is necessarily false; and (3) an omnipotent being exists in every possible world and, hence, (c) is necessarily false.[9] But, again, (a), (b), and (c) do not appear to be necessary falsehoods. Hence, we have reason to deny that God is logically possible."[10]

One reply to this objection is just that, since the proposition that God exists *also* does not appear on its face to be necessarily false, it is as likely not to be necessarily false as (a), (b), and (c); and, hence, it is not *irrational* for the theist to opt for the logical possibility of God, rather than for the contingency of (a), (b), and (c). Plainly, it would be a mistake to argue here that the proposition that God exists is only *one* proposition which is, as it were, epistemically outnumbered by (a), (b), and (c). For the proposition that God exists can be analyzed into at least three propositions, viz., "An omniscient being exists", "An omnipotent being exists" and "A perfectly good being exists". But isn't it true that opting for GLP, rather than for the contingency of (a), (b), and (c) (call this latter alternative '*C*') is epistemically analogous to opting for the proposition that God exists, rather than for the proposition that he does not, when there is no evidence for either proposition, and, hence, no epistemic warrant for believing either of them? It is not clear that the answer is "Yes". No doubt, the fact that we have as much reason to believe C as we do to believe GLP (barring a proof of the latter) diminishes our epistemic warrant for believing GLP. But it is also the case that the fact that we have as much reason to believe GLP as we do to believe C diminishes our epistemic warrant for believing C. Now we have a choice between believing (1) that these facts diminish the credibility of both GLP and C to zero or (2) that, despite C, we have *some* warrant for believing GLP (and, of course, *vice versa*). And surely it would not be irrational for the theist to opt for (2) rather than (1).

But, while it would not be irrational for the theist to opt for (2 and) GLP, neither would it be irrational for the non-theist either to opt for (1) or to suspend judgement about the matter. Hence, if the proponent of M wants to change the mind of the non-theist, then he will want an argument that God is logically possible which is strong enough to offset the present (rather weak) argument that he is not, as well as the (rather weak) arguments considered in 6.2 and 6.3.

6.5. Moreover, there is another criticism which the proponent of M needs to consider: "We are not entitled to affirm of a given complex mathematical or logical formula, F, that F is possibly true even if we know of no proof that it is necessarily false. This is because F, if true, is necessarily true, and, hence, if it is possibly true, then it is (necessarily) true (given S5): the claim that F is possibly true is a very strong claim. But since it is necessarily true that if God exists, then he exists with SS necessity, and, since this proposition, when combined with the claim that God is logically possible, entails that God exists, the claim that God is logically possible is also too strong a claim to be left unsupported."

Now the present objection is right just to the extent that it affirms that there is an onus on the person who claims that F is possibly true to demonstrate that this is the case. But we need to ask here for the explanation of the fact that the claim that F is possibly true (call it 'C_1') differs in the envisaged respect from, e.g., the claim (call it 'C_2') that the proposition (call it 'F'') that Ronald Reagan goes to Jupiter in a space ship is possibly true. Is the explanation just that C_1 entails that F is in fact true, while C_2 does not entail that F' is in fact true? Surely this explanation is inadequate. If we were warranted in rejecting claims just on the ground that they entail 'strong' claims, then we would be warranted in rejecting, e.g., "Socrates is a man and all men are mortal".

Another, better explanation is that if we asserted that all F-like propositions are possibly true, then we would be committed to accepting a myriad of *false* propositions (as well as a myriad of true ones). But we need to ask why the envisaged method would have that result. And surely the correct answer, or, anyway, part of the correct answer, is that the claim that F-like propositions are possibly true is, in the absence of proof, ungrounded and unwarranted.

But now how can this be so if it is also true that the claim that F'-like propositions are possibly true is acceptable, even in the absence of proof? The answer is that there is a relevant, intrinsic difference between F and F', namely, that F''s not appearing on its face to be necessarily false is equivalent to its appearing on its face *not* to be necessarily false, while the same is not true of F (relative to us but not to an omniscient being). It follows that we would be unwarranted in claiming that F is possibly true, not because that entails that F is in fact true but because our claim would not be based on the fact that F appears not to be necessarily false. And, even if that answer were incorrect, there is another one with which we can replace it, viz., we have discovered by (painful) experience that we are apt to be mistaken about the truth, and, hence, the possible truth, of F-like propositions, but have no comparable reason for rejecting the possible truth of F'-like propositions.

Still, in the end, the present objection is not without some cogency. For the defender of GLP must claim at this point that the proposition that God exists belongs to the class of F'-like, rather than F-like, propositions. Now I think that the theist can rationally opt for the claim that the proposition that God exists is more like, e.g., the F'-like proposition that centaurs (or atoms) exist than it is like a complex mathematical or logical formula. But I also think that the non-theist can rationally reject that conclusion. If I am right, then if the proponent of M wishes to convince the non-theist that God exists, he needs at least a moderately plausible argument that God is logically possible. This conclusion is re-enforced by the further (not wholly implausible) criticisms of GLP in Sections 6.2, 6.3, and 6.4.

6.6. I want now to consider one such argument. It is an essentially simple argument, though as we shall see, it requires a relatively lengthy defense. The argument goes as follows:

(1)   It is not possible to experience (i.e., to seem to perceive) what is logically impossible.

(2)   Some people have experienced God.

Hence

(3)   God is logically possible.

I shall begin the critical examination which this argument obviously needs with a discussion of premiss (1). If someone reported that he had visually experienced a square circle, we would be justified in rejecting his report. Not only would we be justified in disbelieving that he had actually seen a square circle, we would be entirely warranted in rejecting the proposition that he had *seemed* to see one, for we know that there are no such things as hallucinations in which people seem to see square circles. And square circles are not unique in the envisaged respect. We know that no one can see, or even seem to see, e.g, an object which is both red and green all over, and we know that no one can hear, or even seem to hear, e.g., the sound of one hand clapping. Now what all these experiences have in common is that they would, if they occurred, be experiences of what is not logically possible. Hence, it is likely that what prevents these experiences from being such that they can occur is precisely that they are experiences of that nature. But then we can generalize: *No* experiences of what is logically impossible are themselves possible.

I do not wish to make the further claim that it is impossible to *believe* that something which is logically impossible exists or occurs or obtains.[11] (E.g., mathematical errors are a counter-example to that claim.) And someone may wish to argue here as follows: "A person's seeming to perceive X is the same thing as his believing, or being inclined to believe, that he veridically perceives X. But it is possible for a person to believe, or to be inclined to believe, that he veridically perceives X even when, since X is not logically possible, his veridical perception of X is itself not logically possible. It follows that it is possible to seem to perceive X even though X is not logically possible."

However, my objector is mistaken in claiming that seeming to perceive X can be adequately analyzed as believing that one veridically perceives X; for a person can have an hallucination which he knows full well to be an hallucination. Perhaps a person cannot suffer an hallucination of X without being *inclined* to believe that he veridically perceives X, but nonetheless, a person's seeming to perceive X cannot be adequately analyzed as his being inclined to believe that he veridically perceives X. For it might be true that I seem to see, e.g., a rat at place P, while being inclined to believe that what I really see there is an old shoe instead. But I could not seem to see a rat at place P while seeming to see an old shoe there instead.[12]

The defense of premiss (2) is simply that many rational and reflective people have sincerely reported having had experiences of God which are somewhat analogous to ordinary sense-experiences.[13] Moreover, rational and reflective people are normally rightly taken to be an authority – and, indeed, the best authority – on the content of their *ordinary* sense-experiences. So anyone who asserts that rational and reflective people are not authorities with respect to their putative God-experiences (i.e., do not know that it is *God*, rather than something else, that they seem to perceive) owes us an explanation of why that should be so. And it is very unlikely that such an explanation is available.

Here someone may say: "The criticisms of GLP which were

presented earlier in this chapter give us reason to believe that God's existence is not logically possible. Hence, if it really is the case that it is not possible to experience what is logically impossible, then we have a good reason for rejecting reports of God-experiences." Now if there were, say, merely five putative God-experiencers, then the envisaged objection might well be cogent. However, a large number of sane and sober people have reported having God-experiences, and have done so independently of one another.[14] So if the present objection is correct, then a large number of sane and sober people have independently confused a mere *belief* that they were having a God-experience with a God-experience *per se*. And, at least, with respect to very *vivid* God-experiences, this looks to be as unlikely as, say, a large number of people confusing a mere belief that they are seeming to see a tree with that seeming perception *per se*. If the arguments against GLP which are found in the earlier sections of this chapter were anything like conclusive, then we *would*, perhaps, have to swallow the contemplated epistemically bitter pill. But, as I have pointed out, none of those arguments does, in fact, provide us with a *very* strong reason for rejecting GLP.

Still, it may be objected that even if premiss (2) is true, it is not a strong enough claim for my purposes. Call the envisaged argument for God's possibility '*M'*'. Then the objection which I have in mind can be formulated as follows: "*M'* does not successfully establish that *M* is sound unless it is the case, not only that people have experienced God, but that they have experienced God *qua* SS necessary being.[15] For, as we have seen, *M*'s first premiss must be taken as affirming in effect that it is true in every possible world that if God exists there, then he exists with SS necessity there. So unless *M* is equivocal, its second premiss (the claim that there is a possible world in which God exists) means that there is a possible world in which God, *qua* SS necessary being, exists. Hence, *M'* requires, not just the truth of the claim that some people have experienced God, but the truth of the stronger claim that some people have experienced God *qua* SS necessary being. And it is far from clear how *that* can be established."

But *is* it the case that M' fails to support M unless it can be shown that God-experiencers seem to perceive God *qua* SS necessarily existent? The following considerations support a negative answer to this question: There is no more doubt that 'God' (and its synonyms), as used by most members of the Judeo-Christian tradition, means 'maximally great being' (and its synonyms) than that 'square' means 'equilateral rectangle' in ordinary English. Hence, it would be as surprising if few or none of the many people, who know what 'God' (and/or its synonyms) mean, and what 'experience' (and/or its synonyms) means, and who have sincerely reported experiencing God, had experienced God *qua* maximally great, as it would be if thousands of people, who know what 'square' means, and what 'experience' means, had sincerely reported experiencing squares, but had not experienced squares *qua* equilateral rectangles. Now I do not wish to insist here that in experiencing a maximally great being, people have also experienced an SS necessary being. SS necessary existence is entailed by maximal greatness, but it seems unlikely that whenever a person experiences something, X, as having some property, P, and having P entails having some further property, Q, then he experiences X *qua* having Q. Thus being the Empire State Building entails being either the Empire State Building or Hamlet or a billion-sided figure, but it is surely implausible that people experience the Empire State Building *qua* having this disjunctive property when they experience the Empire State Building *qua* Empire State Building. Still, if it is logically possible for X to have property P, and being P entails being Q, then it is logically possible for X to be Q. It follows that if (as seems highly likely) people experience God *qua* maximally great being, then, since God *qua* maximally great being is logically possible and being maximally great entails being SS necessary, God *qua* SS necessary being is also logically possible.

Still another criticism of M' needs discussing: "It is well known that some people have reported that they have had experiences of reality *qua* non-personal whole, in which there are no distinct individuals. And if it is true that such experiences (call them '*X*-experiences') have occurred, then, since people can only experience what is logically possible, it is logically possible that there are no persons. But now if God is logically possible, then *M* is sound, and if *M* is sound, then God exists with SS necessity. And, since it is a necessary truth that if God exists, then he is maximally great and also a necessary truth that any maximally great being would be SS necessarily a person, it follows that if God is logically possible, then it is a necessary truth that at least one person exists with SS necessity. But it follows from the latter that it is *not* logically possible that there are no persons. Hence, if God is logically possible, then *X*-experiences have not occurred. But if God-experiences have occurred, then God is logically possible. So if God-experiences have occurred, then *X*-experiences have not, and, hence, if *X*-experiences have occurred, then God-experiences have not. Now there is no more reason to trust reports of God-experiences than to trust reports of *X*-experiences. It follows that reports of *X*-experiences give us reason to hold that reports of God-experiences are mistaken."

One reply to this objection is that, since reports of God-experiences discredit reports of *X*-experiences for the same reason that the latter reports discredit the former ones (namely, that only the members of one of the two kinds of reports can be true), reports of *X*-experiences do not conclusively override reports of God-experiences. But there is a second, stronger reply: Suppose that you say: "While I was asleep and dreaming, I seemed to see everyone who was at Jones's party last night, but I didn't seem to see you there". Then if I respond by saying: "But in fact I was one of the people at Jones's party last night. Indeed I was there all evening", I shall be contradicting you: you did not seem to see *everyone* at Jones's party if *I* was at Jones's party and you did not seem to see *me*. (This fact is compatible with the proposition that might well be expressed by "In my dream, I saw (or seemed to see) everyone who was at Jones's party last night, but I didn't see (or seem to see) you there"; for (1) it is natural to interpret this sentence as meaning "While asleep and dreaming, I *believed* that I saw (or seemed to see) everyone who was at Jones's party last night, but I didn't see (or seem to see) you there", (and (2) (a) as we have seen, seeming to see is not the same as *believing* that one sees, and, of course, (b) neither is it the same as *believing* that one seems to see.) Analogously, if someone says that he has seemed to perceive everything there is and that his experience did not include an experience of persons, then, if in fact there *are* persons, he says something false. It follows that reports of X-experiences are false unless there are in fact no persons. And surely the latter is highly unlikely.

A similar reply to the following criticism is available: "Some people have reported experiencing 'the absence of God' in a sense of those words in which they entail God's non-existence. And if those experiences have occurred, then God's non-existence is possible. But if God is logically possible, and, hence, exists, then God's non-existence is not logically possible and, therefore, absence-of-God-experiences have *not* occurred. So reports of such experiences cast doubt on reports of God-experiences." The reply is that in order to experience 'the absence of God', in the sense in which that entails God's non-existence, one would have to experience all of reality and fail to experience God. But if God exists, then a person who claims to have experienced *all* of reality and not to have experienced God is simply mistaken, just as you are mistaken in case I was at Jones's party last night, and you claim that you seemed to see (as opposed to believed that you saw) everyone at Jones's party, but did not seem to see me there. It follows that a person's claim to have experienced the absence of God (in the requisite sense) *presupposes* that God does not exist: one is not justified in making that claim unless he knows that God does not exist. So, in the context of a criticism of M (*via* a criticism of M'), the envisaged claim is question-begging.

A final objection is that God-experiences are sufficiently out of the ordinary so that it does not follow from the fact that premiss (1) of

M' is true of normal sense-experiences that it is true of God-experiences as well. The answer is that we know,[16] not just that ordinary sense-experiences cannot be experiences of logically impossible things, but that any kind of experience (so long as the word 'experience' truly applies to it) is such that it cannot be an experience of what is logically impossible. The proof of this is simply that if someone claimed to have had an experience of God to which the more detailed description "an experience of God's being red and green all over" or "an experience of God's making the sound of one hand clapping" or "an experience of God's being both a person and not a person", or "an experience of God's being both maximally great and not maximally great", etc., was applicable, then reflective people would not respond by saying that since God-experiences are out of the ordinary, it may well be that these more specific descriptions do in fact apply. We know (upon reflection) that no one can seem to perceive, e.g., the sound of one hand clapping even if that is claimed to be part of an experience of God. (One can, of course, *believe* that he has heard that sound, but, once again, experiences are not beliefs.)

It must, of course, be acknowledged that mystics have typically reported experiencing their identity with God. And it is logically possible for an individual, e.g., Clement Dore, to be identical with God only if it is logically possible that I am SS necessarily existent, etc. But this latter entails that I am indeed God. So it is logically possible for me to be identical with God only if I am God; and since the latter is wildly false, it is not logically possible for me (St. Theresa, Meister Eckhart, etc.) to be identical with God. But we should not draw the conclusion that the reports of mystics discredit my central thesis. If *I* were sincerely to report having experienced a square circle you would surely conclude that *I* mistakenly *believed* that *I* had experienced a square circle, not that *I* had literally seemed to perceive one (in the way that I now literally seem to perceive, say, my hand). And if someone sincerely reported experiencing God as being both God and not God or as being both circular and square (etc.), we would surely draw the conclusion that the report was based on a mistaken belief that its author literally seemed to perceive a violation of the principle of noncontradiction or a square circle (etc.). Hence, to be consistent, we ought to treat the mystic's claim to have experienced her identity with God in the same way, namely, by responding that, though the mystic may well have experienced God, she merely *believed* that she had experienced her *identity* with God, perhaps because some feature of her experience was easily misidentified as union with God.[17] (Indeed, I am told that St. Theresa claimed, not that she experienced herself being identical with God, but that her experience was *like* an experience of union with God.) A good candidate for the envisaged, misleading feature is absorption with the content of the experience to such an extent that one forgets completely about one's self and its problems.

In sum, then, we may conclude that there is reason to hold that God's existence is after all logically possible. It is of note that a similar defense of the logical possibility of Gaunilo-type entities, e.g., super-centaurs and Super-Demon, is not available. For it is highly unlikely that anyone has ever experienced such beings – or, at any rate, experienced them *qua* having some property which entails SS necessary existence.

CHAPTER 7

DESCARTES'S MEDITATION V ARGUMENT

7.1. In Meditation V, Descartes argues that "there is not any less repugnance to our conceiving a God (that is, a Being supremely perfect) to whom existence is lacking (that is to say, to whom a certain perfection is lacking), than to conceive of a mountain which has no valley". And he draws the conclusion that "existence is inseparable from Him, and hence that He really exists".[1]

One interpretation of Descartes's argument can be expressed thusly:

(1)   God is a supremely perfect being.

(2)   Existence is a perfection.

So

(3)   existence is inseparable from God, i.e., God really exists.

Let us begin by examining premiss (2). Existence is not *per se* a perfection; it was not a perfection relative to, e.g., Hitler. So (2) needs to be qualified in some such way as by expanding it to read "Existence is a perfection *relative to God*". I shall have more to say about that qualification shortly. But, even given its acceptability, there is another problem. Nothing can be a perfection relative to a given individual unless it is a property of that individual. And, since Kant, it has been widely held that existence is not a property of things and, hence, that (2) is false.

Now the Frege-Russell analysis of sentences of the form '*X*'s exist' appears to entail that existence is not a property and to make clear precisely what that claim means. On the Frege-Russell analysis, e.g., "Cows exist" means the same as "Some things have the property of being a cow". If this is correct, then "Cows exist" does not attribute the property of existence to cows but rather the property of being a cow to some things. However, though the Frege-Russell analysis looks plausible with respect to such sentences as "Cows exist", it looks quite implausible with respect to existential sentences in which the subject term is a proper name, e.g., "Ronald Reagan exists". On the Frege-Russell analysis, this sentence means the same as "Some thing has the property of being Ronald Reagan"; but it is highly unlikely that there *is* such a property as being Ronald Reagan, i.e., it is highly unlikely that proper names like 'Ronald Reagan' are descriptive terms. The reason is simply that it looks very much as though any sentence of the form "Ronald Reagan is P", where P is some non-vacuous predicate, expresses a contingent truth. (The sentence, e.g., "Ronald Reagan is a non-number" is an exception. 'Non-number' is not (quite) vacuous, since it is false of numbers. But "Ronald Reagan is a non-number" expresses a *de re*, not a *de dicto*, necessary truth: 'Ronald Reagan' plainly does not analytically entail 'non-number', i.e., it does not have that predicate as descriptive content.)

Here someone may propose that "Ronald Reagan exists" means "Some thing is Ronald Reagan", where the 'is' is the 'is' of identity rather than of predication. But the envisaged analysans is equivalent in meaning to "Ronald Reagan is such that some thing is identical with him"; and this latter sentence ascribes to Ronald Reagan the property of being identical with some thing. It follows that the present proposal is equivalent to the thesis that the property of existence can be plausibly explicated as the property of being identical with some thing. Now I think that 'identical', in this context, is sufficiently obscure so that there is a gain in clarity if we explicate "X has the property of being identical with some thing" by "X has the property of existence" rather than *vice versa*. But whether or not I am right in so thinking, Descartes's argument remains essentially unaffected. For if the critic of that argument agrees that existence is a property, though a property which is most perspicuously expressed by a given expression, 'E', other than 'existence', then we can simply replace 'existence', wherever it occurs in Descartes's argument, with 'E', and point out that if the contemplated analysis is correct, then the new version of Descartes's argument is just as apt to be sound as is the old one. (Since I know of no property-expression, 'E', which illuminates the property of existence to a greater extent than does 'existence', I shall in what follows continue to formulate Descartes's argument in terms of the latter expression.)

We have seen in effect that Kant-like critiques of Descartes's argument must rely on a denial of the thesis that existence is a property (of *any* sort). (This would not, of course, have surprised Kant.) Now it seems likely that philosophers who have denied that thesis have been motivated by the commonsense observation that we do not normally use 'exist(s)' as a descriptive term. Thus, if I were asked to give a description of Ronald Reagan, it would certainly be thought odd were I to say that he is, e.g., a male, white, middle class, ex-movie actor, who is the 40th president of the United States and who exists. But I think that all that this indicates is that the activity of describing a thing normally presupposes, rather than makes explicit, that the thing being described is not non-existent. However, it is easy to imagine a set of circumstances in which "It exists" would be obviously descriptive of what it refers to. I have in mind a guessing game, the point of which is to identify what one of the players is thinking about, and in which the players are permitted to think about fictitious, as well as real, entities. Suppose that I say "Is what you are thinking about an animal?" and you say "Yes", and then I say "Is it a horse?" and you say "Yes". And suppose that at that point I say "Does it exist?", having in mind that it might be Pegasus, and you say "Yes, it exists". Surely it looks very much as though 'exists' is functioning here as a descriptive term, like 'animal' and 'horse'. It is doubtful, then, that Descartes's argument can be successfully disposed of by claiming that, since existence is not a property, it is not a perfection (relative to God).

7.2. Still, Descartes's argument is, on the present interpretation, unsuccessful. For nothing can be a supremely perfect being unless it exists. Hence, premiss (1) presupposes that God exists, and so the argument is, as it stands, question-begging. Moreover, "Existence is a perfection relative to God" means or entails either that God actually does possess the perfection of existence, in which case it is question-begging, or that God has the perfection of existence whether or not he exists, in which case it is absurd. A non-question-begging formulation is as follows:

(1')   *If* God exists, *then* he is a supremely perfect being.

(2')   If God exists, then his existence is a perfection.

So

(3')   if God exists, then he exists.

But, of course, (3') is without ontological significance.

But now there is a much more charitable interpretation of Descartes's argument:

(1)   The *concept* of God is the *concept* of a supremely perfect being.

(2)   The *concept* of existence is the *concept* of a perfection relative to God.

Hence

(3)   the concept of God stands to the concept of existence as the concept of a mountain stands to the concept of a valley,[2] i.e., it is a conceptual truth that God exists.

So

(4)   God really exists.

On this interpretation, premiss (1) asserts, not that *God* is a supremely perfect being, but that the *concept* of God is the *concept* of a supremely perfect being, i.e., that it is a necessary truth that what we think about, when we think about God's nature, is a supremely perfect being. And *that* premiss does not, in any obvious way, presuppose God's existence – any more than, e.g., "Necessarily, what we think about, when we think about Zeus, is an Olympian god who hurls thunderbolts" begs the question of whether Zeus exists. (The envisaged premiss *is* part of an argument which demonstrates that God exists, but if *that* entails that it is question-begging, then there are no sound arguments.) Moreover, premiss (2), on its present interpretation, does *not* affirm that God has the perfection of existence but only that the *concept* of existence is the *concept* of a perfection relative to God. And, finally, the argument as a whole has the form of arguments which are obviously sound, e.g.:

(a)   The concept of a square is the concept of a 4-sided figure.

(b)   The concept of a 4-sided figure is the concept of a figure which has more sides than 3.

So

(c)   the concept of a square stands to the concept of a figure which has more sides than 3 as the concept of a mountain stands to the concept of a valley, i.e., it is a conceptual truth that squares have more sides than 3.

Hence

(d)   squares have more sides than 3.

7.3. Still, it may look as though even the present, charitable interpretation is subject to refutation. Consider the following objection: "If it is indeed the case that the concept of God stands to the concept of existence as the concept of a mountain stands to the concept of a valley – or as the concept of a square stands to the concept of a figure which has more sides than 3 – then, *pace* Descartes, it does not follow that God really exists. For it does not follow from the fact that it is a conceptual truth that squares have more sides than 3 that there really are such objects. All that is entailed is that *if* a square exists, *then* it has more sides than 3. (It is a conceptual truth that, say, centaurs are creatures with the torso of a human being and the hind parts of a horse, but it would surely be madness to maintain that this fact warrants us in believing that there really are such creatures. All that follows from the envisaged conceptual truth is that *if* centaurs exist, *then* they are creatures of the contemplated sort.) And, by parity of reasoning, all that follows from the claim that it is a conceptual truth that God exists is that *if* God exists, then he exists, i.e., it does *not* follow that God really exists."

But in fact this objection can be seen to be mistaken. A conceptual-truth-expressing sentence is such that we can give an explanation (and, indeed, a *complete* explanation)[3] of our ability to know that it expresses a truth just in terms of the concepts which it expresses (so that our knowledge that it expresses a truth need not be based on observation). Moreover, it is the mark of a conceptual-truth-expressing sentence that its being truth-expressing is explicable in terms of its expressing *precisely* the concepts which it expresses. Thus, the explanation of the fact that the conceptual-truth-expressing sentence, "Squares are 4-sided figures", expresses a truth has to do with the fact that it is (precisely) about *squares* (and 4-sided figures) rather than some other objects. So the claim that it is a conceptual truth that God exists entails the claim that it is because of the concept of existence and the concept of *God* (and not some other being) that the sentence "God exists" expresses a truth.

But suppose that "God exists" really does mean the same as "If God exists, then he exists". This latter sentence (call it 'ϕ') would continue to express a truth, no matter what proper names, nouns, or definite descriptions we might substitute for 'God': the envisaged sentence expresses a vacuous truth. So it is false that it is because of the concept of *God* that it expresses a truth, and, hence, false that it expresses a conceptual truth. It follows that if "God exists" really does express a conceptual truth, then it does not mean the same as the contemplated, ontologically sterile sentence, ϕ. And it follows in turn that Descartes was right in claiming that the fact that "God exists" expresses a conceptual truth entails that God really exists.

It is of note that similar considerations do not apply to "Squares are 4-sided figures". Though this sentence expresses a conceptual truth, it *is* equivalent in meaning to the conditional sentence, "If squares exist, then they are 4-sided figures"; for this latter sentence does *not* express a vacuous truth, i.e., it would express a falsehood

under most substitutions of plural nouns and definite descriptions for
'squares'. Hence, the fact that it is because of the concept of a square
that "Squares are 4-sided figures" expresses a truth does not entail,
in *this* instance, that it does not mean the same as the envisaged
conditional sentence. However, as we have seen, things are otherwise
with "God exists". This sentence expresses a conceptual truth only
if it is *not* equivalent to ϕ. But now it looks as if Descartes was correct
in claiming that it expresses a conceptual truth. It looks, then, as if
his argument that God really exists is sound.

Here someone may wish to argue as follows: "Consider the concept
of an existent winged horse. It is because of this concept that the
sentence 'Existent winged horses exist' expresses a (necessary)
truth.[4] But this sentence (call it 'ϕ'') is surely equivalent in meaning
to the ontologically sterile sentence 'If existent winged horses exist,
then they exist'. Otherwise existent winged horses (and a myriad of
other such Gaunilo-type entities) really exist. But if 'Existent winged
horses exist' both expresses a conceptual truth and means the same
as the envisaged conditional sentence, why shouldn't 'God exists' be
taken to mean the same as ϕ?"

The answer is that the word "existent" in ϕ' functions as a
(Quinean) logical particle, i.e., ϕ' expresses a logical – and, hence,
vacuous – truth, since it would continue to express a truth, no matter
what plural noun or definite description we might place after the
logical particle 'existent' (so long as the sentence ended with 'exist').
It follows that the fact that ϕ' is truth-expressing can be explained
without referring to precisely the concepts which it expresses. And it
follows in turn that ϕ' does not express a conceptual truth and,
hence, can plausibly be construed as equivalent in meaning to the
ontologically sterile (and vacuous-truth-expressing) sentence "If
existent winged horses exist, then they exist".

At this point, another objection may be raised: "'God' analytically
entails 'an existent, omnipotent, omniscient and perfectly good
being'. Hence, 'God exists' means the same as the vacuous-truth-

expressing sentence 'An existent, omnipotent, omniscient and perfectly good being exists', in which 'existent' figures as a logical particle, as it does in ϕ'. And since the contemplated sentence expresses a vacuous-truth, there is no objection to its being translated into the vacuous truth-expressing conditional sentence, 'If an existent (etc.) being exists, then he exists.' But (3) of Descartes's argument is validly entailed by (1) and (2), and there is no reason to think that either of these turns out false under the present analysis of 'God'. So it is false that if 'God exists' expresses a conceptual truth, then it is not equivalent in meaning to 'If God exists, then he exists'."

One reply to this objection is that (3) does not follow from (1) and (2) as, e.g., p follows from p and q. Whether the concept of God stands to the concept of existence as the concept of a mountain stands to the concept of a valley, depends in part on what 'God' means. And if 'God' has the meaning which is presently contemplated, then in fact it is false that the envisaged analogy holds – since it *is* a conceptual truth that mountains have valleys, but it is *not* (given the present analysis of 'God') a conceptual truth that God exists. Premisses (1) and (2) should be taken as establishing a *prima facie* case for (3), but one which can be overthrown, given that the meaning of 'God' is demonstrably such that it is false that "God exists" expresses a conceptual truth.

In view of this consideration, my interpretation of Descartes's argument can be strengthened as follows:

(1)   The concept of God is the concept of a supremely perfect being.

(2)   The concept of existence is the concept of a perfection relative to God.

(2′)   The concept of God is not such that "God exists" expresses a vacuous logical truth (i.e., it is not like the concept of an existent winged horse in that respect).

So

(3)   it is a conceptual truth that God exists.

Hence

    (4)   God really exists.

But now why should it be thought that 'God' does *not* mean "an existent (etc.) being"? If there is no argument to the contrary, then Descartes's argument is less than compelling. But in fact there *is* an argument which shows that the contemplated analysis of the meaning of 'God' is mistaken: Let us say that for any value of X, "X has actual existence" means that the sentence "X exists" (1) expresses a truth and (2) is not equivalent in meaning to an ontologically sterile conditional sentence. Then we can rephrase Descartes's argument as follows:

    (1)   The concept of God is the concept of a supremely perfect being.

    (2')   The concept of actual existence is the concept of a perfection (relative to God).

Hence

    (3')   the concept of God stands to the concept of actual existence as the concept of a mountain stands to the concept of a valley, i.e., it is a conceptual truth that God has actual existence.

So

    (4')   God has actual existence.

Now it looks to be plainly false that all that *this* argument establishes is the ontologically sterile conclusion that if God exists, then he exists. For it appears that what it shows, if it is sound, is precisely the opposite. (And if "God exists" does *not* mean "If God exists, then he exists", then 'God' does not mean "an existent (etc.) being".) Hence, it looks as though the present argument shows that Descartes's argument is after all sound.

Here someone may say, "The sentence, 'God has actual existence', is equivalent in meaning to 'A being such that it has actual existence and is omnipotent, omniscient and perfectly good has actual existence'; and this sentence expresses a vacuous truth, and, hence, there is no reason to deny that it means the same as the ontologically sterile sentence, 'If a being such that it has actual existence and is omnipotent, omniscient and perfectly good exists, then it has actual existence'. Moreover, the latter sentence expresses a proposition which is compatible with its being the case that 'God exists' means 'If God exists, then he exists'. So the revised argument does not after all show that Descartes's argument has real ontological significance."

But the objection can easily be met. One reply to it is as follows: It is clear that if "God has actual existence" does not express a true proposition which is incompatible with its being the case that "God exists" means "If God exists, then he exists", then no sentence does. So my opponent is arguing in effect that the concept of God is such that it is not possible to express a true proposition which is incompatible with its being the case that "God exists" means the same as "If God exists, then he exists". But this can be seen to be wrong. Let 'a C-concept' = Df "a concept of something, X, such that it is possible to express a true proposition about X which is incompatible with its being the case that 'X exists' means the same as 'If X exists, then it exists'". And consider the following argument:

(1)   The concept of God is the concept of a supremely perfect being.

(2'')   The concept of a supremely perfect being is a C-concept.

So

(3'')   the concept of God is a C-concept.

Now

(4'')   if the sentence "God has actual existence" does not express a true proposition which is incompatible with its being the case that "God exists" means the same as "If God exists, then he exists", then no sentence does.

But

(5'')   if the sentence "God has actual existence" means the same as "A being which has actual existence and is omnipotent, omniscient and perfectly good has actual existence" (call

this sentence 'S'), then the proposition which is expressed
by the former sentence is not incompatible with its being
the case that "God exists" means the same as "If God
exists, then he exists".

Hence

(6'')　"God has actual existence" does not mean the same as S;
so "God exists" does not mean the same as "If God exists,
then he exists".

A second reply to the envisaged objection is this: Let us mean by
"X has real actual existence" that the sentence, "X has actual existence", is (1) true and (2) not equivalent in meaning to any onto
logically sterile conditional sentence. And consider the following
argument:

(1)　The concept of God is the concept of a supremely perfect
being.

(2''')　The concept of real actual existence is the concept of a
perfection (relative to God).

Hence

(3''')　the concept of God stands to the concept of real actual
existence as the concept of a mountain stands to the
concept of a valley, i.e., it is a conceptual truth that God
has real actual existence.

So

(4''')　God has real actual existence.

What this argument shows is that "God has actual existence"
expresses the non-ontologically sterile (non-conditional) truth that
"God exists" expresses a non-ontologically sterile (non-conditional)
truth. Or, at any rate, the contemplated argument establishes this
unless 'God' analytically entails "a being which has real actual
existence and is omnipotent, omniscient and perfectly good", in
which case "God has real actual existence" is equivalent in meaning
to the ontologically sterile, conditional sentence "If a being which has
real actual existence (etc.) exists, then he has real actual existence".

But now this criticism can be countered by (a) introducing the concept of X's having actual real actual existence – i.e., of X's being such that the sentence "X has real actual existence" (1) expresses a truth and (2) is not equivalent in meaning to any ontologically sterile conditional sentence – and (b) pointing out that the concept of God stands to the concept of having actual real actual existence as the concept of a mountain stands to the concept of a valley. It follows from this that "God has real actual existence" expresses the non-ontologically sterile (non-conditional) truth that "God has actual existence" expresses the non-ontologically sterile (non-conditional) truth that "God exists" expresses a non-ontologically sterile (non-conditional) truth. And it would surely be preposterous to claim at this point that 'God' analytically entails "a being who has actual real actual existence", so that "God has actual real actual existence" is equivalent in meaning to "If God exists, then he has actual real actual existence". And, as the regress that we are started on progresses, analytic entailment claims of the envisaged sort would become more and more incredible, i.e., it would become more and more incredible that 'God' has such an immensely bloated meaning.

Or would it? I am claiming that "God exists", "God has actual existence", "God has real actual existence", etc., all express conceptual truths. And this may give rise to the following argument: "Whenever it is a conceptual truth that X's are Y's, this is because the term which stands for X's analytically entails the term which stands for Y's (or vice versa). Thus, it is a conceptual truth that squares are 4-sided figures only because 'squares' analytically entails '4-sided figures'; it is a conceptual truth that bachelors are unmarried adult males only because 'bachelors' analytically entails 'unmarried adult males', and so on. And, by parity of reasoning, it is a conceptual truth that God exists only if 'God' analytically entails 'existent being'; it is a conceptual truth that God has actual existence only if 'God' analytically entails 'a being who has actual existence'; and so on. But now if 'God' analytically entails 'existent being' then 'God exists' is indeed equivalent to 'If God exists, then he exists', (since it means the same as the vacuous sentence, 'An existent (omnipotent, omniscient and perfectly good) being exists'); and if 'God' analytically entails 'a being who has actual existence', then 'God has actual existence' is indeed equivalent to 'If God exists, then he has actual existence', (since it means the same as the vacuous sentence, 'A being who has actual existence (etc.) has actual existence'); and so on."

The reply is simply that there are conceptual truths which are expressed by sentences in which the subject term does *not* analytically entail the predicate term. "Socrates is a non-number" is an example, as is "Mailboxes are non-conscious". Surely both of these sentences express necessary, but non-vacuous (i.e., conceptual) truths, but just as surely 'Socrates' does not analytically entail 'non-number' and 'mailboxes' does not analytically entail 'non-conscious'. And, closer to home, "The number 9 exists" certainly appears to express a conceptual truth, even though it is highly implausible that 'the number 9' analytically entails 'exists'. In short, my objector is overlooking the fact that some conceptual truths are *de re*, rather than *de dicto*, necessary.

7.4. William L. Rowe has presented the following parody of my interpretation of Descartes's argument:[5]

(a)   Let 'minor deity' = Df "a being who possesses all properties which are perfections relative to God, but only a modest degree of perfections which vary in degree, such as knowledge, power and goodness".

Then

(b)   the concept of a minor deity is the concept of a being who possesses such properties.

But

(c)   the concept of existence is the concept of a perfection relative to God.

Hence

(d)   the concept of existence stands to the concept of a minor deity as the concept of a square stands to the concept of a 4-sided figure, i.e., it is a conceptual truth that a minor deity exists.

So

(e)   a minor deity really exists.

We can best dispose of this parody by further strengthening my interpretation of Descartes's argument as follows:

(1)   The concept of God is the concept of a supremely perfect being.

(2)   The concept of existence is the concept of a perfection relative to God.

(2′)   The concept of God is not such that "God exists" expresses a vacuous logical truth (i.e., it does not resemble the concept of an existent winged horse in that respect).

(2′′)   The concept of God is not logically incoherent, i.e., God's existence is not logically impossible.

So

(3)   it is a conceptual truth that God exists.

Hence

(4)   God really exists.

The justification of the explicit addition of (2′′) to my interpretation of Descartes's argument is just that if God's existence were logically impossible, then it would be necessarily false that God exists (in a non-conditional, ontologically significant sense); and, hence, it could hardly be a conceptual truth that God exists.

But the same holds true for minor deities: Rowe's parody needs to be strengthened by the addition of the claim that minor deities are logically possible. And this claim is untenable, since (1) the traditional concept of God is such that it is a necessary truth that if God exists, then he is radically unique, in the sense that it is logically impossible for any other being to rival him with respect to the number and degree of his perfections, and (2) minor deities would, if they existed, have the same number of perfections as does God.

Here someone may wish to redefine 'minor deity' as "a being who possesses *some* properties, *including existence*, which are perfections relative to God". But then 'minor deities' analytically entails 'existent beings', and, hence, "Minor deities exist" does not express a conceptual truth, but rather the logically (and ontologically) vacuous proposition that if minor deities exist, then they exist. (It resembles "Existent winged horses exist" in this respect.) Here my objector may attempt another redefinition, viz., let 'minor deity' = Df "a being who has all of God's perfections (though a lower degree of those that vary in degree) except ..." where the list of exceptions does not include existence. However, it is unlikely that we know *all* the perfections which God possesses, and, hence, it is unlikely that we are in a position to fill in the dots in this latest 'definition'.

7.5. Rowe has also offered the following criticism[6] of my defense of Descartes's argument: "Let 'magican' = Df 'an existing magician'. It follows from this definition that no non-existing object is, or can be, a magican. For, given this definition of 'magican', a non-existing object can be a magican only if a non-existing object can be an existing object; and that is plainly not the case. But now suppose – what is surely possible – that there never have been any magicians. Then no *existing* objects would be magicans either; and so magicans would be neither existing nor non-existing objects.

"Now let us apply this to Dore's defense of Descartes's argument. Even if Dore has established that 'God exists' expresses a conceptual truth and, hence, does not mean the same as the vacuous sentence, 'If God exists, then he exists,' it does not follow that God really does exist. For it is open to us to construe 'God exists' as meaning 'No non-existing object is God'. And just as it does not follow from the fact that no non-existing object is a magican that magicans really do exist, so too, it does not follow from the fact that no non-existing object is God that God really does exist. (However, 'No non-existing object is God' expresses a conceptual – rather than a vacuous – truth, since it would not continue to express a truth no matter what proper names, nouns, or definite descriptions we might substitute for 'God' in that sentence.)"

Rowe's criticism essentially involves the thesis that there are existing and non-existing objects, and, since non-existing objects are notoriously controversial entities, it seems reasonable to try to make sure that talk about them – and their counterparts, existing objects – can be paraphrased into discourse which obeys the laws of logic. The most obvious suggestion for getting a logical handle on sentences of the form, "X is a non-existing object", and sentences of the form, "X is an existing object", is to require that the former sentence means (or, anyway, entails) "X does not exist" and that the latter sentence means (or, anyway, entails) "X does exist". Given that way of construing the former pair of sentences, they express contradictory propositions, from which it follows that if X is not a non-existing object, then it is an existing object. But Rowe evidently does not construe them in the contemplated way, since he claims that, in the event that there were no magicians, magicans would be neither non-existing objects nor existing objects.

Well, then, what is the logical status of objects which are neither existing objects nor non-existing objects? What, on Rowe's view, is the logical status of magicans, given that there are no magicians? The answer is that they are logically impossible objects, since "the set of possible things can be exhaustively divided into those possible things which actually exist and those possible things which do not exist".[7] If Rowe is right, then things are either non-existing objects or existing objects or logically impossible objects, some of which (like Rowe's magicans in the event that there are no magicians) are not also non-existing objects.

Now it is surely a necessary truth that it is logically impossible for an object to be such that it neither exists nor does not exist. And Rowe is presumably trying to conform his view to that fact when he agrees that an object which is neither an existing object nor a non-existing object is a logically impossible object, i.e., he is trying not to lose *all* logical control over objects which are neither existing nor non-existing. Unfortunately, however, in agreeing that objects which are neither existing nor non-existing objects are *ipso facto* logically impossible objects, he runs afoul of a necessary modal truth. Consider magicans again. If Rowe is right, then, given that there are no magicians, magicans are neither existing nor non-existing objects and, hence, are logically impossible objects. But surely, even if there *are* no magicians, it is *logically possible* that there are magicians; and surely it is a necessary truth that if magicians exist, then they are magicans (existing magicians). It follows that, in maintaining that, given that there are no magicians, then magicans are logically impossible objects, Rowe is in effect denying the following necessary truth: when it is logically possible that something, X, (e.g., a magician or a square) exists, and it is logically necessary that if X exists, then it is a Y (e.g., a magican or a 4-sided figure), then it is logically possible that a Y exists.[8] (I am assuming here that sentences of the form, "A Y is a logically impossible object", entail sentences of the form, "It is logically impossible that a Y exists". Rowe can deny this entailment only if he provides us with much more information about the concept of a logically impossible object than in fact he has given us.)

But can we do any better? What *would* be the status of magicans in the event that there were no magicians? Suppose that we tried to get the concept of non-existing objects under logical control by agreeing that sentences of the form "X is a non-existing object" entail sentences of the form "X does not exist". And suppose that we said that, if there were no magicians, then magicans would not exist. Wouldn't that commit us to the unacceptable proposition that there would be at least one non-existing object which is an existing object? But surely it would be just as unacceptable to maintain that magicans *would* exist, even if there were no magicians.

The question before us is "How can magicans be non-existing objects?" Rowe presumably subscribes to the following argument that they cannot be:

(a)   It is a necessary truth that magicans are existing magicians.

(b)   It is a necessary truth that no non-existing object is an existing magician.

So

(c)   it is a necessary truth that no magican is a non-existing object.

But consider the following, analogous argument:

(a′)   It is a necessary truth that dragons are fearsome animals with fiery breaths.

(b′)   It is a necessary truth that no non-existing object has the property of being a fearsome animal with a fiery breath.

Hence

(c′)   it is a necessary truth that no dragon is a non-existing object.

Surely Rowe would not wish to maintain that this latter argument is sound. Any discourse about non-existing objects, the rules of which forbid dragons (and, for an exactly similar reason, centaurs and so on indefinitely) to count among their number, is too logically disreputable to be worthy of serious consideration.

But what is *wrong* with the present argument? One answer is this: To say that dragons are non-existing objects is not to ascribe the property of being a fearsome animal with a fiery breath to some non-existing things. Rather it is to say that *things, which are such that if they exist, then they are fearsome animals with fiery breaths* are non-existing objects. This way of construing the former assertion has the advantage of allowing us to say that dragons are non-existing objects, while making it unnecessary for us to agree that some non-existing objects have the property (remarkable in non-existing objects) of being fearsome animals with fiery breaths. But then consistency obliges us to treat magicans in a similar manner, i.e., given the present reply, we must hold (a) that magicans would be non-existing objects if there were no magicians and (b) that "Magicans are non-existing objects" does not assert that some non-existing objects have the property of being existing objects, but rather that *things, which are such that if they exist, then they are existing magicians,* are non-existing objects.

However, though this approach to the concepts of non-existing dragons and non-existing magicans saves us from logical absurdity, it entails that non-existing objects do in fact have rather remarkable properties. Thus, though the present approach avoids the conclusion that some non-existing objects have the property of being fearsome animals with fiery breaths, it commits us to the conclusion that some non-existing objects have the *dispositional* property of being such that if they exist, then they are fearsome animals with fiery breaths. And, similarly, the present approach commits us to attributing to some non-existing objects the dispositional property of being such that if they exist, then they are existing magicians. But the thesis that non-existing objects can have such dispositional properties is, I think, sufficiently implausible on its face that we need to consider some alternatives to, and/or defenses of, the present, dispositional approach.

A simple alternative is just to deny that there are (and could be) any non-existing objects. I argued in 7.1 that there are contexts in which sentences of the form "*X* exists" are clearly descriptive. But there are no contexts in which sentences of the form "*X* does *not* exist" are obviously descriptive. For (a) many such sentences express truths; (b) it is surely a necessary condition of a descriptive sentence of the form '*Z* is *P*' expressing a truth that the subject term refer to an entity which the predicate is true of; and (c) it looks very much as though sentences of the form "*X* does not exist" entail that there *is* no subject for "does not exist" to be true of. In view of these considerations, it is plausible that "*X* does not exist" is best explicated by "Nothing is (an) *X*", where this sentence is not best explicated by "*X* has the property of being such that nothing is identical with it". (Similar considerations do not apply to sentences of the form "*X* exists", since these sentences posit a subject for 'exists' to be true of.)

But, of course, if "Magicans (existing magicians) do not exist" means simply "Nothing is a magican (an existing magician)", then there is no reason to think that Rowe is right in claiming that magicans would be things which neither exist nor do not exist, in the event that there were no magicians.

There is another approach to non-existence which deserves mention here, namely, taking some sentences of the form "X does not exist" to be elliptical versions of sentences of the form "X exists in some possible worlds but not in the actual one, i.e., X is a possible-but-non-actual object". On this view, there are indeed such things as non-existing objects, namely, possible objects, the positing of which can be defended as follows: (1) Since possible world semantics plays an important role in logical theory and is clearly a deep explication of our ordinary modal concepts, possible worlds are eminently ontologically respectable; (2) possible, but not actual, individuals are as likely to exist (in merely possible worlds) as are possible, but not actual, worlds likely to exist;[9] and, hence, (3) the former provide an ontologically respectable subject for "does not exist (in the actual world)" to be true of. Impossible objects, on the other hand, have nothing to recommend them, since impossible worlds play no role in any respectable theory. It follows that Rowe's impossible objects – objects which are neither existing nor non-existing – are not to be countenanced. (And it follows in turn that, e.g., "Square circles do not exist" should be taken to mean simply "Nothing is a square circle".)

It should be noted that I am not here making the general claim that, for any value of '(logically possible) X', "X does not exist" can plausibly be construed to mean "X is non-actual". For the fact that a possible world, W, is non-actual does not entail that W does not exist. Rather, I am making the more limited claim that "X, a concrete (non-abstract) individual, does not exist" can plausibly be taken to mean "Though X exists in a possible world, it does not exist in the actual one".

It is of note that, if, as seems likely, e.g., a possible dragon is a possible *dragon*, as distinct from, e.g., a possible *unicorn* in virtue of the fact that, if it existed in the actual world, then it would be a dragon there, as opposed to a unicorn, then the earlier dispositional analysis of, e.g., "Dragons are non-existing objects" can, despite *prima facie* implausibility, be defended by reference to the present, possible worlds explication: Possible-but-non-actual dragons (magicans, etc.) are such that they are disposed to be actual dragons (actual magicans, etc.) if actualized. Moreover, if the envisaged, possible worlds explication is correct, then "Dragons are non-existing objects" should be explicated as follows: "Dragons, though possible objects, are not actual objects". And, on the proposed explication, "Magicans are non-existing objects" means "Magicans (existing magicians) are (merely) possible objects". Now there is, or should be, no temptation to think that this latter sentence expresses a logically inconsistent proposition. Hence, even given the possible worlds approach to non-existing objects, Rowe's argument (that there are objects which are neither existing nor non-existing) is a failure. It follows that there is no acceptable alternative to the claim that if "God exists" (1) expresses a truth and (2) is not equivalent in meaning to "If God exists, then he exists", then God, as Descartes says, really does exist.

Michael Scriven has criticised one of St. Anselm's version of the ontological argument as follows:

The sense in which it is true that God 'necessarily exists' is not a sense from which one can conclude that there has to be a God. The first claim is translatable as "Nothing can properly be called God that does not really exist"; the second claim is "God really does exist"; and you cannot get either one from the other.[10]

But now can *anything* that does not really exist be properly called by *any* name? Scriven's argument would be pointless if the answer were "No". So presumably Scriven would say that, e.g., 'Superman' properly names a non-existing object. If this is right, then Scriven is claiming in effect that (unlike Superman) God cannot be a non-existing object, but that the latter proposition is compatible with God's not existing. Scriven's objection, then, amounts to the same thing as Rowe's and can be refuted in an exactly similar manner.

Finally, it should be noticed that my defense of Descartes's argument does not commit me to holding that magicans would exist, even if there were no magicians. An ontological argument for the existence of magicans would have exactly the same dubious status as the Section 7.3 'proof' of the existence of existent winged horses. For just as 'existent' operates as a logical particle in 'Existent winged horses exist", so that the sentence expresses a vacuous, rather than a conceptual, truth, so, too, 'existing' operates as a logical particle in "Magicans (i.e., existing magicians) exist", so that *that* sentence expresses a vacuous, rather than a conceptual, truth, i.e., even though it expresses a necessary truth, it does not entail that magicans really do exist.

CHAPTER 8

AGNOSTICISM

8.1. I hope that many of my readers will think that my Chapter 1 solution of the problem of evil, plus my Chapters 4 through 7 arguments for God's existence, show that there is more evidence for theism than for atheism. But I have no illusions about convincing *all* of my readers of that conclusion. Perhaps some of them will doubt that *any* state of affairs could have sufficient positive value to outweigh the enormous negative value of the sum of all instances of apparently useless, intense and prolonged suffering.[1] And anti-utilitarians will hold that no matter how valuable an end *E* may be, it cannot justify the terrible means which are used to bring it about. However, I think that anyone, no matter how strong a supporter of the argument from suffering he may be, should agree after reading this book (or, at any rate, such an impressive piece of philosophical theology as Plantinga's *Nature of Necessity*) that there is *some* evidence that theism is *true*.

At any rate, I shall, in this chapter, be addressing people who think that there is evidence for God's existence but also evidence (in the form of the argument from suffering) against it. Given that assumption, we are confronted with the following (familiar) argument: "Whenever there is evidence that a given proposition, *p*, is true and also evidence that it is false, and it is not clearly true that the former evidence outweighs the latter or *vice versa*, then the most rational thing for anyone who knows that this is the case is to suspend judgement with respect to *p*. It follows that agnosticism is epistemically preferable to theism and to atheism." I want now to explore the question whether this is a sound argument.

8.2. A famous criticism of the argument can be found in William

James's *The Will to Believe*. James's criticism, briefly stated, is this: When someone cannot decide 'on intellectual grounds' whether a given proposition, p, is true or false, then, if he knows that believing that p will significantly benefit him and that he cannot receive the same benefit by suspending judgement with respect to p, it is rational for him to believe that p. For, whether he believes that p or suspends judgement with respect to p, it is his 'passional nature' which will motivate him, i.e., if he suspends judgement, this will be because he is fearful of making a mistake, and, if he believes that p, this will be because he hopes to achieve the benefits which only belief that p can confer. And suspending judgement because one is fearful of error does not render one's position more rational than it is if he accepts p in the hope that he will gain by accepting it.[2]

The essential principle here (call it 'L') can be formulated as follows: When a person's evidence with respect to p does not enable him to decide, on purely intellectual grounds, whether or not p is true, then it is rational for him to believe that p if he knows that believing that p will significantly benefit him if and only if he believes it. L entails that theism is rational, since theists claim – and presumably have good reason to claim – that believing that God exists is a necessary and sufficient condition of their well-being in this world. (The claim that it is necessary and sufficient for their well-being *in an afterlife* is itself in need of justification.)

Another case to which L would be relevant is the following: Suppose that someone, Z, is captured by a mad tyrant with an accurate lie detector, who commands Z to believe a given proposition, p, which is such that it is not clear that there is more evidence for it than against it. And suppose that Z knows the latter thing, and also knows that the alternative to his believing that p is torture and death; and suppose further that there is some means (e.g., a belief-producing pill) by which Z can bring it about that he believes that p. This is a case in which it is clear that L entails that it is rational for Z to believe that p. And, indeed, it certainly looks as though it *would* be (utterly) rational for Z to believe that p in the envisaged circumstances and, indeed, (utterly) irrational for him not to do so, regardless of what proposition p might be.

But there are two things which should be said about this case: (1) It would be just as rational for Z to take the belief-producing pill even though he knew that not-p was much more plausible than p, i.e., even if the question whether p is true *could* be decided on intellectual grounds.[3] For when saving one's life is at stake, the rational person believes what he must, regardless of how implausible it might be. (2) Still, if p is obviously implausible and Z is rational, then Z must agree that p is implausible regardless of whether it is rational for Z to believe it. (Let us suppose – what is, I think, possible – that the belief-producing pill does not cause Z to be deceived about p's epistemic merit.) But now how can it be rational for Z to believe p even though he knows that it is implausible? The answer is that there are two kinds of rationality: (a) *prudential* rationality, which is based upon its being prudent for Z to believe p, and (b) epistemic rationality, which is a function, not of prudence, but of the degree of epistemic merit which p possesses. Now L is true of prudential rationality, but it is not necessarily true of epistemic rationality. It is not true of the latter when it comes into conflict with prudential rationality, i.e., when, though it is prudent for Z to believe that p, there is good reason to believe that p is false and no reason (or much less reason) to believe that it is true. (Normally, of course, prudential and epistemic rationality do *not* conflict. Indeed, it is normally the case that it is prudentially rational to be epistemically rational, since the latter has a high degree of survival value.)

Now the agnostic will want to say at this point that, since it is not clear that there is more evidence for theism than for atheism and *vice versa*, agnosticism is the most *epistemically* rational position, regardless of whether it is also *prudentially* rational. And I think that many theists, who were aware of the distinction between epistemic and prudential rationality, would not be contented with the claim that agnosticism is more *epistemically* rational than theism, i.e., I think that James's defense of theism can be seen to be far from satisfactory.

8.3. But now *do* theists have to agree that agnosticism is epistemically superior to theism, given that the question whether theism or atheism is true cannot be decided on intellectual grounds? Suppose that the agnostic argues as follows that his position is superior: "The person who claims that it is not known whether a given proposition, *p*, is true does not bear the same onus of proof as does the person who claims to know that *p* is true and the person who claims to know that *p* is false. And, since a person who claims to know that theism is true is confronted with the atheistic argument from suffering, he cannot *adequately* shoulder his burden of proving that theism is true, even if he presents some reasonably plausible arguments for that position. But, by the same token, the atheist cannot adequately shoulder his burden (by advancing the argument from suffering) because of the kind of defense of theism found in some of the earlier chapters of this book. It follows that simply refusing to shoulder any burden at all in this area is the most rational thing to do."

So goes the agnostic's argument. Now one part of it is very plausible, namely, the claim that for any proposition, *p*, there is an onus of proof on the person who claims that it is known that *p* is true (or false) which does not rest on the person who denies this. Thus, the person who claims that it is known that there is life on Mars is epistemically obliged to adduce evidence for his claim, even if there is no evidence that there is no life on Mars, while it is surely false that the person who claims that it is *not* known that there is life on Mars is equally epistemically obliged to adduce evidence for his position, if there is no evidence that there is life there.

But now consider the following three alternatives: (1) There is more evidence for theism than for atheism. (2) There is more evidence for atheism than for theism. (3) There is the same – or almost the same – amount of evidence for both positions. In claiming that it is not

known whether theism or atheism is true, the agnostic can be taken
to be doing one of two things with respect to (1), (2), and (3): (a)
maintaining that (3) is true; (b) maintaining that it is not known
whether (1) or (2) or (3) is true. But if the agnostic is doing the former
thing, then, though he is suspending judgement with respect to theism
and atheism and, hence, avoiding the onus of having to show that
either one of those positions is true, he is *not* suspending judgement
with respect to (3), and, hence, he must accept a certain onus, namely,
that of showing that (3) is true. And it is unlikely that he is prepared
to do so.

But suppose that the agnostic agrees that we ought to suspend
judgement about whether (1) or (2) or (3) is true. Then he will no
longer be able legitimately to claim superiority for his position. For
he would be the first to agree that since we do not know that (1) is
true, it is false that theism is more rational than atheism and agnosticism; and, since we do not know that (2) is true, it is false that atheism
is more rational than theism and agnosticism. And why, then, should
he refuse to accept the analogous conclusion that, since we do not
know that (3) is true, it is false that agnosticism is more rational than
either theism or atheism?

There is an answer which he might wish to give here: "We cannot
agree that there is good reason to reject theism, atheism *and* agnosticism; for we must adopt one position or the other: there is no fourth
alternative. And it cannot be true that we are irrational, no matter
which position we opt for. But, that being so, a suspension of judgement regarding theism and atheism is surely the most rational course.
Consider an analogous case: In the present state of scientific
knowledge, it is not clear whether or not there is intelligent, extraterrestrial life. Or, at any rate, let us assume, for the sake of furthering
the argument, that this is so. And let us also assume (what may well
be the case) that there is not plainly more evidence for one of the
following alternatives than for another: (1′) The thesis (call it 'TH')
that there is intelligent extraterrestrial life is better evidenced than

not-TH; (2′) Not-TH is better evidenced than TH; (3′) TH and not-TH are equally well evidenced. But now, given this assumption, it is surely not just as rational to affirm TH or to affirm not-TH as to suspend judgement about the matter. Surely a scientist who affirmed or denied TH in the envisaged circumstances would be thought to be a very odd scientist indeed."

The reply to this argument is that, though it does sound strange to maintain that affirming or denying TH is, in the circumstances, as rational as suspending judgement, this is not because we subscribe to a sound epistemic principle which dictates that we should suspend judgement in such cases, but rather because *we have no motive* either to affirm or to deny TH and because our psychology is such that, when we are not motivated to affirm or to deny a proposition, we normally do neither. But this is a psychological fact, and epistemic appraisal is out of place here. It follows that, though agnosticism is the position that we are most apt to adopt (barring Jamesean motives) if we do not know whether (1) or (2) or (3) is true, this is not because we think (except in moments of philosophical bemusement) that agnosticism is epistemically superior to theism and atheism in the envisaged circumstances, but because we are so psychologically con-stituted that we are not normally motivated to accept a proposition when we do not know whether it, or its contradictory, is better evidenced. The upshot is that, given that we do not know whether (1) or (2) or (3) is true, theism, agnosticism and atheism are all equally rational positions. (By 'agnosticism' here I mean just a suspension of judgement with respect to theism and atheism, not the additional claim that this is the most rational stance.[4])

8.4. Finally, consider the following passage in Roderick Chisholm's *Theory of Knowledge*:

If withholding [i.e., suspending judgement] is not more reasonable than believing, then believing is more reasonable than disbelieving. Or, more exactly, for any proposition *h* and any subject *S*, if it is not more reasonable for *S* to withhold h than it is for him to believe h, then it is more reasonable for S to believe h than it is for him to disbelieve h. An instance of this principle would be: if agnosticism is not more reasonable than theism, then theism is more reasonable than atheism.[5]

If I am right, then Chisholm is mistaken here.

CHAPTER 9

GOD AND PERCEPTUAL SKEPTICISM

9.1. In the preceding chapter I have addressed myself primarily to those who will reject, on moral grounds, my Chapter 1 solution of the problem of suffering. But these philosophers ought to ask themselves whether they are Kantian absolutists with respect to suffering – whether they hold, e.g., that it would be morally unacceptable to inflict, say, five minutes of intense pain on an innocent person in order to prevent the annihilation of the human species. If they do not, then they have no good reason to reject my Chapter 1 solution. For it is open to us to hold that E is a much *more* valuable end than the preservation of humanity – valuable enough, indeed, to outweigh the negative value of human and animal suffering to a much greater extent than would the preservation of humanity outweigh the negative value of five minutes of intense pain. At any rate, I address myself in this chapter to those who agree that my Chapter 1 solution is successful.

9.2. The following is a familiar argument for perceptual skepticism (which I shall call 'PS'): "Seeming to perceive an object is an essential ingredient in every veridical perception if, indeed, there are veridical perceptions. But seeming perceptions are also essential ingredients in hallucinations and dreams. Hence, hallucinations and dreams resemble veridical perceptions (if there are any). Moreover, the resemblance is such that there is no way of telling, just by examining it, that a seeming perception is part of a veridical perception rather than being a *mere* seeming perception, i.e., a dream or an hallucination. The situation with respect to alleged perception of the external world can be compared to the predicament of a man who sees from a distance something which strongly resembles a duck but who (a) believes it may well be a decoy duck, since he knows that there are decoys in the vicinity and (b) is unable to get close enough to make the kind of examination which would enable him to tell whether the duck-like object is a real, or a decoy, duck. Moreover, let us add that he has no idea of the percentage of decoy ducks in the class of duck-like things, so that he cannot justifiably maintain that there is at least a probability of, say, one-half that what he is seeing is a real duck. Analogously, no one has any grounds for affirming that the percentage of seeming perceptions which are involved in veridical perceptions is such and such. With respect to any seeming perception, we are entirely in the dark as to the probability of its being a component of a veridical perception."

In what follows, I shall first show that PS, thus formulated, must be taken very seriously, and then I shall argue that my Chapter 1 solution of the problem of evil, in conjunction with one or more of the *a priori* arguments for God's existence which I have presented, provides us with the foundation of a refutation of PS.

9.3. The claim that seeming perceptions are essential ingredients in veridical perceptions (if such there be) is central to the skeptic's argument. If it is false, then a person who hallucinates or dreams, but thinks that he veridically perceives something, is profoundly irrational. For, since seeming perceptions are surely the most promising candidates for the respect in which dreams and hallucinations, on the one hand, and veridical perceptions, on the other, are significantly similar, the envisaged person would be claiming (wrongly) that he is veridically perceiving something, though he is hallucinating or dreaming instead, and even though there is no similarity between dreams and hallucinations and veridical perceptions. He would be like a person who thinks that he sees a camel in front of him, even though there is no camel and no facsimile camel there, and even though he is veridically perceiving, say, a typewriter there instead. And if it is that kind of mistake which the perceptual skeptic (call him 'the PS') is imputing to us, then his thesis is so far-fetched that we need not take it seriously.

But in fact it can be shown that seeming perceptions are, indeed, essential ingredients in veridical perceptions (if such there be). I shall now set out an argument to that effect and then defend it against what I take to be the strongest criticisms of it. I shall deal explicitly only with seeming to see, but what I shall say about that will apply in an obvious way to seeming to hear, seeming to feel, etc.

The argument which I have in mind (let us call it 'A') runs as follows:

(a)   Imagine a case in which: (i) someone, Z, sees a puddle of blood on his living room rug; (ii) Z has reason to believe that he does not see blood on the rug; (iii) Z says "I seem to see blood on the rug".

(b)   The fact that Z really does see blood on the rug (though he does not know it) does not make Z mistaken in saying "I seem to see blood on the rug". Z's utterance makes a true statement, therefore. It follows that Z is in a certain state in virtue of which what he says is true, as well as being in that state, in virtue of which it is true that he sees blood on the rug.

(c)   But it is impossible to understand what difference between the case under discussion and any other conceivable instance of Z's seeing anything would be marked by saying that some instance of Z's seeing an object is not an instance in which the state affirmed by "I seem to see ..." is present. (We can of course conceive of a case which differs from the envisaged case in that Z does not seem to see the very same object which he sees. Thus Z might seem to see a rat whereas what he truly sees is an old shoe. However, we cannot conceive of a case which differs from the envisaged case in that Z sees some object at a certain place but fails to seem to see any object of any sort at that place.)

(d)   It follows that "I seem to see ..." affirms the existence of a state which one must, logically, be in if he is to see any-

thing. But "I seem to see ..." does not mean the same as
"I see ...", and, hence, it does not affirm the existence of
precisely the same state, the existence of which is affirmed
by "I see ...". This may be expressed by saying that what
"I seem to see ..." affirms is only a logically necessary, not
a sufficient, condition of what "I see..." affirms.

So much for the exposition of *A*. Let us turn now to a discussion
of some criticisms of it.

9.4. Back in the days when sense-datum theory was frequently
discussed, Gilbert Ryle wrote of sentences of the same sort as "I seem
to see ..." that they are used for the purpose of making "guarded
statements of what I am tempted or inclined to judge to be the case
...".[1] And G. J. Warnock said that "the essential function of the
language of 'seeming' is that it is noncommittal as to the actual facts
...".[2] One plausible interpretation of these remarks is as follows. The
role of 'seems', on all occasions of its use, is exactly similar to the role
of 'maybe': both words, whenever they are uttered, are used solely
for the purpose of asserting a proposition in a guarded or tentative
manner or of indicating a noncommittal attitude toward the proposition.[3]

A criticism of *A* emerges from this analysis of "I seem to see ...".
In step (b) of *A* it is said that *Z*'s utterance makes a true statement.
But, given the similarity of 'seem' to 'maybe', this will not do. Guarded
or noncommittal expressions like *Z*'s cannot be used to make false
statements and therefore they cannot be used to make true ones. The
point may be illustrated by considering a sentence containing
'maybe', e.g., "Maybe it will rain today". What is said by this sentence
is compatible both with its raining today and with its not raining today
and, hence, there is no conceivable state of affairs which can falsify
it.[4] But then, since what is said by "Maybe it will rain today" cannot
be false, it cannot be true either. For what cannot be false can be true
only if it is a necessarily true proposition like that expressed by, e.g.,
"2 + 2 = 4". And it can hardly be maintained that what is expressed

by "Maybe it will rain today" is such a proposition. Exactly similar considerations apply to Z's utterance. But now, since Z's utterance does not make a true statement, it must be a mistake to say – what is also said in (b) – that "Z is in a certain state in virtue of which what he says is true".

Step (d) fares no better in view of the similarity of 'seem' to 'maybe'. Is is a gross mistake to claim that "I seem to see .." is used to affirm the existence of a state of the speaker which is logically necessary, but not sufficient, for his seeing some object. The mistake is exactly similar to that which one would be making were he to claim that "Maybe it will rain today" affirms the existence of something which is logically necessary, but not sufficient, for rain today. The trouble is that "I seem to see x" does not affirm of the speaker something in any way different from what we affirm of him when we say that he sees x, and, hence, it does not affirm the existence of something which is only necessary, not sufficient, for his seeing x. Just in case, and to the extent that, "I seem to see x" is used to affirm anything at all of the speaker, it affirms (in a guarded manner) exactly what we affirm when we say that he sees x.

The criticism of A just presented is based on the claim that 'seem', in all its occurrences (including its occurrences in conjunction with 'see'), behaves like 'maybe'. What may appear to recommend this claim is that, if it were true, then it would be easy to see why "I seem to see x" is not generally uttered when the speaker has no doubt that he sees x. One does not generally make statements in a guarded manner, nor evince a noncommittal attitude toward propositions, when he is certain of their truth. Moreover, it might appear, at least at first glance, that unless we adopt the analysis of "I seem to see x" under discussion, we shall be powerless to explain why "I seem to see x" is not uttered when the speaker is convinced that he sees x. But this, as I shall subsequently try to show, is mere appearance. And, anyway, there are certain considerations which leave us no choice but to repudiate the analysis now in question and, along with it, the criticism of A just considered.

First of all, while it is true that "I seem to see *x*" is not generally uttered by a person who firmly believes that he sees *x*, it is plainly false that it cannot be uttered in perfect propriety by a person who firmly believes that he does not see *x* but suffers an hallucination instead. And this is sufficient to refute the claim that 'seem', like 'maybe', functions in all its occurrences, including its occurrences in connection with forms of the verb 'to see', as a device for enabling the speaker to make a guarded or tentative statement or to evince a noncommittal attitude toward a proposition. For it is less than completely candid for one to assert a proposition tentatively or to evince a noncommittal attitude toward it when one is convinced that the proposition is false, and perceptual propositions are no exception to this rule. *Z* cannot say with perfect candor "Maybe I see blood on the rug" when he firmly believes that he suffers an hallucination. But it would be perfectly proper for him to say "I seem to see blood on the rug" in these same circumstances. It follows that, in case the speaker believes that he hallucinates, "I seem to see ..." does not mean the same as "Maybe I see ...", i.e., it is not used as a guarded or noncommittal utterance.

Someone may wish to reply that at least the analysis under discussion and the criticism of *A* which is based on it hold good for the case in which *Z* is *uncertain* about whether he sees blood on the rug (rather than convinced that he does not). It may be said that, in *this* case, at any rate, *Z* would simply be asserting in a guarded way that he sees blood on the rug or evincing a noncommittal attitude toward that proposition. But I think that it is dubious that *Z* would here mean something quite different by "I seem to see blood on the rug" from what he would mean were he to be convinced that he suffers an hallucination. Suppose that he starts off in a state of doubt and says "I seem to see blood on the rug" and that he subsequently becomes convinced that he hallucinates and says "I still seem to see the blood". Surely he would not be speaking inappropriately in saying the latter, and yet his use of the word 'still' indicates that his second utterance has the same sense as the first one. Moreover, even if we waive this consideration, the reply in question is certainly not sufficient to sustain the proposed criticism of *A*. *Qua* attack on *A*, the reply may be circumvented by the simple expedient of imagining that *Z is* convinced that he suffers an hallucination. It will not do to answer that in that case "I seem to see blood" is used by *Z* to state that he hallucinates and, hence, is plainly not used to affirm that *Z* is in a state which is logically necessary for genuine vision. The claim that *Z* uses "I seem to see blood" to state that he is suffering an hallucination entails that *Z* says what is false (i.e., since *Z* does in fact see blood on the rug). And this last thesis is certainly mistaken. Just as one who says "I seem to see *x*" does not say something which is falsified by the fact that he suffers an hallucination in which he merely seems to see *x*, so too he does not say something which is falsified by the fact that he does not suffer an hallucination but really sees *x* instead.

There is another consideration which has a bearing on the present discussion. If it were really the case that "I seem to see ..." meant the same as "Maybe I see ...", then the criticism of step (b) of *A* given earlier would be accurate, at least to this extent: There would be no conceivable state of affairs in virtue of which what is said by "I seem to see ..." could properly be called false – just as there is no conceivable state of affairs in virtue of which what is said by "Maybe it will rain today" can properly be called false. But in fact this is not the case. Though what is said by "I seem to see *x*" is not incompatible either with the speaker seeing *x* or with his suffering an hallucination in which he merely seems to see *x*, it *is* incompatible with his suffering an hallucination in which he seems to see some object other than *x*. One who says, e.g., "I seem to see a brown horse at place *P*" when in fact he suffers an hallucination in which he seems to see a purple dragon at place *P* tells a falsehood. Moreover, what is said by "I seem to see *x* at *P*" is incompatible with the speaker's seeing (really seeing) some object other than *x* at *P* which does not look like *x* to him. Thus, if I see a cat on the mat and it does not look like a dog to me, I tell a falsehood by saying "I seem to see a dog on the mat". Similar considerations do not hold for "Maybe I see x". States of affairs which involve the speaker suffering an hallucination in which he seems to see some object other than x do not falsify what he says by this utterance. Though what the speaker seems to see is a purple dragon, he would not be speaking falsely – indeed it might be that he would not be speaking insincerely – were he to say "But maybe I see (really see) a brown horse (instead)". Moreover, the state of affairs in which the speaker sees y and it does not look like x to him does not falsify (nor necessarily render insincere) what he says when he says "Maybe what I see (really) is x (which looks like y)".

The essential point here can be put as follows: If I say "I seem to see x at P" and it is later discovered either that I suffered an hallucination in which what I seemed to see at P was not x but y or that I really saw y at P and that it did not look like x to me, then *eo ipso* I am convicted of having said what is false. If, on the other hand, I say "Maybe I see x at P" and these same things are later discovered, then I cannot be accused of having said what is false (nor is it necessarily the case that I can even be accused of being misleading). It follows that "I seem to see ..." does not mean the same as "Maybe I see ...".

A final word in this connexion. I do not wish to deny that a person who says "I seem to see ..." may be either asserting in a guarded way that he sees the object which he mentions or evincing a noncommittal attitude toward the proposition that he sees it. All that I have tried to establish here is that this is never *all* that one does, nor – since "I seem to see ..." has basically the same sense when the speaker is in doubt as when he is convinced that he is hallucinating – the primary thing that one does, when he says "I seem to see ...".[5] If I am right, then the criticism of A which I have been considering is without foundation.

9.5. Another claim about "I seem to see ..." from which it follows that A is not a sound argument is that "I seem to see ..." has the same meaning as "I am inclined to believe that I see ...".[6] At first glance it may appear that this claim does not really differ from the claim that "I seem to see ..." means the same as "Maybe I see ...", since it is tempting to suppose that "I am inclined to believe ..." plays a role exactly similar to 'maybe'. But it is, I think, difficult to reconcile the thesis that "I am inclined to believe ..." has the same use as 'maybe' with the fact that "He is inclined to believe ..." and "You are inclined to believe ..." are not characteristically guarded or noncommittal expressions. I can say of another person that he is inclined to believe a certain proposition, p, even though I am entirely convinced that p is false (or true). When I say "He is (you are) inclined to believe that p", I am not, therefore, asserting p guardedly nor am I evincing a noncommittal attitude toward it. And there is no other proposition which I might be asserting guardedly or toward which I might be evincing a noncommittal attitude. It follows that the expressions in question characteristically affirm something in a non-tentative way about the person to whom they refer. And it is difficult to believe that this is not also the case when 'I' is substituted for 'you' and 'he' in these expressions. I take it, therefore, that "I am inclined to believe that I see ..." typically makes an unguarded affirmation of the existence of a certain state of the speaker – the state of being inclined to believe that he sees the object which he mentions.

The analysis now under consideration, unlike the analysis considered in 9.4, cannot be rejected on the grounds that there are no conceivable states of affairs the existence of which would falsify what is said by "I am inclined to believe that I see x at place P". States of affairs in which the speaker is *not* inclined to believe that he sees x at P but is inclined to believe instead that he sees some object other than x at P would falsify what is said by the utterance in question. And it is not at least immediately obvious that such states of affairs do not coincide with those states of affairs, mentioned in 9.4, in virtue of which what is said by "I seem to see x at P" would be false.

Moreover, some philosophers have argued that it is possible for a person to be inclined to believe that a certain proposition is true, and, at the same time, for him to disbelieve that very proposition.[7] If these philosophers are right, then the present analysis of "I seem to see ...", unlike the analysis considered in 9.4, is not at least plainly incompatible with the fact that I can say "I seem to see x" with perfect propriety even though I disbelieve that I see x.

A criticism of A which may be based on the present analysis is as follows. Though step (b) of A is legitimate (it is perfectly correct to say that "I am inclined to believe that I see blood on the rug" makes a true statement and does so in virtue of a certain state of Z; hence, the same holds for "I seem to see blood on the rug"), steps (c) and (d) are plainly false. We can easily conceive of a case which differs from the envisaged case in that, though Z sees some object at P, he is not in the state affirmed by "I seem to see ...". For this is simply to conceive of a case in which Z is not just inclined to believe that he sees some object at P but has no doubt whatever that he does so.

One approach for the philosopher who wishes to defend A vis-à-vis this criticism is to deny that a person may both be inclined to believe that something is the case and, at the same time, convinced that it is not. For in case this claim is false, then the present analysis of "I seem to see ..." is, like the analysis in 9.4, incompatible with the fact that it is appropriate for one to say "I seem to see ..." when he is convinced that he suffers an hallucination. This much, at least, can be said on behalf of the thesis that disbelieving a proposition is incompatible with being inclined to believe it: One who told us that he was inclined to believe that some proposition was true when in fact he was convinced that it was false would ordinarily seriously mislead us by so doing. To this it may be replied: (a) that, while being inclined to believe p may be incompatible with being fully convinced (firmly believing) that not-p, it is not incompatible with believing not-p with some lesser degree of conviction,[8] and (b) that people who suffer hallucinations are not (and indeed cannot be) fully convinced that they do not see the object which they seem to see. But while (a) is unexceptionable, (b) appears to be false. It appears that the concepts of hallucination and of being fully convinced of something are not such that it is absurd to say of someone that he is fully convinced that he suffers an hallucination. Indeed, it is true as a matter of fact that hallucinogenic drugs produce hallucinations which the subject knows full well to be hallucinations.

But let us waive this rebuttal. Perhaps it is the case that a person's being inclined to believe that he sees x is compatible with his being absolutely certain that he does not see it. There are two further, and, I think, stronger arguments against our accepting the analysis of "I seem to see x" in terms of an inclination on the speaker's part to believe that he sees x. (1) We do not ordinarily say "He seems to see x" or "You seem to see x" when we are convinced that the person to whom we refer really does see x. Just as one who says "I seem to see x" generally indicates that he doubts or disbelieves that he really sees x, so one who utters the second and third person forms of 'seem to see' generally indicates that he, the speaker, doubts or disbelieves that the person to whom he refers really sees x. But, unfortunately for the proponent of the present analysis, similar considerations do not hold for "He is inclined to believe that he sees x" and "You are inclined to believe that you see x". We frequently say of other people (though not of ourselves) that they are inclined to believe some proposition about the truth of which we, the speakers, have absolutely no doubt. (2) As I pointed out in 6.6, I can believe, or be inclined to believe, that I see (really see) an old shoe on my table when it looks to me as though I see (I seem to see) a rat there instead. That is to say, I can believe, or be inclined to believe, that what seems to me to be a rat is in reality an old shoe. I cannot, however, seem to see an old shoe on my table when it looks to me as though I see (I seem to see) a rat there instead. Being inclined to believe that one sees an old shoe cannot, therefore, be the same as seeming to see an old shoe. And of course we may generalize: being inclined to believe that one sees x cannot be the same as seeming to see x.

9.6. The analysis of "I seem to see …" just rejected, like the analysis considered in 9.4, would, if we could accept it, enable us to give an account of the fact that we do not ordinarily say that we seem to see some object when we have no doubt that we do see the object. Whatever may be thought of the claim that a person may be convinced that a certain proposition is *false* and yet inclined to believe it, it is indisputable that one may not be both convinced that a certain proposition is *true* and also inclined to believe it. It would plainly be absurd to say "I am inclined to believe that I see blood on the rug and I have no doubt at all that I do". Exactly similar considerations would, of course, be true of seeming to see some object if (what is not the case) this were the same as being inclined to believe that one sees the object.

Another claim which would, if true, entail that *A* is incorrect and account for the fact that we do not say that we seem to see *x* when we have no doubt that we see *x* is the claim that "I seem to see …" means the same as "I doubt that I see …". If this were so, then (1) "I seem to see *x* and I have no doubt that I do" would be self-contradictory, and (2) step (c) of *A* would be obviously false: since we can easily imagine cases in which a person sees *x* and does not doubt that he does, we can easily imagine cases in which seeing *x* was not accompanied by seeming to see. But the present analysis, like the analysis considered in 9.4, does not accurately represent the meaning of "I seem to see …" in those cases in which the speaker is convinced that he suffers an hallucination. If he is at all concerned to be accurate, one does not say that he doubts that something is the case when he is convinced that it is not the case. It follows that it is unlikely that the present analysis is an adequate analysis of the meaning of "I seem to see …" on *any* occasion of its utterance. Moreover, the present analysis can be rejected on grounds similar to those set out in 9.5. "He doubts that he sees …" and "You doubt that you see …" do not indicate doubt or disbelief on the part of the speaker, while "He seems to see …" and "You seem to see …" do indicate doubt or disbelief. Also, though one can doubt that he sees y at P when he seems to see x at P, one cannot seem to see y at P when he seems to see x at P.

There is still another claim from which it follows that A is not sound and which would, if true, explain why we do not say "I seem to see x" when convinced that we do see x. I have in mind the claim that "I seem to see ..." means the same as "I disbelieve that I see ...". If this analysis were correct, then, once again, "I seem to see x and I have no doubt that I do" would be self-contradictory. Moreover, step (c) of A would be clearly false. But the analysis may be rejected on the grounds: (1) that it cannot account for the fact that people say "I seem to see x" when they strongly suspect that they may in reality be seeing x; (2) that "He disbelieves that he sees x" and "You disbelieve that you see x" do not indicate that the speaker doubts or disbelieves that the person to whom he refers sees x, while this is not true of "He seems to see x", etc.; (3) that one can disbelieve that he sees y at P when he seems to see x at P, but cannot seem to see y at P when he seems to see x at P.

9.6. At this point, it may appear that I have saved A only at the cost of losing any hope of finding an explanation of the fact that we do not ordinarily say that we seem to see an object unless there is at least some doubt that we do. But in fact a very simple and plausible explanation remains open to us. If A has been successfully vindicated, then we must grant that a person who says "I see ..." tells us in part that he seems to see some object. But now, in at least most circumstances in which one believes firmly that he does see the object which he seems to see, it would be pointless for him to withhold the additional information (whatever it may be) conveyed by "I see ...". One who believes that he sees a certain object and says only that he seems to see it, deliberately withholds information from us – tells us part, but only part, of what he believes to be the case. And ordinarily there is simply no reason for one to do this. Of course, one may not be motivated to say anything at all; we do not often find it worthwhile reporting that we see the objects which in fact we see. But when one *is* motivated to report that he sees a certain object, he is generally motivated to tell us what he believes to be the whole story (that he sees the object) and not just a part of it (that he seems to see the object). It is for this reason that one who says "I seem to see ..." is ordinarily understood not to be fully convinced that he sees the object which he mentions.

An analogy may be useful at this point. If I wish to report that I went for a walk this afternoon, I will not, at least ordinarily, say "I moved my legs this afternoon". To say this latter is to tell only part of the story, while to say "I went for a walk" is to tell the part told by "I moved my legs" and more. And ordinarily there would be no reason for me to wish to tell only the part of the story about my moving my legs even though I know that the whole story is true. It is for this reason that, were I to say "I moved my legs this afternoon", I would generally be understood to be indicating that my ability to walk had been in some way impaired (an analogue to the fact that one who says "I seem to see ..." is generally understood to doubt or disbelieve that he really sees the object to which he refers).

It goes without saying that, if the foregoing explanation is correct, then it is not self-contradictory or in any way absurd to say that we seem to see objects whenever we see them. Indeed, my explanation embodies a repudiation of the thesis that it is self-contradictory or absurd to say this, since it involves the claim that seeming to see is a logically necessary condition of seeing. Philosophers who are convinced that "I see ..." says something which is in some sense logically incompatible with what is said by "I seem to see ..." will of course reject the explanation which I have offered (along with *A*). But they cannot argue for their position on the grounds that any of the analyses of "I seem to see ..." which I have been considering are correct. (And if there are other, at least speciously plausible, analyses, we need to be told what they are.) Nor can they argue for their position by saying that unless some such analysis were adequate it would be impossible to present a credible account of the fact that "I seem to see x" is not generally uttered except when the speaker doubts or disbelieves that he really sees x.

9.7. Since one is not correctly called upon to give *evidence* for his sincere assertion that he is seeming to perceive something at a given place, P, and, since it is far from clear what such evidence would look like (i.e., that there *could* be such evidence), we may conclude that we are *non-inferentially* aware of our seeming perceptions. Now the PS is committed to the thesis that *all* that one is non-inferentially aware of when (and if) he veridically perceives things are the seeming perceptions which are ingredients in veridical perceptions. For, needless to say, if I am non-inferentially aware of my veridical perceptions *qua* veridical, as well as being non-inferentially aware of my seeming perceptions, then the thesis that all veridical perceptions involve seeming perceptions has no skeptical bite. (Of course, some skeptics may want to maintain that I have no reason to believe in even what I am non-inferentially aware of, but we have again a version of skepticism which is too implausible to be taken seriously.)

However, given the first skeptical thesis (that seeming to perceive is necessary for perceiving), the second one (that only seeming to perceive is known non-inferentially) is easily demonstrated. One argument for it is as follows: I have established that seeing a puddle of blood on the rug normally involves seeming to see a puddle of blood there (and *necessarily* involves seeming to see *something* there). But now when (or if) I really do see a puddle of blood, I am not non-inferentially aware of two things – my veridical perception of the blood as well as my seeming perception of it. Hence, we need an answer to the question, "Which *am* I non-inferentially aware of?" If one of the two is such that, even if I am rational, I can be persuaded that it is false, whereas this is *not* true of the other member of the pair, then the latter is plainly a much more promising candidate for being the object of non-inferential awareness. Suppose, then, that I veridically see a puddle of blood. Even if I am entirely rational, I can be persuaded that it is false that I do so, by trumped-up evidence that I am hallucinating. However, I cannot, if I am entirely rational, be persuaded that I do not even *seem* to see a puddle of blood. It follows that the member of the pair which I am non-inferentially aware of is my *seeming* perception of the blood. Hence, I am only *inferentially* aware of my *veridical* perception.

Other arguments for the same conclusion are as follows: Suppose that I see (really see) a puddle of blood at place P at time t. We know that this veridical perception essentially involves my *seeming* to see *something* at place P. And, for simplicity, let us imagine that what I seem to see at P is blood. Now suppose (what is entirely possible) that even though I believe truly that I veridically see blood at time t and even though I am entirely rational, I am given a good reason at time t_1 to believe (what is false) that I am in fact suffering an hallucination in which I merely seem to perceive the blood. Still I would be entitled to assert at t_1 that at least I *seem* to see blood, even though I do not *really* see it. But now, so far as non-inferential awareness is concerned, nothing would have changed between t and t_1. (Let us, for simplicity, keep my other putative perceptions constant.) However, if I were non-inferentially aware of my veridical perception of the blood at time t, then, assuming that I am rational, things *would* have changed between t and t_1. For if I were non-inferentially aware of my veridical perception of the blood at t_1, then, if I were rational, I would *know* this to be the case and, hence, could not be taken in by the evidence that I am hallucinating. So if I had been non-inferentially aware of my veridical perception of the blood at t, then, from a phenomenological point of view, things would after all have changed between t and t_1. But, again, no such change would have taken place. So I was *not* non-inferentially aware of my veridical perception *qua* veridical at t. And, of course, we can generalize: I am *never* non-inferentially aware of my veridical perceptions *qua* veridical.

Another, similar argument for the same conclusion is as follows:

Suppose that at t I am having an hallucination in which I merely seem to see blood, but that I nonetheless believe that I really do see blood. And suppose further (what is surely possible in the circumstances) that I am rational. (Imagine, for example, that my hallucination is due to post-hypnotic suggestion, but that I have no reason to suspect that I have been hypnotized.) Then if, in cases in which I really do see blood, I were non-inferentially aware of my veridical perceptions, I would recognize that the case under discussion (in which I am hallucinating blood) is *different* from the former cases, since *ex hypothesi* I am *not*, in the envisaged case, non-inferentially aware of a veridical perception of blood. But then I could not, if I were rational, be fooled by the hypnotist. And, of course, I *could* be thus fooled even if I were rational. So cases of veridically perceiving blood are not phenomenologically distinguishable from cases of merely seeming to perceive it. And that entails that the former cases do not differ from the latter, in that in the former cases, but not in the latter, I am non-inferentially aware of my veridical perception of blood. And, again, we can generalize. *No* instance of veridical perception (given that there are such things) is an instance of non-inferential awareness of that perception *qua* veridical.

9.8. The following is an epistemic principle (call it 'R'), which has been advanced, in one version or another, by such philosophers as Broad and Chisholm[9]: "When someone, Z, seems to perceive something, x, there is an onus on anyone who maintains that Z does not really perceive x to justify his claim, though there is no onus on Z to justify the positive claim that he *does* perceive x, except in cases where there is evidence that he does *not* perceive it." Though some philosophers believe that R refutes PS,[10] this is in fact very doubtful. For even if all rational people would accept R, the *skeptic* can cheerfully accept it as well and add that he *can* shoulder the burden of providing evidence that there are no veridical perceptions by claiming that there is always a good reason to reject any veridical perception claim, namely, that from a purely phenomenological point of view, there is no difference between merely seeming to perceive and perceiving, and, hence, that the alleged veridical perceiver is of necessity in the same kind of predicament as the man who cannot get close enough to the duck-like object which he is perceiving to tell whether it is a real or a decoy duck and who is not in a position to determine the odds against its being a decoy.

Robert Nozick has recently argued in effect that a person is being perfectly consistent if he asserts (1) that he knows that he veridically perceives objects in his environment at time t and also knows that the proposition that he does so entails that he is neither dreaming nor hallucinating at t and (2) that he does not *know* that he is neither dreaming nor hallucinating at t.[11] Nozick's argument is roughly that the claim that Z knows that he veridically perceives something, x, at t entails that if Z were not veridically perceiving x at t, then he would not believe that he was, and that the latter proposition might well be true, even if it is not the case that Z knows that he is neither dreaming nor hallucinating at t, because even if he were in fact doing so, Z would continue to believe otherwise (since, from a phenomenological point of view, things would remain the same). If Nozick is right, then PS – the claim that I cannot know, on any given occasion, that I am neither dreaming nor hallucinating – does *not* entail that I cannot know, on any given occasion, that I am veridically perceiving objects in my environment, and, hence, is really quite innocuous.

Unfortunately, however, Nozick's defense against PS is unsuccessful. For barring some other refutation of PS, it is not enough to say just that Z does not know that he is neither dreaming nor hallucinating. (Call the thesis that he is doing neither one 'N'.) Rather, barring another refutation of PS, what is actually the case is that Z has *reason to doubt N*. Moreover if Z knows (a) that a given proposition, p, entails another proposition, q, and (b) that q is doubtful, then, if he is rational, Z knows (c) that p is doubtful as well. The reason is that if Z knows that it is doubtful that q, and also knows that if p is true, then (what is doubtful) q is true nonetheless, then Z knows (if he is rational) that p is doubtful to exactly the same extent as q is. (The case in which there is doubt-dispelling evidence for p is not a counter-example, since, if p entails q, then doubt-dispelling evidence for p is doubt-dispelling evidence for q.) Suppose, then, that Z has no reason to believe that N is true. Then since Z knows, if he is rational and reflective, (1) that "Z is veridically perceiving x" entails that N is true, and (2) that unless there is evidence for N, then that proposition is doubtful, Z knows that the claim that he is veridically perceiving x is also doubtful. And if Z knows that a given proposition, p, is doubtful, then Z knows that he does not know that p.[12]

On Saul Kripke's interpretation of Wittgenstein,[13] the only criterion of my following mathematical, logical and semantical rules correctly is the conformity of my rule-following procedures to that of most (or all?) other members of the symbol-using community. Thus, if I used 'green' in the past to mean 'grue' (where something is grue if and only if it was green in the past and is blue in the present[14]) the only standard, by which I can be judged wrong on that account, are the speech habits of my fellow language-users. There is no such thing as a mental act of mine of intending to use 'green' to apply to all and only things which are green *simpliciter*. And the only plausible alternative candidate for a constraint on my rule-following is that it conform to the rule-following of others. Moreover, if there were no such constraint then, of course, 'rule-following' would be wildly arbitrary and, hence, there would be no rules and no correct use of language and, also, no correct mathematical and logical computations.

However, PS entails that it is at the very least not unlikely that I, in my egocentric predicament, am using 'rules' without recourse to a community of fellow rule-users and, hence, that in fact my speech does not conform to any rules and is really just nonsense. It follows that PS is either false or is nonsense.

Now I think that Kripke's interpretation of Wittgenstein's strictures concerning a privatelanguage is by far the most charitable and plausible interpretation of Wittgenstein's views on private languages.

But if I am right here, then Wittgenstein is mistaken. We cannot avoid rule-skepticism simply by appealing to the community of symbol-users, since, even given that I know that such a community exists, I do *not* know that the object before me, which was once green and is now (painted) blue, is not green = grue, since I am presently alone, and, hence, do not know at present that most members of the symbol-using community have not been using 'green' all along to mean the same as 'grue'. (Or, at any rate, this is true on Wittgenstein's account of the matter. The fact that most symbol-users share a common interpretation of a semantical, logical or mathematical rule at a given time is simply a brute fact, not one which can be predicted and explained on the basis of past observations.[15]) Moreover, even if I know that my fellow English-speakers would still call this blue thing 'blue' (instead of 'green' = 'grue'), I have no way of telling, on the Kripke-Wittgenstein account of the matter, that they will not start calling green things 'green' = 'grue', say, an hour hence. (I cannot discover this by interviewing some of them, since each of them is just as much in the dark about the matter as I.)

Kripke-Wittgenstein discuss the question whether I have "in the past … used 'plus' and ' + ' to denote a function which [Kripke calls] 'quus' and symbolize[s] by '$\oplus$'. It is defined by

$$x \oplus y = x + y, \text{ if } x, y < 57$$
$$= 5 \quad \text{otherwise}".[16]$$

(The example contains an unrealistically low number, but, of course, that can easily be fixed by substituting a very large number.) The answer to the present question is that, apart from other users of 'plus' and ' + ', there is no fact of the matter, no mental state of intending *not* to use 'plus' to mean 'quus' and ' + ' to mean '$\oplus$'. The only constraint on the use of 'plus' and ' + ' is how the community of arithmetic users in fact employs them. But surely this is a legitimate constraint on *my* use of 'plus' and ' + ' only if there is some legitimate constraint on the *community's* use of 'plus' and ' + '. Perhaps *they* have been using the quus function all along and this will become plain as soon as we get to large enough numbers. But Kripke-Wittgenstein leave us in the dark as to what a constraint on the community's interpretation of rules might be like.

My central concern about Kripke-Wittgenstein on rules can be expressed in the form of a question: If any interpretation of a rule by the linguistic community is *ipso facto* correct, no matter how different the moves which count as following the rule are in the present from the way they were in the past and the way they will be in the future, then why should it not be the case that my individual interpretation of a rule is also correct, no matter what kind of seemingly bizarre behavior results from my interpretation? We are surely justified in being skeptical about Kripke-Wittgenstein on private languages until this question is answered.

In the meanwhile we have no reason to reject PS on the ground that it presupposes the possibility of a private (and *bona fide*) language – or, at any rate, no reason to reject it, except on the ground of an *unqualified* rule-skepticism which entails that *all* symbol-using results only in nonsense – a kind of skepticism which is beyond the scope of the present chapter.

9.9. At this point, it will be convenient to proceed for awhile by imagining the following dialogue between the perceptual skeptic and his adversary (call him 'A').

A. It is irrational to deny that things have a sound explanation. But the claim that there are sound explanations entails that the external world of science and scientifically informed common sense (call it '*W*') exists. For the claim just that there *are* any explanations entails that there is an external world of *some* kind; and the *best* explanations available are those of science and scientifically informed common sense, which entail that the external world is in fact pretty much the way it appears to be.

PS. Why do you hold that there being any explanations entails that there is an external world?

A. Explanations assign causes. But we would have no good reason to believe that there *are* any causes unless we had established that there is frequently a constant, or near constant, conjunction between members of one class of things and members of another. And I do not find such constant conjunctions in my phenomenal world. E.g., phenomenal smoke is frequently not conjoined with phenomenal fire, the sound of a passing train is frequently not conjoined with a visual experience of the train, etc. If I am justified in believing that the external world exists, then I can explain these facts by claiming that there was, indeed, fire, a passing train, etc., etc., but that I was *not in a position to observe them*. However, talk about unobserved parts of my *phenomenal* world is logically inconsistent. It follows that the claim that there are (at least speciously plausible) explanations entails that there is an external world. But surely it is rational to believe the former claim. Hence, it is rational to believe that there is an external world and, what is more, that it is identical with *W*.

PS. You are arguing in effect that, since it is doubtful that there are no sound explanations, it is not doubtful that *W* exists. But one man's *modus ponens* is another man's *modus tollens*. What *I* maintain is that, since it is doubtful that *W* exists, it is doubtful that there are any sound explanations. Moreover, my argument is stronger than yours, since I can provide *a reason* (which involves the decoy duck analogy or some other resembling analogy) for my claim that it is doubtful that the external world exists, while you have yet to furnish evidence that there are sound explanations.

A. You are in effect denying that I am warranted in believing that things have causes. Now I must admit that (barring that I am justified in believing that the external world exists) I cannot provide evidence for that belief. But I do not *need* evidence, since the following principle is properly basic: things which do not exist with SS necessity have causes.

PS. Surely it is *not* properly basic. Quantum theory entails that it is false. And it is very implausible that indeterminists with respect to free will can be refuted just by the claim that determinism is properly basic.

A. Let me, then, affirm the following, less vulnerable *a priori* principle (call it 'PR'): for any given thing, X, which does not exist with SS necessity, it is *prima facie* rational to believe that it has a cause, i.e., it is rational so to believe unless or until evidence that it is uncaused is revealed. PR entails that my seeming perceptions have causes; and since (for a reason presented earlier) it is very doubtful that seeming perceptions are the sole causes of one another, the causes of my seeming perceptions must be parts of the external world. But now, given that there is an external world, it is most likely to be W. (An argument for this conclusion will subsequently emerge.)

PS. I doubt that PR is properly basic. Rather (*pace* Kant) it looks very much like a principle which must be inferred from alleged *observations* of the external world. But set that aside. PR entails that my seeming perceptions have an external cause *only if* I have no reason to doubt that claim. And it is precisely my thesis that I *do* have such a reason, i.e., my phenomenal world is phenomenologically indistinguishable from the way the external world would appear if it existed.

9.10 End of dialogue. PS's argument is formidable. But we need not despair. Parts of my phenomenal world, namely, instances of my suffering, plus at least one of the two *a priori* arguments for God's existence which I have examined, plus my rebuttal of the atheistic argument from suffering in Chapter 1, give me a way out of the contemplated epistemic predicament. Consider an instance of my suffering, e.g., my phenomenal stomach-ache at time t. I cannot assign a phenomenal cause of my phenomenal stomach-ache, since I have not observed anything like a constant conjunction between my phenomenal stomach-aches and other phenomena and, more generally, such is the flux of phenomena that it is doubtful that there are any purely phenomenal causes and effects. Hence, my phenomenal stomach-ache must have an external cause, if it has any cause at all. But I have good reason to believe that it *does* have a certain cause, namely, a cause which is also a cause of E (the enormously valuable end of Chapter 1) or (as I shall presently argue) an *effect* of that cause. For I have reason to believe that God exists, in the form of *a priori* arguments for his existence, and I have reason, based on my Chapter 1 solution of the problem of evil, to believe that if God exists, then my suffering is caused by the cause of E or (as I shall argue) that it is caused by an *effect* of the cause of E.

What, then, are we to make of this extra-phenomenal cause? Well, in the absence of any *better* explanation of my phenomenal stomach-ache, I should surely accept the *scientific* explanation of it in terms of, e.g., stomach acid. And, given that much of W, we can pass very rapidly to the whole of W (with which the S of Chapter 1, the for the most part unimpeded operation of scientific laws on the matter which the universe contains, can be equated.)

This latter claim needs elaboration. The best explanation of a given thing, X, will conform more closely to the following criteria than any other putative explanations of X: It will be (a) relatively simple, (b) predictively fruitful, (c) wide in scope and (d) itself explicable by such explanations. (If an infinite regress of explanations is impossible, then the ultimate explainers will not be subject to (d). But, for simplicity, I shall, for the most part, ignore ultimate explanations. Their existence would not undermine my present argument.) The explanation of my phenomenal stomach-ache in terms of stomach acid conforms to these criteria to a greater extent than any alternative explanations.[17] And, in particular, it conforms to criterion (d), i.e., it is itself explicable by sound explanations which are themselves explicable by sound explanations and so on. But the best explanations along the way are those offered by science and scientifically informed common sense; so the envisaged series of explanations takes us to $W\ (=S)$. Moreover, in explaining stomach acid and the cause of stomach acid, etc., science, and scientifically informed common sense, will have to utilize information which it could not have unless there are frequent veridical perceptions. Hence, I have reason to believe that many of my seeming perceptions are ingredients in veridical perceptions, i.e., I have reason to believe that PS is false.

This last step needs to be discussed in greater detail. The best explanations of my phenomenal stomach-ache, of the stomach acid which is causing it, and of the cause of that stomach acid, etc., are the explanations of science and scientifically informed common sense. (Call these "*B*-explanations".) But I know, via *B*-explanations, that a *B*-explainer would not have the information necessary to construct *B*-explanations unless some of his seeming perceptions were ingredients in veridical perceptions, e.g., unless his seeming perception of a metre reading *M* were caused by the metre's pointing to *M*. However, if one argues that *some* seeming perceptions are trustworthy, then it would be irrationally arbitrary for him to maintain that *only* those seeming perceptions are trustworthy. Rather, he should trust all seeming perceptions that conform to scientific laws (unlike the seeming perceptions which are involved in dreams and hallucinations) and are such that *B*-explanations can be causally based on them. (People who are not themselves scientists will be much better able to understand their phenomenal world if they take non-dreamlike seeming perceptions of scientific testimony to be veridical.)

My perceptual situation is not, therefore, like the predicament discussed in the original duck example, but is, rather, like the following case: A man who has proven himself an expert at distinguishing real ducks from decoys at a distance, on the basis of criteria $C_1 .. C_n$, encounters a new duck-like object about which he can make out that *it* satisfies those criteria. Under these circumstances, skepticism about the true nature of the duck-like object would be misplaced. And analogously, since we can know that *some* seeming perceptions must be veridical, we are warranted in inferring that *relevantly similar* seeming perceptions are also veridical and, hence, that PS is false.

My argument can be summarized as follows: The PS argues that since the (non-self-evident) claim that there are sound explanations entails that W exists, and since the latter claim is doubtful, so is the former one. But, given that we can know that there is at least one best – and, hence, sound – explanation, it would be irrationally arbitrary to maintain that it is the *only* sound explanation, i.e., that there is just *one* extra-phenomenal cause of just *one* effect, e.g., my phenomenal stomach-ache. And, indeed, a greater mistake would be involved, namely, admitting that the envisaged explanation is sound, while denying in effect that it conforms to the criteria for a sound explanation. For if there were only *one* explanation of *one* phenomenal event, or, at any rate, just a *few* such explanations, then they would be neither predictively fruitful, nor wide in scope, nor themselves explicable in terms of other sound explanations, i.e., they could not successfully compete with *other* explanations which *did* satisfy those criteria. But the *latter* explanations entail that $W(=S)$ exists. Hence, we arrive at the Cartesian conclusion[18] that an *a priori* knowledge of God's existence will enable us to overcome PS: I suffer and God is good; therefore, the world exists.

Another analogy may be useful here. I know scientists who say that science is the only sound intellectual discipline and that *a fortiori* all philosophy (including even Quinean philosophy) is unsound. But it is doubtful that this thesis is *entailed* by any theory which they would be willing to call 'scientific'. So, paradoxically, they have made a *start* at doing philosophy, and, hence, must (1) qualify their original claim in such a way as to avoid inconsistency ('*Most* philosophical theorizing is unsound') and (2) conform their philosophical defense of their thesis to the criteria for sound philosophizing, as I must conform my explanations to the criteria for sound theorizing about the nature of $W(=S)$.

9.11. The preceding refutation of PS presupposes that my Chapter 1 solution of the problem of evil is the only correct one. And someone may object that I have not fully considered the most promising alternatives, the soul-making theodicy and the free will defense,[19] i.e., the claim that suffering is the result of wrong, free choices, but that free will is nonetheless sufficiently valuable to outweigh the negative value of the suffering to which it gives rise, so long as it also gives rise to many morally right choices. Now in fact I have explicitly repudiated the former theory in 1.2, on the ground that (a) it is highly counter-intuitive that charitable responses to intense and prolonged pain (e.g., of the burn victim or the cancer patient) are sufficiently valuable to outweigh the negative value of the pain and (b) that some suffering (e.g., the suffering of wild animals) only very rarely evokes virtuous responses. And there is another objection to the soul-making theodicy, which is also an objection to the free will defense, namely, that having a capacity for serious wrongdoing is a very dubious blessing. (See my argument for this conclusion in 5.6.) The reason that this objection applies to both theodicies is that the soul-making theodicy overlaps the free will defense. The advocate of the former theory must account for the fact that we often fail to respond virtuously in situations which call for a virtuous response. And his answer is that God cannot be blamed for these omissions, since (1) they are the result of the misuse of our power of free choice and (2) the latter is (allegedly) a highly valuable thing to have.

9.12. Another criticism of my rebuttal of PS arises from the consideration that it contains as an essential premise the claim that I know the criteria to which an explanation must, to some extent, conform if it is to be a serious candidate for being the best explanation of a given phenomenon. (It is because I know what these criteria are that I know that science and scientifically informed common sense give us the best explanations with respect to the workings of the extra-phenomenal world.) But at this point the PS may wish to claim that my knowledge of the contemplated criteria (given that I have it) is not *a priori*, i.e., that it must be based on observations of the external world. And if the PS is right about this, then, since my argument has as its *conclusion* the claim that there is an external world, the argument is plainly circular.

Let us consider, then, the envisaged criteria one by one. It is surely

very doubtful that the claim that, *ceteris paribus*, the simplest explanation is the best one, is an empirically based theory. Indeed, it is widely
acknowledged that all sound empirical theory-formation presupposes
that simplicity is a valid criterion, but that the latter proposition is *not*
an empirical theory which (untenably) presupposes itself. Moreover,
the requirement that (barring ultimate explanations) a given explanation be such that the explanatory entities which it posits are themselves explicable (or, at any rate, promising candidates for explica-
bility) is surely one that can be known *a priori*. We do not require
empirical evidence to know that we are better off with an explanation,
the components of which are themselves explicable, than with an
explanation of which this is not true. (If there are sound ultimate
explanations, then they have some feature in virtue of which they
stand to explanations of themselves as properly basic propositions
stand to evidence. I shall not pause to discuss the question of what
such a feature might be.) Similar considerations obviously hold for
wideness of scope. And, finally, so far as predictive fruitfulness is
concerned, it is plainly a necessary truth, which is known *a priori*, that,
ceteris paribus, for any putative explanation, EX, that explanation is
more likely to be true, given that it accurately predicts events which
are such that they are unlikely to occur if EX is false, than is an alleged
explanation which is *not* thus predictively fruitful.

9.13. My rebuttal of PS depends on my having *a priori* knowledge
that God exists. Arguments for God's existence which are based on
premisses which imply that *W* exists would, in the present context,
be question-begging. But now *do* I have *a priori* knowledge of God's
existence? The arguments which I considered in Chapters 5 and 7
contain as an essential premiss the claim that God's existence is
logically possible; and it will be remembered that in 6.6 I based an
argument for that premiss on the claim that there are religious
experiences. But the latter claim cannot be known to be true prior to
knowledge of the external world (unless, indeed, *I* have had a religious
experience. And the non-theist can be excused if he rejects that

autobiographical claim as too thin a reed to support the argument in question. Moreover, since *he* has probably *not* had a religious experience, it is likely that he, at least, cannot extricate himself from the grip of PS via the argument of 6.6.).

But, in fact, I argued in Chapter 6 that the criticisms of God's possibility are not so convincing that the theist would be irrational in accepting the possibility premiss without the defense of it in 6.6. *That* argument was meant to persuade the non-theist. But now we have in effect another means of persuading him. Since it is not irrational to believe that God is logically possible, even in the absence of the kind of evidence for that claim which is found in 6.6, and since that claim is an essential premiss in a plausible refutation of PS, it has consider-able pragmatic value, and, for that reason, should be embraced by everyone who does not have a stake in PS, even without the *a posteriori* considerations set forth in 6.6. (Atheists sometimes claim that atheism is subject to a pragmatic justification as well – that, from the atheist's point of view, the actual world is a much better place if God does not dwell in it. However, this claim is generally based on the mistaken belief that if God exists, then he punishes all non-believers just for their non-belief, i.e., that if God exists, then he is not a morally perfect being.)

But does not the unevidenced claim that W exists have as much pragmatic value as the claim that God's existence is logically possible? And, if so, is not the latter claim merely superfluous, so far as the former claim is concerned? The answer is that the defense of PS, which I offered earlier in this chapter, makes it plain that belief that W exists is not properly basic, i.e., that we need evidence for that belief. However, I pointed out in 6.1 that the assertion that it is logically possible that a given proposition, p, is true, is, when p is not a mathematical or logical proposition, *prima facie* properly basic, i.e., that it is rational to reject that assertion only if there is evidence *against* it. Moreover, I argued throughout Chapter 6 that the criti-cisms of the claim that it is logically possible that God exists (GLP) are *not* such that it is irrational to accept that claim, even given that there is no evidence for it. In short, it is rational to believe that GLP is properly basic, while it is not rational to believe that about the proposition that W exists. It follows that, though both propositions get high marks from a pragmatic point of view, whether or not they are unevidenced, the proposition that W exists has low *epistemic* credibility unless there is evidence for it, while this is not true of GLP. Indeed, GLP has a pragmatic justification which the former proposition *per se* lacks, since (a) GLP is a premiss in a plausible argument that W exists and, hence, provides a basis for rational belief that it exists, and (b) rationality is highly desirable. It follows that my rebuttal of PS, based as it is on GLP, is not rendered superfluous by the fact that the unevidenced denial of PS is itself pragmatically justifiable.

Exactly similar considerations apply to the claim (call it 'C') that God exists. Even unevidenced, C is pragmatically justifiable (at least for many people).[20] However, from an *epistemic* point of view, GLP is properly basic, while C is not (or, at any rate, even if it is properly basic relative to *some* people, there are many people to whom it is not properly basic). It follows that GLP is a premiss in arguments for God's existence (i.e., those of Chapters 5 and 7 and the subsequent arguments in the Appendix) in which the premisses are all epistemically prior to the conclusion. And, indeed, since GLP thus contributes to the (desirable) rationality of theism, it has a pragmatic justification which C *per se* does not have.

Finally, if the claim that the external world exists must be justified by reference to the unevidenced, but properly basic, proposition, GLP, then the argument of 6.6, which *presupposes* that the external world exists, cannot bestow any more credibility on GLP than it possesses independently of that argument. Nonetheless, the argument of 6.6 is not superfluous if there is *another* argument for the existence of W which does not include GLP as an essential premiss. And I am not prepared to show that there is not.

TWO ARGUMENTS OF ST. ANSELM

1. In Proslogium II, St. Anselm argues as follows:

And assuredly that than which no greater being can be conceived, cannot exist in the understanding alone. For suppose it exists in the understanding alone: then it can be conceived to exist in reality; which is greater.

Therefore, if that than which nothing greater can be conceived exists in the understanding alone, the very being than which nothing greater can be conceived, is one, than which a greater can be conceived. But obviously this is impossible. Hence, there is no doubt that there exists a being, than which nothing greater can be conceived, and it exists both in the understanding and in reality.[1]

I shall take "exists in the understanding alone" to mean "is logically possible but not actual", and I shall take "a being than which no greater can be conceived" to mean "a being than which no greater being is logically possible", i.e., "a maximally great being". Moreover, I shall take "[If X] exists in the understanding alone, [then] it can be conceived to exist in reality, which is greater" to mean "If X is merely logically possible, then it would be greater if it were actual"; and I shall take it that the bearer of the predicate "would be greater if it were actual" is, at least, a logically possible object.

Given these interpretations, Anselm's argument can be restated as follows:

(1)   If there were a logically possible object which is a maximally great being and it were *merely* logically possible (rather than *both* logically possible *and* actual), then it would be greater if it were actual.

But

(2)   "X is a logically possible object which is maximally great" entails "X could not (and would not) be greater under *any* conditions, including its actuality".

So

   (3)   there is no logically possible object which is both maximally great and *merely* logically possible.

But

   (4)   there is in fact a logically possible object which is maximally great (namely, God).

Hence

   (5)   there is a logically possible object (i.e., God) who is not *merely* logically possible but both logically possible and actual as well.

2. Premisses (1) and (4) of this argument are, of course, controversial. Premiss (4) is false unless (a) there are logically possible objects and (b) God is among their number. However, I have defended the thesis that there are logically possible objects in 7.5, and I have discussed the question whether God is logically possible in Chapters 6 and 9; so I shall say no more about premiss (4) here.

But now what are we to make of premiss (1) – the claim that if there were a *merely* logically possible object which is maximally great, then it would be greater if it were actual? Isn't that claim suspiciously similar to the claim that, e.g., a merely logically possible glass of beer would, *ceteris paribus*, contain more beer if it were actual? Reflection will show that the answer is "No". *Qua* glass of beer, the *only* difference between a merely logically possible glass of beer and an actual one is *just* that the former is merely logically possible and the latter is actual. Actuality is not a beer-increasing property and being merely logically possible is not a beer-diminishing property. However, things are otherwise with respect to greatness. Actuality *is* a greatness-increasing property relative to God, as the following will show.

We can say with perfect propriety about some individuals (e.g., St. Francis) that it is better than not that they are (or were) actual. And it is even clearer that it is better than not that God, a maximally great being, be actual. But maximal greatness entails having every property which is such that it is better than not that an omnipotent, omniscient and perfectly good being have it. Hence, even though, for most predicates, it is false that the actuality of the object which bears them increases the amount or degree in which they are possessed, actuality *is* a greatness-increasing property relative to God (though not relative to, say, Hitler). But now it is surely a necessary truth that if an individual, X, lacks a given greatness-increasing property, G, then, *ceteris paribus*, it would be greater if it possessed G. It follows that if God is merely logically possible, then he would be greater if he were actual.

It is of note that, even if we subscribe to a relativistic interpretation of actuality – even if we hold that "X is actual" always expands into "X is actual relative to a given possible world, W" and that, hence, the possible world, which is actual *from our point of view*, has no privileged status with respect to actuality, my argument will still hold. For, whatever may be thought of *other* possible worlds, it is plainly better than not that God exist in the world which is actual from our point of view. And, again, it is a necessary truth that a maximally great being would have every property which is such that it is better than not that he possesses it.

But, finally, *does* God exist, not only in our world, but in every possible world? Anselm's Proslogium II argument does not require this to be the case; but if it is not the case, then God does not exist with SS necessity. And it is not, perhaps, just *intuitive* that God occupies every possible world. (Aren't there possible worlds in which, e.g., the only non-divine things are mud and rain? And if so, is it really better than not that God occupy those worlds?) But fortunately we need not simply rely on our intuitions here, since Chapter 5 provides us with a *demonstration* that if God exists in one possible world, then he exists, with SS necessity and *qua* maximally great, in all possible worlds, including our own. (If it is clear that God would not inhabit worlds in which the only non-divine things were, e.g., mud and rain, then, if God exists in *some* possible world, so much the worse for mud-and-rain 'worlds'. They are demonstrably not possible.)

3. In *Responsio* I, Anselm presents the following argument:

> Furthermore, if it can be conceived at all, it must exist. For no one who denies or doubts the existence of a being than which a greater is inconceivable [i.e., God] denies or doubts that if it did exist, its non-existence would be impossible. For otherwise it would not be a being than which a greater cannot be conceived. But as to whatever can be conceived but does not exist – if there were such a being, its non-existence ... would be possible. Therefore if a being than which a greater is inconceivable can even be conceived, it cannot be non-existent.[2]

Norman Malcolm has written as follows about this argument:

> Let me summarize the proof. If God, a being greater than which cannot be conceived, does not exist then He cannot *come* into existence. For if He did He would either have been *caused* to come into existence or have *happened* to come into existence, and in either case He would be a limited being, which by our conception of Him He is not. Since He cannot come into existence, if He does not exist His existence is impossible. ... Thus God's existence is either impossible or necessary. It can be the former only if the concept of such a being is self-contradictory or in some way logically absurd. Assuming that this is not so, it follows that He necessarily exists.[3]

What Malcolm writes here is a considerable departure from what Anselm actually says. Anselm does not claim, in the envisaged argument, that if God does not exist, then his existence is impossible. This is in fact demonstrable. (One way of demonstrating it is to point out that (1) the denial of the conclusion of modal argument *M* (Chapter 5), namely, that God exists, entails the denial of one of *M*'s premises and (2) the premiss which affirms God's logical possibility is the best candidate for being rejected.) But Anselm does not demonstrate it – at least not in connexion with the present proof.[4] Another defect in Malcolm's interpretation is that Anselm evidently intends to reach his conclusion via *modus tollens*, but there is no hint of this in Malcolm's interpretation.[5]

4. Let me say more about the *modus tollens* character of Anselm's proof. One not implausible interpretation of the proof is as follows:

(1)   If God does not exist, then if God existed, his non-existence would be possible.

But

(2)   if God existed, then his non-existence would *not* be possible.

So

(3)   the antecedent of (1) is false, i.e., God exists. (From (1) and (2) by *modus tollens*.)

On this interpretation, Anselm holds that "If God existed, his non-existence would be possible" is contradicted by "If God existed, his non-existence would *not* be possible". But in fact it is doubtful that these are contradictories. For, again, it is demonstrable that if God does not exist, then it is logically impossible that he exists. So if God does not exist, the antecedents of the allegedly contradictory conditionals are neessary falsehoods. But then, if we treat them as counterfactual conditionals, they are, if David K. Lewis is right,[6] both vacuously true and, hence, not contradictories. And, of course, the same is true of them if we take them to be material conditionals. But Anselm cannot *presuppose* that it is *false* that God does not exist without begging the question. So, on the present interpretation, Anselm's argument is a spectacular failure.

But there is another, more charitable interpretation of Anselm, on which it turns out to be true that if God does not exist, then it is possible that his non-existence is both possible and not possible. And the (necessarily true) denial of *this* consequent entails, by *modus tollens*, the denial of the antecedent, i.e., it entails that God exists. On this interpretation, we capture the *modus tollens* character of Anselm's argument, while avoiding the mistake which is embodied in the first interpretation. In presenting the new interpretation, I shall avoid using counterfactual conditionals, since the argument really does not need them. I have the following interpretation in mind:

(1)   It is necessarily true that if God exists, then his non-existence is logically impossible.

Hence

(2)   if God does not exist, then it is necessarily true that if God exists, then his non-existence is logically impossible. (Since the consequent of the conditional is necessarily true, it is entailed by every proposition, including the antecedent.)

So

(3)   if God does not exist, then each possible world is such that if God exists there, then his non-existence is logically impossible there.

(4)   There is a possible world in which God exists.

So

(5)   if God does not exist, then there is a possible world in which his non-existence is logically impossible. (From (3) and (4) by *modus ponens*.)

But now assume that

(6)   God does not exist.

Then

(7)   there is a possible world in which God does not exist and, hence, in which God's non-existence is logically possible.

But

(8)   what is logically possible in one possible world is logically possible in all possible worlds: every possible world is such that God's non-existence is logically possible there.

Hence

(9)   if God does not exist, then there is a possible world in which God's non-existence is both logically impossible and logically possible. (From (5) and (8).)

But

(10)   the consequent of (9) is false.

So

(11)   the antecedent of (9) is false, i.e., God exists. (From (9) and (10) by *modus tollens*.)

5. So goes the charitable interpretation of Anselm's argument. The

only controversial premisses are (1), (4), and (8). (1) and (4) have been defended in Chapters 5, 6, and 9; and the following is a proof of (8): If a philosopher claims that some proposition, p, which is possibly true in the actual world is necessarily false in another possible world, then he owes us an example of such a proposition; and it is very unlikely that such an example can be cited. So what is possibly true in the actual world is possibly true in all other possible worlds. And if someone claims that our world is special in that respect, then he owes us an explanation of why that should be so; and it is very doubtful that he can produce such an explanation.

Actually, as we saw in Chapter 5, premisses (1) and (4) alone entail that God exists: Anselm's argument is unnecessarily complicated. But the surprising thing is not Anselm's lack of elegance, but the essential soundness of his 11th century modal intuitions.

NOTES

PREFACE

[1] Plantinga, *The Nature of Necessity* (Oxford: The Clarendon Press, 1974).

[2] See, for example, Plantinga, 'Is Belief in God Properly Basic?', *Nous* **XV** (March, 1981), and 'Is Belief in God Rational?' in *Rationality and Religious Belief*, ed. C. Delaney (Notre Dame: University of Notre Dame Press, 1979).

CHAPTER 1

[1] I have discussed this topic in detail in 'An Examination of the 'Soul-Making' Theodicy', *Amercan Philosophical Quarterly* **7** (1970) and 'Do Theodicists Mean What They Say?' *Philosophy* **49** (1974).

[2] Another way of meeting the objection is just to affirm that all that God has brought about with respect to nature is the 'singularity' which gave rise to the big bang, and that it is doubtful that any scientific laws were in effect at that time and *a fortiori* doubtful that God's actions violated any scientific laws. However, I prefer the approach which I present in the text, since (1) it is unwise for religionists to commit themselves to scientific hypotheses which are far from certain and, indeed, in a state of flux, and (2) my approach in the text explains how God could have sometimes intervened in nature *after* the big bang; and this will be welcomed by the many theists who believe, or would like to believe, that he has done so.

[3] Someone may wish to say here that God's not making us clairvoyant is itself logically necessary for *E*. But the person who makes this claim in effect abandons the envisaged attempt to specify *E*'s nature. I shall, for simplicity, henceforth ignore this complication.

[4] See W. V. Quine, *The Ways of Paradox*, (New York: Random House, 1966), p. 4.

CHAPTER 2

[1] William L. Rowe, *The Cosmological Argument* (Princeton, N.J.: Princeton University Press, 1975). All Chapter 2 references to Rowe's writing but one will be to this book.

[2] It should be pointed out that Clarke would not be satisfied with the thesis that, since, e.g., sets are logically necessary beings, all of reality does *not* consist merely

of contingent things. For Clarke wants to establish the conclusion, not just that there is a logically necessary being, but a logically necessary being who is a *cause* of contingent things.

[3] See Rowe, pp. 222–269.

[4] For simplicity, I am assuming, throughout my discussion of Clarke's argument, that all contingent things are subject to causal explanation, i.e., I am ignoring, for the time being, the exceptions which are found in quantum mechanics.

[5] Rather than states of affairs. The reason for this qualifier can be found on pp. 97–114. See also pp. 149–151.

[6] See note 5.

[7] William L. Rowe, *Philosophy of Religion, An Introduction* (Belmont, California: Dickenson, 1978), p. 57.

[8] There is a question which even more obviously does not have a true answer, given that the only true answer would refer to a cause outside the envisaged set, viz., "Why are there any *causes* at all?"

[9] Actually, however, Clarke's subsequent argument for the infinity of the logically necessary cause (pp. 227–233), which is in essence an argument of St. Anselm which I shall discuss in Chapter 6, should, for a reason I shall present there, be taken as an argument that God *is* in fact essentially disembodied.

[10] Perhaps it would be better to say that there is a *prima facie* case against the existence of the envisaged series, but one which can, in the end, be overthrown by science.

CHAPTER 3

[1] Though, instead of considering the more specific claim that the eye is camera-like, Plantinga considers the claim that the *universe* resembles "the productions of human contrivance" (p. 97), inasmuch as "it exhibits curious adaptation of means to ends" (p. 101). See Alvin Plantinga, *God and Other Minds* (Ithaca: Cornell University Press, 1967), Chapters 4 and 10.

[2] David Hume, *Dialogues Concerning Natural Religion* in *The Empiricists* (Garden City, New York: Doubleday, 1974), pp. 466–469.

[3] *Ibid.*, pp. 459–461.

[4] *God and Other Minds*, p. 104.

[5] *Ibid.*, pp. 104–106.

[6] *Ibid.*, p. 102.

Another pseudo-argument which this description fits (which is cited by Plantinga on pp. 101–102) is:

(1) Every member of the class of Chevrolets plus the universe, of which we know whether or not it is the product of intelligent design, is indeed the product of intelligent design.

(2) The universe is a member of the class of Chevrolets plus the universe. So

(3) probably the universe is the product of intelligent design.

[7] A similar argument shows that what is wrong with the pseudo-argument cited in note 6 is that there are some members of the class of Chevrolets plus the universe (namely, the random configurations cited above) about which we know that they are *not* the products of design; so we know that there is no nomic connexion between being a member of that class and being designed.

CHAPTER 4

[1] Kurt Baier, *The Moral Point of View*, abridged edition (New York: Random House, 1965), p. 150.

[2] *Ibid.*, p. 156.

[3] Actually, things are a bit more complicated. The suicidally depressed patient harms himself by committing suicide if, even though he does not desire continued life at the time of his suicide, he would, in the normal course of events, have come to desire (and acquire) continued life in the future. Hence the reader should add to my subsequent definition of 'hedonist', "a person about whom it is false that he *would* have come to desire (and acquire) moral innocence, were it not for his present misdeeds". Whether there are in fact such people is not crucial to my central argument, for a reason which will shortly emerge.

[4] The entailment does not go the other way. A child is not harmed by the boredom which sometimes accompanies his piano practice, even though he strongly desires its absence as an end-in-itself.

[5] See David K. Lewis, *Counterfactuals* (Cambridge: Harvard University Press, 1973), pp. 24–26.

[6] I have in mind Lewis's possible world analysis of counterfactuals. See the book referred to in the preceding note.

[7] According to *The Compact Edition of the Oxford English Dictionary* (p. 1964), 'oblige' means "to bind by ... a moral ... tie, to render liable ...".

According to *The Random House Dictionary of the English Language* (p. 917), 'oblige' means (1) "to require or constrain" and (2) "to bind morally ...".

There are, of course, other senses of 'oblige'. The latter dictionary gives these alternative senses: "(a) to make (an action, policy, etc.) necessary ...: 'Your recalcitrance obliges firmness on my part'; (b) to place under a debt of gratitude: obligate; (c) to favor or accommodate: 'Mr. Weems will oblige us with a song'; (d) to be kindly accommodating; help out).

It is plain, however, that none of these alternative senses is at all a plausible candidate for the meaning of 'morally oblige(d)'. A review of various major dictionaries reveals no ambiguity in the term 'morally obliged' which is analogous to, e.g., the ambiguity of 'theory' which fundamentalists trade on when they say of evolutionary theory that "it is only a theory". (*The Random House Dictionary of the English Language* gives, as one sense of 'theory', "a proposed explanation whose status is still conjectural, in contrast to well-established propositions that are regarded as reporting matters of actual fact". But, of course, another definition which it gives is "a coherent group of general propositions used as principles of explanation for a class of phenomena".)

[8] The standard dictionary definition does *not* entail that Z's doing what he is morally obliged to do is of *overriding* importance to Z. And how do we know that this *is* of overriding importance to Z, if it is not analytically entailed by our obligation claims? (It cannot be an empirical truth, since we do not, or should not, allow observations to count against it.) The answer is simply that the envisaged thesis is best construed as a non-analytic necessary truth, which is known *a priori*.

[9] The leading proponent of prescriptivism, R. M. Hare, does recognize that overridingness has some kind of connexion with moral obligation. But he claims that this is best explained as its being the case that the concept of morality is such that some moral obligation prescriptions, from which all other such prescriptions are derivable, take action-guiding precedence over any other prescriptions. See Hare's *Moral Thinking* (Oxford: Clarendon Press, 1981), pp. 49–61. But whatever may be thought of this account, Hare's prescriptivism certainly does not yield as a consequence that S's fulfilling his moral obligations is of overriding importance *to S*, in the sense that his interests will be substantially adversely affected if he fails to fulfill them. Moreover, it is demonstrable that prescriptivism is fundamentally mistaken. We say with warrant, not only that particular individuals are morally obliged to perform certain actions, but in the case of some actions, that *every* person is obliged to perform them. And it is highly implausible that, though "Z (an individual person) is morally obliged to do X" is essentially prescriptive, "*Everyone* who bears a certain description, D, is morally obliged to do X" is not. Hare agrees, and calls utterances of the latter sort 'universal prescriptions'. (See, for example, *Moral Thinking*, p. 60.) But surely it is true that if, e.g., "Everyone who can do so ought to practice self-control" is a universal prescription, it is, in view of the fact that the vast majority of the audience to whom it is addressed is (normally) not reached by it, remarkably infelicitous (in J. L. Austin's sense). (I am assuming – what seems clearly true – that in prescribing things, we prescribe them *to* people and, hence, that a universal prescription prescribes something to everyone and so is intended to address everyone.) My prescribing self-control to all human beings who can exercise it, even though most of them will never know what I said, is rather like a doctor prescribing vitamin C tablets to all mankind when, in so doing, he reaches only one other person. Needless to say, however, "Everyone who can do so ought to exercise self-control" is, in many contexts, perfectly felicitous.

[10] *Moral Thinking*, p. 70.

[11] *Ibid.*, p. 71.

[12] Another redefinition of '*A*' on which "*Z* is morally obliged to refrain from doing *A*" turns out true, even in the case envisaged in the counter-example, is "the action of *wrongly* promoting one's self at the considerable expense of another". But, on this definition, "*Z* is morally obliged to refrain from doing *A*" reduces to a tautology. And, though that is compatible with the main thrust of my argument, I think it worthwhile to show that at least some ethical language expresses necessary, but non-trivial, truths.

[13] See note 5.

CHAPTER 5

[1] Very similar arguments would, of course, show that if *p* is possibly true in *W*, then it is possibly true in *W'*, and that if *p* is contingent in *W*, then it is contingent in *W'*. For more on this topic see Plantinga, *The Nature of Necessity*, pp. 51–54.

[2] I shall, for simplicity, omit the further characteristic, "creator of the universe". If maximal greatness does not entail that characteristic, then the present argument does not establish the existence of (the full-fledged) God. However, it comes close enough to doing so that the non-irrationalist theist should certainly be satisfied with it.

[3] The paradox of the stone can be viewed as a special case of God's not being able to diminish his power. God's having the power to make a stone which he cannot move would be *eo ipso* God's having the power to create a state of affairs at a given time, *t*, in which there is a stone which God cannot move, even though there was no such stone before *t*. And God's having that power would be a case of his having the power to diminish his power.

[4] For an alternative approach, see my 'Examination of an Ontological Argument', *Philosophical Studies* **28** (1975), pp. 347–350.

CHAPTER 6

[1] Alvin Plantinga, ed., *The Ontological Argument from St. Anselm to Contemporary Philosophers* (New York: Doubleday, 1965), p. 157.

[2] Complex mathematical and logical formulae are an exception to the present thesis. I shall say more about this in 6.5.

[3] The proposition that God exists is also an exception, if it is, as Plantinga has recently argued, properly basic. (See the relevant references in the Preface.) However, there are many people with respect to whom it is not properly basic, and for *those* people, at least, God's logical possibility is arguably epistemically prior to God's existence.

[4] Needless to say, there are values of '*X*' such that "*X* is maximal with respect to property *P*" does *not* entail "*X* is absolutely preeminent with respect to *P*".

[5] Maximal greatness in, e.g., a flute player is being a maximally great *flute player*, which does not entail being absolutely preeminently powerful. And, in general, when we are dealing with things or persons *qua* having some specific function like flute playing, it is not at all clear that maximal greatness in such things entails omnipotence. However, the word 'person' does not entail having a specific function, nor does, e.g., the word 'centaur'. And, when qualifying 'person', 'maximal greatness' does appear to entail omnipotence, (etc.). Moreover, given that, e.g., 'maximally great centaur' has a meaning, then it looks as if a maximally great centaur would be a maximally great person, and, hence, omnipotent (omniscient and perfectly good).

[6] Plantinga, p. 15.
It is of note that Samuel Clarke uses the very same argument to establish the omnipresence of God. See Rowe, *The Cosmological Argument*, pp. 222–235.

[7] Plantinga, p. 15.

[8] Plantinga, p. 157.

[9] Pavel Tichy has recently argued in effect that, since propositions like (a), (b), and (c) are obviously possibly true, SS necessary existence is incompatible with necessarily possessing greatness-making properties like omnipotence, omniscience and perfect goodness. See Pavel Tichy, 'Existence and God', *Journal of Philosophy* **LXXVI** (1979), pp. 19–20.

[10] For a discussion of a similar argument against God's logical possibility, see Plantinga, *The Nature of Necessity*, pp. 217–221.

[11] In commenting on their dreams, people sometimes make such claims as that they dreamed that they were identical with the number 9. But it is surely much more likely that a person who makes this report *believed* in his dream that he was identical with the number 9 than that he had a *sense-experience* of his identity with the number 9.

[12] For much more extensive comments on this matter, see my article, 'Seeming to See', *American Philosophical Quarterly* **2** (1965), pp. 312–318 and see Chapter 9 of this book.

[13] See, for example, William James, *The Varieties of Religious Experience* (New York: Random House, 1929), pp. 58–77. On p. 63, James comments on the various reports of God-experiences which he has cited as follows: "We may now lay it down as certain that in the distinctively religious sphere of experience, many persons ... possess the objects of their beliefs, not in the form of mere conceptions, which their intellect accepts as true, but rather in the form of quasi-sensible realities directly apprehended".

[14] *Ibid.*

[15] And *qua* SS necessarily maximally great being I shall, for simplicity, omit this qualifier, though the reader should keep it in mind.

[16] We know *a priori* that, e.g., "Z experiences a square circle" is false. Hence, it is likely that it is *necessarily* false, i.e., it is likely that it is *logically* impossible to experience what is logically impossible.

[17] Since the claim that, e.g., St. Theresa is God is much more apt to be false than is GLP (even given the earlier criticisms of it), we are much more warranted in rejecting the claim that St. Theresa has experienced (as opposed to believing in) her identity with God than we are in rejecting reports of more ordinary God-experiences.

CHAPTER 7

[1] Haldane and Ross, *The Philosophical Works of Descartes*, Vol. 1 (New York: Dover Publications, Inc., 1955), p. 181.

[2] Anthony Kenny points out that Descartes explained to a critic that by "a mountain without a valley", he meant an uphill slope without a downhill slope. Anthony Kenny, *Descartes, A Study of His Philosophy* (New York: Random House, 1968), p. 156.

[3] When *any* sentence expresses a truth, this is at least *in part* explicable by reference to the concepts which it expresses.

[4] Descartes claims that the idea of God – like the idea of geometrical figures – is not *made* by the mind, but rather *discovered* to be part of its contents. He says of his idea of God, "I discern ... that this idea is not something factitious, and depending solely on my thought. ..." (Haldane and Ross, p. 182). And he says of his idea of a certain fiction – namely, a winged horse – which he has invented, that "just as I may imagine a winged horse, although no horse with wings exists, so I could perhaps attribute existence to God, although no God existed. But a sophism is concealed in this objection. ... For it is not within my power to think of God without existence ... though it is in my power to imagine a horse either with wings or without wings." (*Ibid.*, pp. 181-2). Here it appears that Descartes believes that there are no necessary truths about fictitious beings. But that is a mistake. Though winged horses are fictitious, the sentence "Winged horses are winged" surely expresses a necessary truth, as does "Existent winged horses exist". Still – as the above will make plain – Descartes need not have worried about such Gaunilo-type entities.

[5] At a 1981 Notre Dame Conference on the Philosophy of Religion. The objection considered in the next section was also presented at that conference.

[6] In formulating this objection, I have drawn on Rowe's critique of Anselm's *Proslogium* II proof in Rowe's *Philosophy of Religion: An Introduction*, pp. 41–46.

[7] *Ibid.*, p. 43.

[8] There is another objection to Rowe's approach to magicans: Since magicans exist in the actual world, they are logically possible in the actual world. But, if Rowe is

right, in possible worlds in which there are no magicians, magicans are logically impossible. So there are some possible worlds (e.g., the actual world) in which magicans are logically possible and some in which they are not. Hence, Rowe's argument entails the denial of the intuitive (S5) thesis that what is logically possible is necessarily logically possible.

[9] If we are going to subscribe to possible world theory, and yet deny that there are objects which, though they do not exist in the actual world, exist in *some* possible worlds, then, in order to deal with, e.g., Pegasus, we shall have to adopt one or other of the following, unpalatable theses: (a) Pegasus is not logically possible. (b) Though Pegasus exists in at least one possible world, he is identical with some inhabitant of the actual world, even though he is very different in the former world from the being which he is in the latter one. (The trouble with (b) is that it appears not to be even in principle possible to specify the individual (horse?) in the actual world with whom Pegasus is allegedly identical.)

[10] Michael Scriven, *Primary Philosophy* (New York: McGraw Hill, 1966), pp. 146–147.

CHAPTER 8

[1] Ivan Karamazov doubts that any state of affairs could compensate even for a single instance of a child's intense and prolonged suffering: "I renounce the higher harmony altogether. It's not worth the tears of that one tortured child. ..." Dostoyevsky, *The Brothers Karamazov*, translated by Constance Garnett, (New York: Random House, 1950), p. 290.

[2] The exact words of James are these: "Our passional nature not only lawfully may, but must, decide an option between propositions, whenever it is a genuine option which cannot be decided on intellectual grounds; for to say, under such circumstances, 'Do not decide, but leave the question open', is itself a passional decision – just like deciding yes or no – and it is attended with the same risk of losing the truth." William James, 'The Will to Believe', *Essays in Pragmatism* (New York: Hafner, 1957), p. 95.

James sometimes says that it is a necessary condition of the theist benefitting from his belief that it be true (*Ibid.*, p. 106). But in another place (*Ibid.*, p. 108) he maintains that "the whole defense of religious faith hinges upon action", and I take it that here he is claiming that theism results in conduct which benefits both the theist and others. But it is not clear why theism must be true in order to have this consequence (unless having good consequences is *ipso facto* a sufficient condition of the truth of a belief).

[3] I gather that James would say that the question of whether p is true is "decided on intellectual grounds" if there is significantly more reason to believe p than to believe not-p or *vice versa*.

[4] Someone may wish to say at this point that the theist who claims to know that (1) is true and the atheist who claims to know that (2) is true are in as precarious an epistemic position as is the agnostic who claims to know that (3) is true. However, even given that theism is not clearly better evidenced than atheism and *vice versa*, neither the contemplated theist nor the contemplated atheist is subject to the dialectical point that the agnostic, who claims that his position is superior because suspending judgement in the envisaged circumstances is the epistemically preferable thing to do, cannot in consistency claim to know that (3) is true.

[5] Roderick Chisholm, *Theory of Knowledge*, second edition, (Englewood Cliffs, N.J.: Prentice-Hall, 1977), p. 13.

CHAPTER 9

[1] Gilbert Ryle, 'Sensation', *Contemporary British Philosophy*, 3rd series, H. D. Lewis, ed., (New York: Macmillan, 1956), p. 435.

[2] G. J. Warnock, *Berkeley* (London: Penguin Books, 1953), p. 186.

[3] Unless, of course, they are placed in quotation marks and used to refer to word types or tokens.

[4] It might be thought that the speaker's being sure that it will rain falsifies what he says, as would his being certain that it will not rain. But this is a mistake, since "Maybe it will rain today" does not, strictly speaking, *assert* that the speaker is uncertain about whether it will rain. The speaker is, of course, being *insincere* (hiding his real belief about the matter) if he is convinced that it will rain or convinced that it will not.

[5] It may be objected that Ryle and Warnock possibly did not intend to adopt the strong position which I have been attacking but simply the weaker one mentioned above. But if Warnock would admit that it is neither the sole nor primary function of 'seem', in all its occurrences, to enable the spekar to evince a non-committal attitude toward a proposition, then he would be admitting in effect that his argument against Berkeley's idealism is without force. (It would take us too far afield were I to substantiate that claim. But I invite the reader to examine *Berkeley*, pp. 181–189.) As for Ryle, he appears to believe that his analysis of statements of the same sort as "I seem to see ..." entails that these locutions are not used to report the occurrence of sense-data. It is not at all plain that this follows, however, if "I seem to see ..." is typically *more* than a guarded assertion that the speaker veridically sees an object or a device for evincing a non-committal attitude toward this proposition.

[6] D. M. Armstrong says, "To say 'It looks oval to me' usually means that I have some inclination to believe that I am seeing something oval". *Perception and the Physical World* (London: Routledge and Kegan Paul, 1961), p. 92. No doubt Armstrong is willing to extend this type of analysis to, e.g., "I seem to see ...".

[7] See, for example, Alan R. White, 'The Causal Theory of Perception', *Proceedings*

of the Aristotelian Society, Supplementary Volume **XXXV** (1961), p. 165. White appears to wish to defend the claim that locutions like "I seem to see *x*" mean the same as "I am inclined to think that *x* has such and such visual characteristics", (*Ibid.*, p. 167). That claim is false, however. A person who is blind from birth can be inclined to think that *x* has such and such visual characteristics, but he cannot truthfully say that he seems to see *x*. Similar considerations apply to another analysis of "I seem to see *x*" which White appears to find adequate, viz., "I am inclined to think that what is before my eyes is *x*", (*Ibid.*, p. 167).

It should be pointed out that the analysis being considered above is not subject to this same criticism. A person who is blind from birth can truthfully say neither that he seems to see *x* nor that he is inclined to believe that he sees it.

[8] Possibly this is White's position in the paper which I cited in the preceding footnote.

[9] C. D. Broad, 'Arguments for the Existence of God II', *The Journal of Theological Studies* **XL** (1939), p. 163, and Roderick Chisholm, *Theory of Knowledge*, second edition, pp. 74–77.

[10] It is doubtful, however, that *Chisholm* would accept this characterization. For he claims in effect that he is not so much trying to refute PS as trying to formulate what we must know *if* we know that PS is false. However, I think that Chisholm underestimates the difficulty of coming to know that PS is false.

[11] Robert Nozick, *Philosophical Explanations* (Cambridge: Harvard University Press, 1981), pp. 211–247.

Actually, Nozick's (playful) example of his dreaming or hallucinating is his floating in a tank, being stimulated by electrochemical means to have seeming perceptions which give rise to his mistaken belief that he is veridically perceiving objects in his environment. However, it is surely the case that if one's seeming perceptions have *any* explanation, then it is *very unlikely* that Nozick's explanation (as opposed to the scientific one) is the best explanation. I shall discuss this point at length in 9.10.

[12] A more detailed exposition of Nozick's argument is as follows: Nozick asks us (*Ibid.*, p. 207) to consider two propositions which are roughly equivalent to the following ones:

p = I am awake and sitting on a chair in New York.

q = I am not floating in a tank, being electrochemically stimulated by deceiving scientists to believe that p.

Nozick points out that I know that p and not-q are logically incompatible, agrees with the skeptic that I do not know that q, and yet argues roughly as follows that my not knowing that q is compatible with my knowing that p: "Assume that I know that p is true. A necessary condition (call it 'ϕ') of my knowing that a given proposition, Q, is true is that if Q were false, then I would not believe that it is true, i.e., in the closest possible worlds in which Q is false, I do not believe that it is true. Now since I know that p, it is true that in the closest not-p worlds, I do not believe that p. ('If p were false, I would be standing or lying down in the same city, or perhaps sleeping there, or perhaps in a neighboring city or town' (p. 207). And, under those circumstances, I would not believe that p.) However, if q were false – if I were floating in the tank – then I would still believe that q, since *ex hypothesi* the scientists who are stimulating my brain are bent on deceiving me. In short, I know that p because (among other things) condition ϕ is satisfied with respect to my belief that p, even though I do not know that q, since condition ϕ is *not* satisfied with respect to my belief that q."

Nozick's main thesis (call it 'T') can be expressed as follows: Proposition q is such that not-q *entails* that, in the closest not-q worlds, I still believe that q. Hence, q is not the kind of proposition that can be known to be true (since my belief that q cannot satisfy ϕ); and so it should not, upon reflection, be surprising that, even when I know that p and that p entails q, I do not know that q.

However, even if we set the above criticism of Nozick aside, it can be shown that T has a consequence which is not compatible with Nozick's explanation of how, given skepticism, I can nonetheless know that p is true. Suppose that I know that I know that p (that Kp), and since I know that Kp entails that my belief that p satisfies ϕ, I know that this latter proposition (call it 'r') is true. Then I know that the closest possible worlds are not tank-worlds, since I know that if they were tank-worlds, then *ex hypothesi* the scientists who are bent on deceiving me would cause me not to disbelieve that p. But if T is true, I cannot know that the closest possible worlds are not tank-worlds, since I cannot know that q is true, i.e., I cannot know that the *actual* world is not a tank-world. (If it *is* a tank-world, then the closest possible worlds are also tank-worlds.) It follows that T entails that, for any p-like proposition, p', which I know to be true, either (1) I cannot know that Kp' or (2) even though I know that Kp' and that Kp' entails r, I cannot know that r.

Let us look first at disjunct (1) – the claim that, though I can know that a myriad of p-like propositions are true, none of these propositions is such that I can know that I know it. Not only is (1) implausible on its face, it is inconsistent with Nozick's explanation of how I can know that p, even though I do not know that q. For that explanation surely presupposes that I know that I know that p. Nozick can deny this only at the cost of having to admit that what he is explaining, namely, knowledge of p-like propositions, is something which we do not, and cannot, know to exist.

Well, then, can Nozick fall back on disjunct (2) – the claim that we cannot know that r-like propositions are true? Actually, Nozick is *committed* to accepting disjunct (2). For consider the closest possible worlds in which r is false, i.e., in which, though p is false, I still believe it. If I am rational and believe that p, then my belief that p is caused and warranted by my seeming perceptions. So any close world, in which p is false and yet, though I am rational, I believe that p, is a world in which despite my rationality, I am being deceived by delusory seeming perceptions. Now Nozick thinks that, since any close world in which q is false is a tank-world, I cannot know that q is true. Hence, consistency dictates that Nozick agree to the conclusion that, since any close world in which r is false and I am rational, is a world in which I am suffering from delusory seeming perceptions, I cannot know that r is true.

But that is not a conclusion which Nozick can embrace. The claim that my belief that p satisfies ϕ is central to Nozick's explanation of how I can know that p, even though I do not know that q. So if I do not *know* that my belief that p-like propositions are true satisfies ϕ (while my belief that q does not) then *eo ipso* I do not know that Nozick's explanation is plausible.

[13] Saul A. Kripke, *Wittgenstein on Rules and Private Language* (Cambridge: Harvard University Press, 1982).

[14] *Ibid.*, p. 20, note 5.

[15] Let me say in passing that I find *this* thesis very hard to swallow.

[16] *Ibid.*, pp. 8–9.

[17] Again, Nozick's playful 'explanation' of my phenomenal world in terms of evil scientists who are bent on deceiving me is surely vastly inferior to the explanations of science and scientifically informed common sense.

[18] However, Descartes's attempt to justify belief in the external world by citing God's goodness clearly fails. God's goodness is compatible with my being deceived sometimes, so why not always (as is, indeed, the case with the severely mentally ill)? Moreover, blaming all instances of mistaken belief on the misuse of free will implies – what is surely implausible – that if I am fooled by a nightmare, this is my own fault, and that the mentally ill have it in their power to cure themselves.

[19] The Biblical explanation in terms of punishment for sin cannot account for the suffering of human infants and non-human animals.

[20] A powerful motive for accepting theism on non-epistemic grounds, is the desire to believe that justice is finally done, no matter how the unjust may prosper in this world. (Strictly speaking, *God* is not required to play this role. See 4.7. But, such is our religious heritage, that many of us would find it very difficult to believe in supernatural reward and punishment if we did not believe that (precisely) God exists.)

APPENDIX

[1] Plantinga, *The Ontological Argument*, p. 4.

[2] Plantinga, p. 14.

[3] Plantinga, p. 146.

[4] An immediately preceding argument is as follows:

> That than which a greater is inconceivable cannot be conceived except as without a beginning. But whatever can be conceived to exist, and does not exist, can be conceived to exist through a beginning. Hence, what can

be conceived to exist, but does not exist, is not the being than which a greater cannot be conceived. Therefore, if such a being can be conceived to exist, necessarily it does exist. (Plantinga, p. 14).

This argument is subject to the following interpretation:

(1)   If there is a logically possible object which is a maximally great being, then it is not such that it is logically possible that it has a beginning in actuality.

But

(2)   if there is a *merely* logically possible object, then it *is* such that it is logically possible that it has a beginning in actuality.

So

(3)   if there is a logically possible object which is a maximally great being (i.e., if God's existence is logically possible), then it is not a *merely* logically possible object (i.e., God (actually) exists).

(3) is logically equivalent to the proposition that if God does not (actually) exist then his existence is not logically possible. (There are other ways in which this conclusion can be demonstrated, but I shall leave it to the reader to explore them.)

[5] Robert Merrihew Adams's interpretation of the proof also suffers from this defect. See Adams, 'The Logical Structure of Anselm's Arguments', *Philosophical Review* **80** (1971), pp. 43–44.

[6] David K. Lewis, *Counterfactuals*, pp. 24–26.

If Lewis is right, then my argument on behalf of premiss (1) of Anselm's Proslogium II proof – "If there were a merely logically possible maximally great being then it would be greater if it existed" – is in effect part of an argument for the conclusion that (1) is vacuously true.

A RESEARCH BIBLIOGRAPHY

PREPARED BY P. HOLLEY ROBERTS

This bibliography contains sources for topics covered in the chapters of this book. Most of the sources appeared after 1977. For sources prior to 1978, see the bibliography prepared by William J. Wainwright, *Philosophy of Religion: An Annotated Bibliography of Twentieth-Century Writings in English* (New York: Garland Press, 1978). A more recent bibliography covering a wide range of topics in the philosophy of religion is the bibliography for Chapter 5, 'The Problem of Justifying Belief in God', in James W. Cornman, Keith Lehrer, and George S. Pappas, *Philosophical Problems and Arguments: An Introduction*, 3rd ed. (New York: MacMillan, 1982), pp. 341-348. Other recent bibliographies have been noted in the relevant sections below.

CHAPTER 1.
DOES SUFFERING SERVE VALUABLE ENDS?

I. Historical sources

Plato: *Laws*, Book X.
Hume, David: *Dialogues Concerning Natural Religion*.
Hume, David: *Enquiry Concerning Human Understanding*, Section X.
Mill, John Stuart: 'Nature', *Three Essays on Religion*.

II. Contemporary sources
A. Books

Feinberg, John S.: *Theologies and Evil*. Washington, D. C.: University Press of America, 1979.

B. Chapters of books, selections from collected essays

Plantinga, Alvin: 'The Free Will Defense', *Philosophy in America: Essays*, ed. Max Black. London: George Allen & Unwin Ltd., 1965.
Plantinga, Alvin: Chapter IX, 'God, Evil, and the Metaphysics of Freedom'. *The Nature of Necessity*. Oxford: Clarendon Press, 1974.
Rowe, William L.: Chapter 6, 'The Problem of Evil', *Philosophy of Religion: An Introduction*. Belmont, Calif.: Wadsworth, 1978.

161

Swinburne, Richard: Chapter 11, 'The Problem of Evil', *The Existence of God.* Oxford: Clarendon Press, 1979.

Watson, S. Youree: 'The Other Face of Evil', *Essays in Morality and Ethics*, ed. James Gaffney. New York: Paulist Press, 1980.

Hick, John H.: 'An Irenaean Theodicy', *Encountering Evil*, ed. Stephen T. Davis. Atlanta: Knox Press, 1981.

Mackie, J. L.: Chapter 9, 'The Problem of Evil', *The Miracle of Theism*: *Arguments For and Against the Existence of God.* Oxford: Clarendon Press, 1982.

C. Journal articles

Basinger, David: 'Evil as Evidence Against the Existence of God: A Response', *Philosophy Research Archives* **4** (1978), no. 1275.

Böer, Steven E.: 'The Irrelevance of the Free Will Defense', *Analysis* **38** (1978), 110–112.

Byrne, Peter: 'Miracles and the Philosophy of Science', *Heythrop Journal* **19** (April 1978), 162–170.

Gregory, Donald R.: 'Would a Satanic Resurrection World Falsify Christian Theism: A Reply to Gregory S. Kavka', *Religious Studies* **14** (1978), 69–72.

Hill, John: 'Natural Sanction and Philosophical Theology', *Sophia* **17** (July 1978), 27–34.

King-Farlow, John: 'Cacodaemony and Devilish Isomorphism', *Analysis* **38** (1978), 59–61.

Martin, Michael: 'Is Evil Evidence Against the Existence of God?', *Mind* **87** (1978), 429–432.

Mohr, Richard: 'Plato's Final Thoughts on Evil: *Laws* **X**, 899–905', *Mind* **87** (1978), 572–575.

Moore, Harold F.: 'Evidence, Evil and Religious Belief', *International Journal for Philosophy of Religion* **9** (1978), 241-245.

Moore, Harold F.: 'Evidence – Once More: Reply to E. Wierenga's "Reply to H. Moore's Evidence, Evil and Religious Belief"', *International Journal for Philosophy of Religion* **9** (1978), 252–253.

Ramberan, Osmond G.: 'Evil and Theism', *Sophia* **17** (April 1978), 28–36.

Swinburne, Richard: 'Natural Evil', *American Philosophical Quarterly* **15** (1978), 295–301.

Wierenga, Edward: 'Reply to Harold Moore's "Evidence, Evil and Religious Belief"', *International Journal for Philosophy of Religion* **9** (1978), 246–251.

Adams, Robert: 'Existence, Self-Interest, and the Problem of Evil', *Nous* **13** (1979), 53–65.

Coughlan, M. J.: 'Moral Evil Without Consequences?', *Analysis* **39** (1979), 58–60.

Kellenberger, J.: 'Miracles', *International Journal for Philosophy of Religion* **10** (1979), 145-162.

Peterson, Michael L.: 'Evil and Inconsistency', *Sophia* **18** (July 1979), 20–27.

Peterson, Michael L.: 'God and Evil: Problems of Consistency and Gratuity', *Journal of Value Inquiry* **13** (Winter 1979), 305–313.

Pike, Nelson: 'Plantinga on Free Will and Evil', *Religious Studies* **15** (1979), 449–473.

Rowe, William L.: 'The Problem of Evil and Some Varieties of Atheism', *American Philosophical Quarterly* **16** (1979), 335–341.

Wall, George B.: 'A New Solution to an Old Problem', *Religious Studies* **15** (1979), 511–530.

Wood, Forrest, Jr.: 'Some Whiteheadian Insights into the Problem of Evil', *Southwestern Journal of Philosophy* **10** (Spring 1979), 147–155.

Allen, Diogenes: 'Natural Evil and the Love of God', *Religious Studies* **16** (1980), 439–456.

Anglin, W. S.: 'Can God Create a Being He Cannot Control?', *Analysis* **40** (1980), 220–223.

Basinger, David: 'Christian Theism and the Free Will Defence', *Sophia* **19** (July 1980), 20–23.

Chernoff, Fred: 'The Obstinance of Evil', *Mind* **89** (1980), 269–273.

Davies, Martin: 'Determinism and Evil', *Australasian Journal of Philosophy* **58** (June 1980), 116–127.

Kane, G. Stephen: 'Evil and Privation', *International Journal for Philosophy of Religion* **11** (1980), 43–58.

Lafollette, Hugh: 'Plantinga on the Free Will Defense', *International Journal for Philosophy of Religion* **11** (1980), 123–132.

Langston, Douglas: 'The Argument from Evil: Reply to Professor Richman', *Religious Studies* **16** (1980), 103–113.

Miller, Randolph Crump: 'Process, Evil and God', *American Journal of Theology & Philosophy* **1** (May 1980), 60–70.

Reichenbach, Bruce R.: 'The Inductive Argument from Evil', *American Philosophical Quarterly* **17** (1980), 221–227.

Ross, James F.: 'Creation', *Journal of Philosophy* **77** (October 1980), 614–629.

Sainsbury, R. M.: 'Benevolence and Evil' *Australasian Journal of Philosophy* **58** (June 1980), 128–134.

Tooley, Michael: 'Alvin Plantinga and the Argument from Evil', *Australasian Journal of Philosophy* **58** (December 1980), 360–376.

Young, Robert: 'Miracles and Credibility', *Religious Studies* **16** (1980), 465–468.

Anderson, Susan: 'Plantinga and the Free Will Defense', *Pacific Philosophical Quarterly* **62** (June 1981), 274–281.

Basinger, David: 'Evil as Evidence Against God's Existence: Some Clarifications', *Modern Schoolman* **58** (March 1981), 175–184.

Basinger, David: 'Plantinga's "Free Will Defense" as a Challenge to Orthodox Theism', *American Journal of Theology & Philosophy* **3** (May 1981), 35–41.

Basinger, David and Randall Basinger: 'Divine Omnipotence: Plantinga vs. Griffin', *Process Studies* **11** (Spring 1981), 11–24.

Berthold, Fred Jr.: 'Free Will and Theodicy in Augustine: An Exposition and Critique', *Religious Studies* **17** (1981), 525–536.

Fitzpatrick, F. J.: 'The Onus of Proof in Arguments About the Problem of Evil', *Religious Studies* **17** (1981), 19–38.

Forrest, Peter: 'The Problem of Evil: Two Neglected Defences', *Sophia* **20** (April 1981), 49–54.

Hasker, William: 'On Regretting the Evils of This World', *Southern Journal of Philosophy* **19** (Winter 1981), 425–438.

Kroon, Frederick W.: 'Plantinga on God, Freedom, and Evil', *International Journal for Philosophy of Religion* **12** (1981), 75–96.

Paulsen, David: 'Divine Determinateness and the Free Will Defence', *Analysis* **41** (1981), 150–153.

Pielke, Robert G.: 'Recent Science Fiction and the Problem of Evil', *Philosophy in Context* **11** (1981), 41–50.

Plantinga, Alvin: 'Reply to the Basingers on Divine Omnipotence', *Process Studies* **11** (Spring 1981), 25–29.

Ratzsch, Del: 'Plantinga's Free Will Defense', *International Journal for Philosophy of Religion* **12** (1981), 235–244.

Reichenbach, Bruce R.: 'The Deductive Argument from Evil', *Sophia* **20** (April 1981), 25–42.

Runzo, Joseph: 'Omniscience and Freedom for Evil', *International Journal for Philosophy of Religion* **12** (1981), 131–148.

Stearns, J. Brenton: 'Divine Punishment and Reconciliation', *Journal of Religious Ethics* **9** (Spring 1981), 118–130.

Vertin, Michael: 'Philosophy-of–God, Theology, and the Problems of Evil', *Laval Theologique et Philosophique* **37** (February 1981), 15–32.

Yandell, Keith E.: 'The Problem of Evil', *Philosophical Topics* **12** (1981), 7–38.

Ackerman, Robert: 'An Alternative Free Will Defence', *Religious Studies* **18** (1982), 365–372.

Anglin, Bill and Stewart Goetz: 'Evil Is Privation', *International Journal for Philosophy of Religion* **13** (1982), 3–12.

Basinger, David: 'Anderson on Plantinga: A Response', *Philosophy Research Archives* **8** (1982), no. 1499.

Basinger, David: 'Determinism and Evil: Some Clarifications', *Australasian Journal of Philosophy* **60** (June 1982), 163–164.

Basinger, David and Randall Basinger: 'Divine Determinateness and the Free Will Defense: Some Clarifications', *Philosophy Research Archives* **8** (1982), no. 1517.

Colwell, Gary: 'On Defining Away the Miraculous', *Philosophy* **57** (1982), 327–337.

Dilley, Frank B.: 'A Modified Flew Attack on the Free Will Defense', *Southern Journal of Philosophy* **20** (Spring 1982), 25–34.

Dilley, Frank B.: 'Is the Free Will Defense Irrelevent?', *Religious Studies* **18** (1982), 355–364.

Fern, Richard L.: 'Hume's Critique of Miracles: An Irrelevant Triumph', *Religious Studies* **18** (1982), 337–354.

Fulmer, Gilbert: 'John Hick's Soul-Making Theodicy', *Southwest Philosophical Studies* **7** (April 1982), 170–179.

Gan, Barry L.: 'Plantinga's Transworld Depravity: It's Got Possibilities', *International Journal for Philosophy of Religion* **13** (1982), 169–177.

King-Farlow, John: 'Historical Insights on Miracles: Babbage, Hume, Aquinas', *International Journal for Philosophy of Religion* **13** (1982), 209–218.

Lugenbehl, Dale: 'Can the Argument from Evil Be Decisive After All?' *Religious Studies* **18** (1982), 29–35.

Morriston, Wesley: 'Gladness, Regret, God and Evil', *Southern Journal of Philosophy* **20** (Fall 1982), 401–407.

Pargetter, Robert: 'Evil as Evidence', *Sophia* **21** (July 1982), 11–15.

Pentz, Rebecca D.: 'Rules and Values and the Problem of Evil', *Sophia* **21** (July 1982), 23–29.

Plantinga, Alvin: 'Tooley and Evil: A Reply', *Australian Journal of Philosophy* **60** (March 1982), 66–75.

Walker, Ian: 'Miracles and Violations', *International Journal for Philosophy of Religion* **13** (1982), 103–108.

Cooper, Keith J.: 'Here We Go Again: Pike vs. Plantinga on the Problem of Evil', *International Journal for Philosophy of Religion* **14** (1983), 107–116.

Evans, Jonathan A.: 'Lafollette on Plantinga's Free Will Defense', *International Journal for Philosophy of Religion* **14** (1983), 117–121.

Fischer, John Martin: 'Freedom and Foreknowledge', *Philosophical Review* **92** (January 1983), 67–79.

Flint, Thomas P.: 'The Problem of Divine Freedom', *American Philosophical Quarterly* **20** (1983), 255–264.

Gordon, David: 'Paulsen on the Free Will Defence', *Analysis* **43** (1983), 63–64.

Guleserian, Theodore: 'God and Possible Worlds: The Modal Problem of Evil', *Nous* **17** (1983), 221–238.

Hasker, William: 'Concerning the Intelligibility of "God Is Timeless"', *Modern Schoolman* **57** (1983), 170–195.

Kondoleon, Theodore J.: 'More on the Free Will Defense', *Thomist* **47** (January 1983), 1–42.

Lewis, Delmas: 'The Problem with the Problem of Evil', *Sophia* **22** (April 1983), 26–35.

O'Connor, David: 'Swinburne on Natural Evil', *Religious Studies* **19** (1983), 65–73.

O'Connor, David: 'Theism, Evil and the Onus of Proof – Reply to F. J. Fitzpatrick', *Religious Studies* **19** (1983), 241–247.
Perkins, R. K., Jr.: 'An Atheistic Argument from the Improvability of the Universe', *Nous* **17** (1983), 239–250.
Stump, Eleonore: 'Knowledge, Freedom and the Problem of Evil', *International Journal for Philosophy of Religion* **14** (1983), 49–58.

CHAPTER 2. THE COSMOLOGICAL ARGUMENT

For sources before 1978 see the bibliography prepared by Terry L. Miethe, 'The Cosmological Argument', *New Scholasticism* **52** (1978), 285–305. For sources on Thomas Aquinas see the relevant entries in the bibliography prepared by Terry L. Miethe and Vernon L. Bourke, *Thomist Bibliography, 1940–1978* (Westport, Conn.: Greenwood Press, 1980).

I. Historical sources

Plato: *Laws*, Book X.
Aristotle: *Metaphysics*, Book XII.
Thomas Aquinas: *Summa Theologica*, Part I, Question 2, Article 3.
Descartes, René: *Meditations* III.
Locke, John: *Essays Concerning Human Understanding*, Book IV, Chapter 10.
Hume, David: *Dialogues Concerning Natural Religion*.
Hume, David: *Enquiry Concerning Human Understanding*, Section XI.
Kant, Immanuel: *Critique of Pure Reason*, Transcendental Dialectic, Book II, Chapters 2 and 3.
Mill, John Stuart: 'Theism', *Three Essays on Religion*.

II. Contemporary sources
A. Books

Reichenbach, Bruce R.: *The Cosmological Argument*: *A Reassessment*. Springfield, Ill.: Charles C. Thomas, 1972.
Rowe, William L.: *The Cosmological Argument*. Princeton, N.J.: Princeton University Press, 1975.
Burrell, David: *Aquinas*: *God and Action*. Notre Dame, Ind.: University of Notre Dame Press, 1979.
Craig, William Lane: *The Cosmological Argument from Plato to Leibniz*, ed. John Hick. New York: Barnes & Noble, 1980.
Kenny, Anthony: *The Five Ways to St. Thomas Aquinas' Proofs*. Notre Dame, Ind.: University of Notre Dame Press, 1980.
Bertocci, Peter A.: *The Goodness of God*. Washington, D. C.: University Press of America, 1981.

Meynell, Hugo A.: *The Intelligible Universe*: *A Cosmological Argument*. Totowa, N. J.: Barnes & Noble, 1982.

Torrance, Thomas F.: *Divine and Contingent Order*. New York: Oxford University Press, 1982.

B. Chapters of books, selections from collected essays

Rowe, William L.: Chapter 2, 'The Cosmological Argument', *Philosophy of Religion*: *An Introduction*. Belmont, Calif.: Wadsworth, 1978.

Swinburne, Richard: Chapter 7, 'The Cosmological Argument', *The Existence of God*. Oxford: Clarendon Press, 1979.

Mackie, J. L.: Chapter 5, 'Cosmological Arguments', *The Miracle of Theism*: *Arguments For and Against the Existence of God*. Oxford: Clarendon Press, 1982.

C. Journal articles

Bobik, Joseph: 'The Sixth Way of St. Thomas Aquinas', *Thomist* **42** (July 1978), 373–399.

Cox, L. Hughes: 'On Extending Mavrodes' Analysis of the Logic of Religious Belief', *Religious Studies* **14** (1978), 99–111.

Craig, William Lane: 'A Further Critique of Reichenbach's Cosmological Argument', *International Journal for Philosophy of Religion* **9** (1978), 53–60.

De Nys, Martin L.: 'The Cosmological Argument and Hegel's Doctrine of God', *New Scholasticism* **52** (1978), 343–372.

Dinan, Stephen A.: 'Sartre: Contingent Being and the Non-Existence of God', *Philosophy Today* **22** (Summer 1978), 103–118.

Geisler, Norman L.: 'The Missing Premise in the Cosmological Argument', *Modern Schoolman* **56** (November 1978), 31–45.

Knasas, John F. X.: '"Necessity" in the *Tertia Via*', *New Scholasticism* **52** (1978), 373–394.

Leslie, John: 'Efforts to Explain All Existence', *Mind* **87** (1978), 181–194.

Quinn, John M.: 'The Third Way to God: A New Approach', *Thomist* **42** (January 1978), 50–68.

Satre, Thomas W.: 'Necessary Being and the Question-Blocking Argument', *International Journal for Philosophy of Religion* **9** (1978), 158–170.

Stove, D. C.: 'Part IX of Hume's *Dialogues*', *Philosophical Quarterly* **28** (October 1978), 300–309.

Craig, William Lane: 'Dilley's Misunderstandings of the Cosmological Argument', *New Scholasticism* **53** (1979), 388–392.

Craig, William Lane: 'Wallace Matson and the Crude Cosmological Argument', *Australasian Journal of Philosophy* **57** (June 1979), 163–170.

Craig, William Lane: 'Whitrow and Popper on the Impossibility of an Infinite Past', *British Journal for the Philosophy of Science* **30** (June 1979), 165–170.

Dewan, Lawrence: 'St. Thomas and the Possibles', *New Scholasticism* **53** (1979), 76–85.

Garrett, Don: 'Spinoza's "Ontological" Argument', *Philosophical Review* **88** (April 1979), 198–223.

Nieznanski, E.: 'A Formalization of Thomistic Foundations of a Proof for the Existence of a Necessary First Being', *Studia Philosophiae Christiane* **15** (1979), 163–180.

Quinn, Philip L.: 'Divine Conservation and Spinozistic Pantheism', *Religious Studies* **15** (1979), 289–302.

Torrance, T. F.: 'God and the Contingent World', *Zygon* **14** (December 1979), 329–348.

Wainwright, William J.: 'Causality, Necessity and the Cosmological Argument', *Philosophical Studies* **36** (October 1979), 261–270.

White, David E.: 'An Argument for God's Existence', *International Journal for Philosophy of Religion* **10** (1979), 101–115.

Armour, Leslie: 'Ideas, Causes and God', *Sophia* **19** (April 1980), 14–21.

Baumer, Michale R.: 'Possible Worlds and Duns Scotus's Proof of the Existence of God', *New Scholasticism* **54** (1980), 182–188.

Bench–Capon, T.: 'Reinterpreting the Proofs of the Existence of God ', *Religious Studies* **16** (1980), 299–306.

Byrne, Peter: 'Arguing About the Reality of God', *Sophia* **19** (October 1980), 1–9.

Crawford, Dan D.: 'The Cosmological Argument, Sufficient Reason, and Why-Questions', *International Journal for Philosophy of Religion* **11** (1980), 111–122.

Delahunty, Robert: 'Descartes' Cosmological Argument', *Philosophical Quarterly* **30** (January 1980), 34–46.

Dewan, Lawrence: 'The Distinctiveness of St. Thomas' "Third Way"', *Dialogue* (Canada) **19** (June 1980), 201–218.

Franklin, James: 'More on Part IX of Hume's *Dialogues'*, *Philosophical Quarterly* **30** (January 1980), 69–71.

Knasas, John F. X.: 'Making Sense of the *Tertia Via*', *New Scholasticism* **54** (1980), 476–511.

Kondoleon, Theodore: 'The Third Way: Encore', *Thomist* **44** (July 1980), 325–356.

Leslie, John: 'The World's Necessary Existence', *International Journal for Philosophy of Religion* **11** (1980), 207–224.

Marmura, Michael E.: 'Avicenna's Proof from Contingency for God's Existence', *Mediaeval Studies* **62** (1980), 337–352.

Maydole, Robert E.: 'A Modal Model for Proving the Existence of God', *American Philosophical Quarterly* **17** (1980), 135–142.

Morreall, John: 'God as Self–Explanatory', *Philosophical Quarterly* **30** (July 1980), 206–214.

Oakes, Robert A.: 'A New Argument for the Existence of God', *New Scholasticism* **54** (1980), 213–223.

Oakes, Robert A.: 'Classical Theism and Pantheism: A Reply to Professor Quinn', *Religious Studies* **16** (1980), 353–356.

Owens, Joseph: *'Quandoque* and *Aliquando* in Aquinas's *Tertia Via*', *New Scholasticism* **54** (1980), 447–475.

Sadowsky, James A.: 'The Cosmological Argument and the Endless Regress', *International Philosophical Quarterly* **20** (December 1980), 465–467.

Crawford, Patricia A.: 'Is the Cosmological Argument Dependent Upon the Ontological Argument?', *Sophia* **20** (October 1981), 27–31.

Kelly, Charles J.: 'Some Fallacies in the First Movement of Aquinas's Third Way', *International Journal for Philosophy of Religion* **12** (1981), 39–54.

Kraft, Michael: 'Thinking the Physico–Teleological Proof', *International Journal for Philosophy of Religion* **12** (1981), 65–74.

Zedler, Beatrice H.: 'Why Are the Possibles Possible?", *New Scholasticism* **55** (1981), 113–130.

Bartel, Timothy W.: 'Cosmological Arguments and the Uniqueness of God', *International Journal for Philosophy of Religion* **13** (1982), 23–32.

Brown, Robert F.: 'A Reply to Kelly on Aquinas's Third Way', *International Journal for Philosophy of Religion* **13** (1982), 225–227.

Hill, Christopher S.: 'On a Revised Version of the Principle of Sufficient Reason', *Pacific Philosophical Quarterly* **63** (1982), 236–242.

Immerwahr, John: 'Descartes' Two Cosmological Proofs', *New Scholasticism* **56** (1982), 346–354.

Keating, B. F.: 'Rowe, Self-Existence, and the Cosmological Argument', *Analysis* **42** (1982), 99–102.

Kelly, Charles J.: 'The Third Way and the Possible Eternity of the World', *New Scholasticism* **56** (1982), 273–291.

Kondoleon, Theodore J.: 'Oakes' New Argument for God's Existence', *New Scholasticism* **56** (1982), 100–109.

LaCroix, Richard R.: 'Aquinas on God's Omnipresence and Timelessness', *Philosophy and Phenomenological Research* **42** (March 1982), 391–399.

Miller, Barry: 'Wainwright on Causeless Beings: An Ontological Disproof?', *Sophia* **21** (October 1982), 49–56.

Quinn, John M.: 'A Few Reflections on "The Third Way: Encore"', *Thomist* **46** (January 1982), 75–91.

Calvert, Brian: 'Another Problem About Part IX of Hume's *Dialogues*', *International Journal for Philosophy of Religion* **14** (1983), 65–70.

Clarke, Bowman L.: 'Natural Theology and Methodology', *Modern Schoolman* **57** (1983), 233–252.

Conway, David A.: 'Concerning Infinite Chains, Infinite Trains, and Borrowing a Typewriter', *International Journal for Philosophy of Religion* **14** (1983), 71–86.

Dore, Clement: 'Rowe on the Cosmological Argument', *International Journal for Philosophy of Religion* **14** (1983), 25–31.

Eslick, Leonard J.: 'From the World to God: The Cosmological Argument', *Modern Schoolman* **60** (March 1983), 145–169.

Oakes, Robert: 'Does Traditional Theism Entail Pantheism', *American Philosophical Quarterly* **20** (1983), 105–112.

Rowe, William L.: 'Self-Existence and the Cosmological Argument', *Analysis* **43** (1983), 61–62.

CHAPTER 3. THE DESIGN ARGUMENT

I. Historical sources

Thomas Aquinas: *Summa Theologica*, Part I, Question 2, Article 3.

Hume, David: *Dialogues Concerning Natural Religion*.

Kant, Immanuel: *Critique of Pure Reason*, Transcendental Dialectic, Book II, Chapter 3.

Paley, William: *Natural Theology: Or,Evidence and Attributes of the Deity, Collected from the Appearences of Nature*.

Mill, John Stuart: 'Theism', *Three Essays on Religion*.

II. Contemporary sources
A. Books

Turner, Dean: *Commitment to Care*. Old Greenwhich, Ct.: Devin-Adair, 1978.

Horigan, James E.: *Chance or Design?* New York, N. Y.: Philosophical Library, 1979.

Bertocci, Peter A.: *The Goodness of God*. Washington, D. C.: University Press of America, 1981.

Schlesinger, George: *Metaphysics: Problems and Method*. Totowa, N. J.: Barnes & Noble, 1983.

B. Chapters of books, selections from collected essays

Rowe, William L.: Chapter 4, 'The Teleological Argument', *Philosophy of Religion: An Introduction*. Belmont, Calif.: Wadsworth, 1978.

Hambourger, Robert: 'The Argument from Design', *Intention and Intentionality: Essays in Honour of G. E. M. Anscombe*, ed. Cora Diamond and Jenny Teichman. Ithaca, N. Y.: Cornell University Press, 1979.

Swinburne, Richard: Chapter 8, 'Teleological Arguments', *The Existence of God*. Oxford: Clarendon Press, 1979.

Mackie, J. L.: Chapter 8, 'Arguments for Design', *The Miracle of Theism: Arguments For and Against the Existence of God*. Oxford: Clarendon Press, 1982.

C. Journal articles

Ameriks, Karl: 'Plantinga and Other Minds', *Southern Journal of Philosophy* **16** (Winter 1978), 285–291.

Cartwright, Nancy: 'Comments on Wesley Salmon's "Science and Religion"', *Philosophical Studies* **33** (1978), 177–183.

Cox, L. Hughes: 'On Extending Mavrodes' Analysis of the Logic of Religious Belief', *Religious Studies* **14** (1978), 99–111.

Dinan, Stephen A.: 'Sartre: Contingent Being and the Non-Existence of God', *Philosophy Today* **22** (Summer 1978), 103–118.

Leslie, John: 'God and Scientific Verifiability', *Philosophy* **53** (1978), 71–79.

Nelson, Kenneth V.: 'Evolution and the Argument from Design', *Religious Studies* **14** (1978), 423–443.

Salmon, Wesley: 'Religion and Science: A New Look at Hume's *Dialogues*', *Philosophical Studies* **33** (February 1979), 143–176.

Friquegnon, Marie-Louise: 'God and Other Programs', *Religious Studies* **15** (1979), 83–89.

Tweyman, Stanley: 'The Vegetable Library and God', *Dialogue* (Canada) **18** (December 1979), 517–527.

Bench-Capon, T.: 'Reinterpreting the Proofs of the Existence of God', *Religious Studies* **16** (1980), 299–306.

Burch, Robert: 'Bayesianism and Analogy in Hume's *Dialogues*', *Hume Studies* **6** (April 1980), 32–44.

Byrne, Peter: 'Arguing About the Reality of God', *Sophia* **19** (October 1980), 1–9.

Clarke, Bowman L.: 'The Argument from Design', *American Journal of Theology & Philosophy* **1** (Summer 1980), 98–108.

Doore, Gary: 'The Argument from Design: Some Better Reasons for Agreeing with Hume', *Religious Studies* **16** (1980), 145–161.

Tweyman, Stanley: 'Remarks on P. S. Wadia's "Philo Confounded"', *Hume Studies* **6** (November 1980), 155–161.

Whittaker, John A.: 'Hume's Forgotten Fallacy', *Sophia* **19** (July 1980), 1–8.

Prado, C. G.: 'Hume and the God-Hypothesis ', *Hume Studies* **7** (November 1981), 154–163.

Priest, Graham: 'The Argument from Design', *Australasian Journal of Philosophy* **59** (December 1981), 422–431.

Rohatyn, Dennis: 'Resurrecting Peirce's "Neglected Argument" for God', *Transactions of the Charles S. Peirce Society* **18** (Winter 1981), 66–74.

Duerlinger, James: 'Unspoken Connections in the Design Argument', *Philosophy and Phenomenological Research* **42** (June 1982), 519–529.

Leslie, John: 'Anthropic Principle, World Ensemble, Design', *American Philosophical Quarterly* **19** (1982), 141–152.

Lewis, Delmas: 'On Salmon's Attempt to Redesign the Design Argument', *International Journal for Philosophy of Religion* **13** (1982), 77–84.
Tweyman, Stanley: 'The Articulate Voice and God', *Southern Journal of Philosophy* **20** (Summer 1982), 263–275.
Forrest, Peter: 'Priest on the Argument from Design', *Australasian Journal of Philosophy* **61** (March 1983), 84–87.
Schlesinger, George N.: 'Theism and Confirmation', *Pacific Philosophical Quarterly* **64** (1983), 46–56.

CHAPTER 4. A MORAL ARGUMENT

I. Historical sources

Kant, Immanuel: *Critique of Practical Reason*.
Kant, Immanuael: *Critique of Pure Reason*, Transcendental Doctrine of Method, Chapter 2.
Kant, Immanuel: *Religion Within the Limits of Reason Alone*.

II. Contemporary sources
A. Books

Muyskens, James L.: *The Sufficiency of Hope*: *The Conceptual Foundations of Religion*. Philadelphia, Penn.: Temple University Press, 1979.
Bertocci, Peter A.: *The Goodness of God*. Washington, D. C.: University Press of America, 1981.
Hare, R. M.: *Moral Thinking*: *Its Levels, Method, and Point*. New York: Oxford University Press, 1981.
Auxter, Thomas: *Kant's Moral Teleology*. Macon, Ga.: Mercer University Press, 1982.

B. Chapters of books, selections from collected essays

Adams, Robert M.: 'Moral Arguments for Theistic Belief', *Rationality and Religious Belief*, ed. C. F. Delaney. Notre Dame, Ind.: University of Notre Dame Press, 1979.
Swinburne, Richard: Chapter 9, 'Arguments from Consciousness and Morality', *The Existence of God*. Oxford: Clarendon Press, 1979.
Mackie, J. L.: Chapter 6, 'Moral Arguments for the Existence of God', *The Miracle of Theism*: *Arguments For and Against the Existence of God*. Oxford: Clarendon Press, 1982.

C. Journal articles

Carney, Frederick: 'On McCormick and Teleological Morality', *Journal of Religious Ethics* **6** (Spring 1978), 81–107.

Gregory, Donald R.: 'Would a Satanic Resurrection World Falsify Christian Theism: A Reply to Gregory S. Kavka', *Religious Studies* **14** (1978), 69–72.

Hill, John: 'Natural Sanction and Philosophical Theology', *Sophia* **17** (July 1978), 27–34.

Leslie, John: 'Efforts to Explain All Existence', *Mind* **87** (1978), 181–194.

Leslie, John: 'God and Scientific Verifiability', *Philosophy* **53** (1978), 71–79.

Stearns, J. Brenton: 'The Moral Argument', *Idealistic Studies* **8** (September 1978), 193–205.

Abugattas, Juan A.: 'On the Relation Between Morality and the Notion of God', *Auslegung* **7** (November 1979), 47–81.

Griffin, David Ray: 'The Holy, Necessary Goodness, and Morality', *Journal of Religious Ethics* **8** (Fall 1980), 330–349.

Kohl, Marvin and Joseph Fletcher: 'Morality Without Religion', *Free Inquiry* **1** (Winter 1980/1981), 28–29.

McDermott, John M.: 'A New Approach to God's Existence', *Thomist* **44** (April 1980), 219–250.

Roth, Robert J.: 'Moral Obligation and God', *New Scholasticism* **54** (1980), 265–278.

Sessions, Wiliam Lad: 'Kant and Religious Belief', *Kantstudien* **71** (1980), 455–468.

Rossi, Philip J.: 'Kant as a Christian Philosopher: Hope and the Symbols of Christian Faith', *Philosophy Today* **25** (Spring 1981), 24–33.

Soffer, Walter: 'Kant on the Tutelage of God and Nature', *Thomist* **45** (January 1981), 26–40.

Ewbank, Michael B.: 'Where to Begin in Thinking About Obligation', *Modern Schoolman* **56** (1982), 480–489.

Gellman, Jerome: 'God and Theoretical Entities', *International Journal for Philosophy of Religion* **13** (1982), 131–141.

Rossi, Philip: 'Kant's Doctrine of Hope: Reason's Interest and the Things of Faith', *New Scholasticism* **56** (1982), 228–238.

Rossi, Philip: 'Moral Autonomy, Divine Transcendence, and Human Destiny: Kant's Doctrine of Hope as a Philosophical Foundation for Christian Ethics', *Thomist* **46** (July 1982), 441–458.

Talbott, Thomas B.: 'Quinn on Divine Commands and Moral Requirements', *International Journal for Philosophy of Religion* **13** (1982), 193–208.

Ferreira, M. Jamie: 'Kant's Postulate: The Possibility or the Existence of God?', *Kantstudien* **74** (1983), 75–80.

Nielsen, Kai: 'Hobbesist and Humean Alternatives to a Religious Morality', *International Journal for Philosophy of Religion* **14** (1983), 33–47.

CHAPTER 5. A MODAL ARGUMENT

I. Historical sources

Anselm of Canterbury: *Proslogion*, Chapters 2–4.
Hume, David: *Dialogues Concerning Natural Religion*.

II. Contemporary sources
A. Books

Hartshorne, Charles: *The Logic of Perfection, and Other Essays in Neoclassical Metaphysics*. La Salle, Ill.: Open Court, 1962.
Hartshorne, Charles: *Anselm's Discovery*. La Salle, Ill.: Open Court, 1965.
Barnes, Jonathan: *The Ontological Argument*. London: Macmillan Press, 1972.
Goodwin, George L.: *The Ontological Argument of Hartshorne*. Missoula, Mont.: Scholars Press, 1978.
Torrance, Thomas F.: *Divine and Contingent Order*. New York: Oxford University Press, 1982.

B. Chapters of books, selections from collected essays

Hartshorne, Charles: 'Introduction', *St. Anselm: Basic Writings*, 2nd ed., trans. S. N. Deane. La Salle, Ill.: Open Court, 1962.
Plantinga, Alvin: Chapter X, 'God and Necessity', *The Nature of Necessity*. Oxford: Clarendon Press, 1974.
Rowe, William L.: Chapter 3, 'The Ontological Argument', *Philosophy of Religion: An Introduction*. Belmont, Calif.: Wadsworth, 1978.
Mackie, J. L.: Chapter 3, 'The Ontological Arguments', *The Miracle of Theism: Arguments For and Against the Existence of God*. Oxford: Clarendon Press, 1982.

C. Journal articles

Malcolm, Norman: 'Anselm's Ontological Arguments', *Philosophical Review* **69** (1960), 41–62.
Dore, Clement: 'Examination of an Ontological Argument', *Philosophical Studies* **28** (1975), 345–356.
Brown, Charles D.: 'The Ontological Theorem', *Notre Dame Journal of Formal Logic* **19** (October 1978), 591–592.
Dinan, Stephen A.: 'Sartre: Contingent Being and the Non-Existence of God', *Philosophy Today* **22** (Summer 1978), 103–118.
Hopkins, Jasper: 'On Understanding and Preunderstanding St. Anselm', *New Scholasticism* **52** (1978), 243–260.
Kielkopf, Charles F.: 'Dun Scotus's Rejection of "Necessarily Exists" as a Predicate', *Journal of the History of Philosophy* **16** (January 1978), 13–21.

Knasas, John F. X.: '"Necessity" in the *Tertia Via*', *New Scholasticism* **52** (1978), 373–394.

Lansing, John W.: 'Necessity, Possible Worlds, and Whitehead's God', *Modern Schoolman* **55** (March 1978), 223–240.

McAllister, Alan: 'Two Errors in Assessing the Ontological Argument', *International Journal for Philosophy of Religion* **9** (1978), 171–178.

Bedell, Gary: 'The Many Faces of Necessity in the Many-Faced Argument', *New Scholasticism* **53** (1979), 1–21.

Englebretsen, George: 'The Powers and Capabilities of God', *Sophia* **18** (April 1979), 29–31.

Gellman, Jerome: 'On Arguing from God's Possibility to His Necessity', *Logique et Analyse* **22** (December 1979), 525–526.

Grim, Patrick: 'Plantinga's God', *Sophia* **18** (October 1979), 35–42.

Grim, Patrick: 'Plantinga's God and Other Monstrosities', *Religious Studies* **15** (1979), 91–97.

Hoffman, Joshua: 'Can God Do Evil?', *Southern Journal of Philosophy* **17** (Summer 1979), 213–220.

Nasser, Alan G.: 'Divine Independence and the Ontological Argument: A Reply to James M. Humber', *Religious Studies* **15** (1979), 391–397.

Nielsen, Kai: 'Necessity and God', *International Journal for Philosophy of Religion* **10** (1979), 1–23.

Parsons, J. E., Jr.: 'Hume's *Dialogues Concerning Natural Religion*: II', *Independent Journal of Philosophy* **3** (1979), 119-126.

White, John D.: 'God and Necessity', *International Journal for Philosophy of Religion* **10** (1979), 177–187.

Whittaker, John H.: 'Kierkegaard on Names, Concepts, and Proofs for God's Existence', *International Journal for Philosophy of Religion* **10** (1979), 117–129.

Baker, John Robert: 'What Is Not Wrong with a Hartshornean Modal Proof', *Southern Journal of Philosophy* **18** (Spring 1980), 99–106.

Byrne, Peter: 'Arguing About the Reality of God', *Sophia* **19** (October 1980), 1–9.

Friedman, Joel I.: 'Necessity and Ontological Argument', *Erkenntnis* **15** (November 1980), 301–331.

Leslie, John: 'The World's Necessary Existence', *International Journal for Philosophy of Religion* **11** (1980), 207–224.

Maydole, Robert E.: 'A Modal Model for Proving the Existence of God', *American Philosophical Quarterly* **17** (1980), 135–142.

Rosenkrantz, Gary: 'The Omnipotence Paradox, Modality, and Time', *Southern Journal of Philosophy* **18** (Winter 1980), 473–479.

Shields, George W.: 'Hartshorne's Modal Ontological Argument', *Dialogue* (Phi Sigma Tua) **22** (April 1980), 45–56.

Walker, Ian: 'The Logical Status of "God"', *Religious Studies* **16** (1980), 217–228.

Grim, Patrick: 'Plantinga, Hartshorne, and the Ontological Argument', *Sophia* **20** (July 1981), 12–16.

Kordig, Carl R.: 'A Deontic Argument for God's Existence', *Nous* **15** (1981), 207–208.

Rosenberg, Shalom: 'On the Modal Version of the Ontological Argument', *Logique et Analyse* **24** (March 1981), 129–133.

Tatarkiewicz, Wladyslaw: 'Ontological and Theological Perfection', *Dialectics and Humanism* **8** (Winter 1981), 187–192.

Tooley, Michael: 'Plantinga's Defence of the Ontological Argument', *Mind* **90** (1981), 422–427.

Carter, W. R.: 'Omniscience and Sin' *Analysis* **42** (1982), 102–105.

Grim, Patrick: 'Against a Deontic Argument for God's Existence', *Analysis* **42** (1982), 171–174.

Gutting, Gary: 'Can Philosophical Beliefs Be Rationally Justified?', *American Philosophical Quarterly* **19** (1982), 315–330.

Hasker, William: 'Is There a Second Ontological Argument?', *International Journal for Philosophy of Religion* **13** (1982), 93–102.

LaCroix, Richard R.: 'Aquinas on God's Omnipresence and Timelessness', *Philosophy and Phenomenological Research* **42** (March 1982), 391–399.

Mason, David R.: 'Can God be Both Perfect and Free?', *Religious Studies* **18** (1982), 191–200.

Quinn, Philip L.: 'Metaphysical Necessity and Modal Logics', *Monist* **65** (1982), 444–455.

Rohatyn, Dennis: 'Anselm's Inconceivability Argument', *Sophia* **21** (October 1982), 57–63.

Surin, Kenneth: 'The Self Existence of God: Hartshorne and Classical Theism', *Sophia* **21** (October 1982), 17–36.

Guleserian, Theodore: 'God and Possible Worlds: The Modal Problem of Evil', *Nous* **17** (1983), 221–238.

Morris, Thomas V.: 'Impeccability', *Analysis* **43** (1983), 106–112.

Pottinger, Garrell: 'A Formal Analysis of the Ontological Argument', *American Philosophical Quarterly* **20**, (1983), 37–46.

CHAPTER 6.
IS GOD'S EXISTENCE LOGICALLY POSSIBLE?

I. Historical sources

Anselm of Canterbury: *Proslogion*, Chapters 2–4.
Anselm of Canterbury: *Reply to Gaunilo*.
Gaunilo: *A Reply on Behalf of the Fool*.
Hume, David: *Dialogues Concerning Natural Religion*.
James, William: *The Varieties of Religious Experience*.

II. Contemporary sources
A. Books

Barnes, Jonathan: *The Ontological Argument*. London: Macmillan Press, 1972.
Donceel, Joseph F.: *The Searching Mind: An Introduction to a Philosophy of God*. Notre Dame, Ind.: University of Notre Dame Press, 1979.
Kenny, Anthony: *God of the Philosophers*. Oxford: Clarendon Press, 1979.

B. Chapters of books, selections from collected essays

Plantinga, Alvin: Chapter X, 'God and Necessity', *The Nature of Necessity*. Oxford: Clarendon Press, 1974.
Rowe, William L.: Chapter 3, 'The Ontological Argument', *Philosophy of Religion: An Introduction*. Belmont, Calif.: Wadsworth, 1978.
Swinburne, Richard: Chapter 13, 'The Argument from Religious Experience', *The Existence of God*. Oxford: Clarendon Press, 1979.
Mackie, J. L.: 'The Problem of Evil', *The Miracle of Theism: Arguments For and Against the Existence of God*. Oxford: Clarendon Press, 1982.

C. Journal articles

Blumenfeld, David: 'On the Compossibility of the Divine Attributes', *Philosophical Studies* **34** (July 1978), 91–103.
Edwards, Rem B.: 'The Pagan Dogma of the Absolute Unchangeableness of God', *Religious Studies* **14** (1978), 305–313.
Factor, R. Lance: 'Newcomb's Paradox and Omniscience', *International Journal for Philosophy of Religion* **9** (1978), 30–40.
Frankenberry, Nancy: 'The Empirical Dimension of Religious Experience', *Religious Studies* **8** (1978), 259–276.
Jantzen, Grace M.: 'On Worshipping an Embodied God', *Canadian Journal of Philosophy* **8** (September 1978), 511–519.
Khamara, Edward J.: 'In Defense of Omniscience', *Philosophical Quarterly* **28** (July 1978), 215–228.
Knasas, John F. X.: '"Necessity" in the *Tertia Via*', *New Scholasticism* **52** (1978), 373–394.
Lansing, John W.: 'Necessity, Possible Worlds, and Whitehead's God', *Modern Schoolman* **55** (March 1978), 223–240.
Londey, David: 'Concepts and God's Possibility', *Sophia* **17** (April 1978), 15–19.
Quinn, Philip L.: 'Divine Foreknowledge and Divine Freedom', *International Journal for Philosophy of Religion* **9** (1978), 219–240.
Sutherland, Stewart R.: 'God, Time and Eternity', *Proceedings of the Aristotelian Society* **79** (1978), 103–121.
Wainwright, William J.: 'The Ontological Argument, Question-Begging and Professor Rowe', *International Journal for Philosophy of Religion* **9** (1978), 254–257.

178   A RESEARCH BIBLIOGRAPHY

Wainwright, William J.: 'Unihorses and the Ontological Argument', *Sophia* **17** (October 1978), 27–32.

Bedell, Gary: 'The Many Faces of Necessity in the Many-Faced Argument', *New Scholasticism* **53** (1979), 1–21.

Burch, Robert: 'Plantinga and Leibniz's Lapse', *Analysis* **39** (1979), 24–29.

Francks, Richard: 'Omniscience, Omnipotence and Pantheism', *Philosophy* **54** (1979), 395–399.

Gellman, Jerome: 'On Arguing from God's Possibility to His Necessity', *Logique et Analyse* **22** (December 1979), 525–526.

Grim, Patrick: 'Plantinga's God', *Sophia* **18** (October 1979), 35–42.

Grim Patrick: 'Plantinga's God and Other Monstrosities', *Religious Studies* **15** (1979), 91–97.

Hoffman, Joshua: 'Mavrodes on Defining Omnipotence', *Philosophical Studies* **35** (April 1979), 311–313.

Joy, Glenn C.: 'The Perfection of Perfection: On How Not to Improve the Ontological Argument', *Journal of Thought* **14** (January 1979), 42–44.

King-Farlow, John: 'Nielsen and Penelhum on Agents Outside Space', *Religious Studies* **15** (1979), 79–82.

Knasas, John F. X.: 'Aquinas and Finite Gods', *Proceedings of the American Catholic Philosophical Association* **53** (1979), 88–97.

La Croix, Richard R.: 'Is There a Paradox of Omniscience?', *Modern Schoolman* **56** (March 1979), 251–265.

Lackey, Douglas: 'The Epistemology of Omnipotence', *Religious Studies* **15** (1979), 25–30.

Morreall, John S.: 'Aquinas's Fourth Way', *Sophia* **18** (April 1979), 20–28.

Oakes, Robert A.: 'Religious Experience, Self-Authentication, and Modality *De Re*: A Prolegomenon', *American Philosophical Quarterly* **16** (1979), 217–224.

Parsons, J. E., Jr.: 'Hume's *Dialogues Concerning Natural Religion*: II', *Independent Journal of Philosophy* **3** (1979), 119–126.

Schrader, David E.: 'A Solution to the Stone Paradox', *Synthese* **42** (October 1979), 255–264.

Tatarkiewicz, Wladyslaw: 'Perfection: The Term and the Concept', *Dialectics and Humanism* **6** (Fall 1979), 5–10.

Teske, Roland J.: 'Omniscience, Omnipotence, and Divine Transcendence', *New Scholasticism* **53** (1979), 277–294.

Tichy, Pavel: 'Existence and God', *Journal of Philosophy* **76** (August 1979), 403–420.

White, John D.: 'God and Necessity', *International Journal for Philosophy of Religion* **10** (1979), 177–187.

Whittaker, John H.: 'Kierkegaard on Names, Concepts, and Proofs for God's Existence', *International Journal for Philosophy of Religion* **10** (1979), 117–129.

Wierenga, Edward: 'Intrinsic Maxima and Omnibenevolence', *International Journal for Philosophy of Religion* **10** (1979), 41–50.

Wilson, Margaret D.: 'Possible Gods', *Review of Metaphysics* **32** (June 1979), 717–733.

Baumer, Michale R.: 'Possible Worlds and Duns Scotus's Proof of the Existence of God', *New Scholasticism* **54** (1980), 182–188.

Byrne, Peter: 'Arguing About the Reality of God', *Sophia* **19** (October 1980), 1–9.

Duncan, Roger: 'Analogy and the Ontological Argument', *New Scholasticism* **54** (1980), 25–33.

Helm, Paul: 'God and Spacelessness', *Philosophy* **55** (1980), 211–223.

Maloney, J. Christopher: 'On What Might Be', *Southern Journal of Philosophy* **18** (Fall 1980), 313–322.

Maydole, Robert E.: 'A Modal Model for Proving the Existence of God', *American Philosophical Quarterly* **17** (1980), 135–142.

Meierding, Loren: 'The Impossibility of Necessary Omnitemporal Omnipotence', *International Journal for Philosophy of Religion* **11** (1980), 21–26.

Reichenbach, Bruce R.: 'Mavrodes on Omnipotence', *Philosophical Studies* **37** (February 1980), 211–214.

Rosenkrantz, Gary and Joshua Hoffman: 'What an Omnipotent Agent Can Do', *International Journal for Philosophy of Religion* **11** (1980), 1–19.

Tatarkiewicz, Wladyslaw: 'Paradoxes of Perfection', *Dialectics and Humanism* **7** (Winter 1980), 77–80.

DePaul, Michael R.: 'The Rationality of Belief in God', *Religious Studies* **17** (1981), 343–356.

Hunt, W. Murray: 'Some Remarks About the Embodiment of God', *Religious Studies* **17** (1981), 105–108.

Oakes, Robert: 'Religious Experience, Sense-Perception and God's Essential Unobservability', *Religious Studies* **17** (1981), 357–368.

Tatarkiewicz, Wladyslaw: 'Ontological and Theological Perfection', *Dialectics and Humanism* **8** (Winter 1981), 187–192.

Tooley, Michael: 'Plantinga's Defence of the Ontological Argument', *Mind* **90** (1981), 422–427.

Carter, W. R.: 'Omniscience and Sin', *Analysis* **42** (1982), 102–105.

Davies, Brian: 'Kenny on God', *Philosophy* **57** (1982), 105–118.

Grim, Patrick: 'In Behalf of "In Behalf of the Fool"', *International Journal for Philosophy of Religion* **13** (1982), 33–42.

Gutting, Gary: 'Can Philosophical Beliefs Be Rationally Justified?', *American Philosophical Quarterly* **19** (1982), 315–330.

Keller, James A.: 'The Basingers on Divine Omnipotence: A Further Point', *Process Studies* **12** (1982), 23–25.

Kvart, Igal:'The Omnipotence Puzzle', *Logique et Analyse* **25** (March 1982), 75–81.

LaCroix, Richard R.: 'Aquinas on God's Omnipresence and Timelessness', *Philosophy and Phenomenological Research* **42** (March 1982), 391–399.

Menne, Albert: 'Concerning the Logical Analysis of "Existence"', *Monist* **65** (1982), 415–419.

Miller, Barry: 'Wainwright on Causeless Beings: An Ontological Disproof?', *Sophia* **21** (October 1982), 49–56.

Quinn, Philip L.: 'Metaphysical Necessity and Modal Logics', *Monist* **65** (1982), 444–455.

Rowe, William L.: 'Religious Experience and the Principle of Credulity', *International Journal for Philosophy of Religion* **13** (1982), 85–92.

Basinger, David: 'In What Sense Must God be Omnibenevolent?', *International Journal for Philosophy of Religion* **14** (1983), 3–15.

Flint, Thomas P.: 'The Problem of Divine Freedom', *American Philosophical Quarterly* **20** (1983), 255–264.

Grim, Patrick: 'Some Neglected Problems of Omniscience', *American Philosophical Quarterly* **20** (1983), 265–276.

Guleserian, Theodore: 'God and Possible Worlds: The Modal Problem of Evil', *Nous* **17** (1983), 221–238.

Hasker, William: 'Concerning the Intelligibility of "God Is Timeless"', *Modern Schoolman* **57** (1983), 170–195.

Levine, Michael P.: 'Can There Be Self-Authenticating Experiences of God?', *Religious Studies* **19** (1983), 229–234.

Morris, Thomas V.: 'Impeccability', *Analysis* **43** (1983), 106–112.

Oakes, Robert: 'Reply to Michael Levine', *Religious Studies* **19** (1983), 235–239.

Taliaferro, Charles: 'The Magnitude of Omnipotence', *International Journal for Philosophy of Religion* **14** (1983), 99–106.

Wierenga, Edward: 'Omnipotence Defined', *Philosophy and Phenomenological Research* **43** (March 1983), 363–375.

Zeis, John and Jonathan Jacobs: 'Omnipotence and Concurrence', *International Journal for Philosophy of Religion* **14** (1983), 17–23.

CHAPTER 7.
DESCARTES'S MEDITATION V ARGUMENT

I. Historical sources

Descartes, René: *Meditations* III, V.

Descartes, René: *Principles of Philosophy*, I, xviii.

Descartes, René: *Objections to the Meditations,* Part II, Objection II and Reply.

Spinoza, Benedict: *Ethics*, Part I.

Leibniz, Gottfried Wilhelm: *New Essays Concerning Human Understanding*, Book IV, Chapter 10 and Appendix X.

Leibniz, Gottfried Wilhelm: *Monadology*, Sections 44–45.

Kant, Immanuel: *Critique of Pure Reason*, Transcendental Dialectic, Book II, Chapter 3.

II. Contemporary sources
A. Books

Barnes, Jonathan: *The Ontological Argument*. London: Macmillan Press, 1972.

Curley, E. M.: *Descartes Against the Skeptics*. Cambridge, Mass.: Harvard University Press, 1978.

Wilson, Margaret Dauler: *Descartes*. London: Routledge & Kegan Paul, 1978.

Plantinga, Alvin: *Does God Have a Nature?* Milwaukee, Wi.: Marquette University Press, 1980.

Cassidy, Laurence L.: *Existence and Presence: The Dialectics of Divinity*. Washington, D. C.: University Press of America, 1981.

Schlesinger, George: *Metaphysics: Problems and Method*. Totowa, N. J.: Barnes & Noble, 1983.

B. Chapters of books, selections from collected essays

Plantinga, Alvin: Chapter X, 'God and Necessity', *The Nature of Necessity*. Oxford: Clarendon Press, 1974.

Rowe, William L.: Chapter 3, 'The Ontological Argument', *Philosophy of Religion: An Introduction*. Belmont, Calif.: Wadsworth, 1978.

Doney, Willis: 'Spinoza's Ontological Proof', *The Philosophy of Baruch Spinoza*, ed. Richard Kennington. Washington, D. C.: Catholic University of America Press, 1980.

Hooker, Michael: 'The Deductive Character of Spinoza's Metaphysics', *The Philosophy of Baruch Spinoza*, ed. Richard Kennington. Washington, D. C.: Catholic University of America Press, 1980.

Parsons, Terrence: Chapter 8, Section 1, 'Traditional Issues from the Present Perspective', *Nonexistent Objects*. New Haven, Conn.: Yale University Press, 1980.

Mackie, J. L.: Chapter 3, 'The Ontological Arguments', *The Miracle of Theism: Arguments For and Against the Existence of God*. Oxford: Clarendon Press, 1982.

Dore, Clement: 'Descartes's Meditation V Proof of God's Existence', *The Existence and Nature of God*, ed. Alfred J. Freddoso. Notre Dame, Ind.: University of Notre Dame Press, 1983.

C. Journal articles

Dreisbach, Donald F.: 'Circularity and Consistency in Descartes', *Canadian Journal of Philosophy* 8 (March 1978), 59–78.

Ebersole, Frank B.: 'Everyman's Ontological Argument', *Philosophical Investigations* 1 (Fall 1978), 1–15.

Elliot, Robert and Michal Smith: 'Descartes, God and the Evil Spirit', *Sophia* 17 (October 1978), 33–36.

Kielkopf, Charles F.: 'Duns Scotus's Rejection of "Necessarily Exists" as a Predicate', *Journal of the History of Philosophy* **16** (January 1978), 13–21.

Knasas, John F. X.: '"Necessity" in the *Tertia Via*', *New Scholasticism* **52** (1978), 373–394.

Loewer, Barry: 'Leibnitz and the Ontological Argument', *Philosophical Studies* **34** (July 1978), 105–109.

McGinley, John: 'Does God Exist?', *Philosophy Today* **22** (Summer 1978), 168–171.

Norton, David Fate: 'A Reply to Professor Stevens "Unknown Faculties and Descartes" First Proof of the Existence of God", *Journal of the History of Philosophy* **16** (July 1978), 338–341.

Seeskin, Kenneth R.: 'Is Existence a Perfection: A Case Study in the Philosophy of Leibniz', *Idealistic Studies* **8** (May 1978), 124–135.

Soffer, Walter: 'Descartes, Rationality, and God', *Thomist* **42** (October 1978), 666–691.

Stevens, John C.: 'Unknown Faculties and Descartes's First Proof of the Existence of God', *Journal of the History of Philosophy* **16** (July 1978), 334–338.

Joy, Glenn C.: 'The Perfection of Perfection: On How Not to Improve the Ontological Argument', *Journal of Thought* **14** (January 1979), 42–44.

O'Briant, Walter H.: 'Is Descartes' Evil Spirit Finite or Infinite?', *Sophia*, **18** (July 1979), 28–32.

Tatarkiewicz, Wladyslaw: 'Perfection: The Term and the Concept', *Dialectics and Humanism* **6** (Fall 1979), 5–10.

Tichy, Pavel: 'Existence and God', *Journal of Philosophy* **76** (August 1979), 403–420.

Young, J. Michael: 'Existence, Predication, and the Real', *New Scholasticism* **53** (1979), 295–323.

Anderson, Daniel E.: 'Descartes and Atheism', *Tulane Studies in Philosophy* **29** (December 1980), 11–24.

Bakhle, S. W.: 'Predicate and Property', *Indian Philosophical Quarterly* **7** (July 1980), 463–470.

Doney, Willis: 'Curley and Wilson on Descartes', *Philosophy Research Archives* **6** (1980), no. 1376.

Heaney, James J.: 'The Logic of Questions and the Existence of God', *Religious Studies* **16** (1980), 203–216.

Schneier, Cheri K.: 'Descartes' Proof for the Existence of God: Comparison and Contrast', *Dialogue* (Phi Sigma Tau) **23** (October 1980), 22–26.

Hintikka, Jaakko: 'Kant on Existence, Predication, and the Ontological Argument', *Dialogue* **35** (1981), 128–146.

Holt, Dennis C.: 'Timelessness and the Metaphysics of Temporal Existence', *American Philosophical Quarterly* **18** (1981), 141–156.

Loewer, Barry: 'Descartes' Skeptical and Antiskeptical Arguments', *Philosophical Studies* **39** (February 1981), 163–182.

Tatarkiewicz, Wladyslaw: 'Ontological and Theological Perfection', *Dialectics and Humanism* **8** (Winter 1981), 187–192.

Wippel, John F.: 'The Reality of Nonexisting Possibles According to Thomas Aquinas, Henry of Ghent, and Godfrey of Fontaines', *Review of Metaphysics* **34** (June 1981), 729–758.

Friedman, Joel I.: 'Was Spinoza Fooled by the Ontological Argument?', *Philosophia* **11** (July 1982), 307–344.

Immerwahr, John: 'Descartes' Two Cosmological Proofs', *New Scholasticism* **56** (1982), 346–354.

Kalin, Martin: 'Is a Proof for God Still Possible?', *Philosophy Today* **26** (Spring 1982), 76–84.

Menne, Albert: 'Concerning the Logical Analysis of "Existence"', *Monist* **65** (1982), 415–419.

Peetz, Vera: 'Is Existence a Predicate?', *Philosophy* **57** (1982), 395–401.

Sievert, Donald: 'Descartes on Theological Knowledge', *Philosophy and Phenomenological Research* **43** (December 1982), 201–219.

Ferreira, M. Jamie: 'Kant's Postulate: The Possibility Or the Existence of God?', *Kantstudien* **74** (1983), 75–80.

Sen, Sushanta: 'The Ontological Argument Revisited', *Indian Philosophical Quarterly* **10** (January 1983), 219–242.

CHAPTER 8. AGNOSTICISM

I. Historical sources

Hume, David: *Dialogues Concerning Natural Religion*.

Mill, John Stuart: *Three Essays on Religion*.

James, William: *The Varieties of Religious Experience*.

James, William: *The Will to Believe*.

II. Contemporary sources
A. Books

Evans, C. Stephen: *Subjectivity and Religious Belief: An Historical, Critical Study*. Grand Rapids, Mich.: Christian University Press, 1978.

Green, Ronald M.: *Religious Reason: The Rational and Moral Basis of Religious Belief*. New York: Oxford University Press, 1978.

Bonansea, Bernardino M.: *God and Atheism: A Philosophical Approach to the Problem of God*. Washington, D. C.: Catholic University of America Press, 1979.

Smith, George H.: *Atheism: The Case Against God*. Buffalo, N. Y.: Prometheus Books, 1979.

Swinburne, Richard: *The Existence of God*. Oxford: Clarendon Press, 1979.

Kung, Hans: *Does God Exist?*: *An Answer for Today*, trans. Edward Quinn. New York: Vintage Press, 1981.

Swinburne, Richard: *Faith and Reason*. Oxford: Clarendon Press, 1981.

Whittaker, John H.: *Matters of Faith and Matters of Principle*. San Antonio, Tex.: Trinity University Press, 1981.

Mackie, J. L.: *The Miracle of Theism*: *Arguments For and Against the Existence of God*. Oxford: Clarendon Press, 1982.

B. Chapters of books, selections from collected essays

Mavrodes, George I.: 'Rationality and Religious Belief – A Perverse Question', *Rationality and Religious Belief*, ed. C. F. Delaney. Notre Dame, Ind.: University of Notre Dame Press, 1979.

Plantinga, Alvin: 'Is Belief in God Rational?', *Rationality and Religious Belief*, ed. C. F. Delaney. Notre Dame, Ind.: University of Notre Dame Press, 1979.

C. Journal articles

Burrell, David: 'The Performative Character of the "Proofs" for the Existence of God', *Listening* 13 (Winter 1978), 20–26.

Dinan, Stephen A.: 'Sartre: Contingent Being and the Non-Existence of God', *Philosophy Today* 22 (Summer 1978), 103–118.

Gellman, Jerome: 'The Religious Option Is a Genuine Option', *Religious Studies* 14 (1978), 505–514.

King-Farlow, John: 'Faith and a Failure of Arguments Against Scepticism', *Sophia* 17 (July 1978), 10–15.

Loughran, James N.: 'Another Look at Mavrodes' "Simple Argument"', *New Scholasticism* 52 (1978), 548–557.

Sullivan, Denis F.: 'Vagueness and the Verifiability of Ordinary Faith', *Religious Studies* 14 (1978), 459–467.

Craft, J. L.: 'Is Belief in God Rational?', *Personalist* 60 (July 1979), 298–304.

Creel, Richard E.: 'A Realistic Argument for Belief in the Existence of God', *International Journal for Philosophy of Religion* 10 (1979), 233–253.

Ommen, Thomas B.: 'Verification in Theology: A Tension in Revisionist Method', *Thomist* 43 (July 1979), 357–384.

Parsons, J. E., Jr.: 'Hume's *Dialogues Concerning Natural Religion*: II', *Independent Journal of Philosophy* 3 (1979), 119–126.

Plantinga, Alvin: 'The Probabilistic Argument from Evil', *Philosophical Studies* 35 (January 1979), 1–53.

Pojman, Louis P.: 'Rationality and Religious Belief', *Religious Studies* 15 (1979), 159–172.

Rowe, William L.: 'The Problem of Evil and Some Varieties of Atheism', *American Philosophical Quarterley* 16 (1979), 335–341.

Salmon, Wesley: 'Experimental Atheism', *Philosophical Studies* **35** (January 1979), 101–104.

Duncan, Roger: 'Analogy and the Ontological Argument', *New Scholasticism* **54** (1980), 25–33.

Heaney, James J.: 'The Logic of Questions and the Existence of God', *Religious Studies* **16** (1980), 203–216.

Londis, James J.: 'God, Probability and John Hick', *Religious Studies* **16** (1980), 457–463.

Sessions, William L.: 'William James and the Right to Over-Believe', *Philosophy Research Archives* **7** (1981), no. 1420.

Winetrout, Kenneth and William H. Fisher: 'On Pragmatism and Existentialism: A Response to Professor Duncan', *Journal of Thought* **15** (Spring 1980), 7–10.

Blackham, H. J.: 'What is Agnosticism?', *Free Inquiry* **1** (Summer 1981), 31–33.

DePaul, Michael R.: 'The Rationality of Belief in God', *Religious Studies* **17** (1981), 343–356.

Duncan, Elmer H.: 'Existentialism, Pragmatism and Atheism', *Journal of Thought* **16** (Spring 1981), 7–10.

Kellenberger, J.: 'Belief in God and Belief in the Devil', *Sophia* **20** (October 1981), 3–15.

Nielsen, Kai: 'Does God Exist: Reflections on Disbelief', *Free Inquiry* **1** (Spring 1981), 21–26.

Perrett, Roy W.: 'Solipsism and Religious Belief', *Sophia* **20** (October 1981), 17–26.

Plantinga, Alvin: 'Is Belief in God Properly Basic?', *Nous* **15** (1981), 41–52.

Smith, John E.: 'The Tension Between Direct Experience and Argument in Religion', *Religious Studies* **17** (1981), 487–498.

Dore, Clement: 'Agnosticism', *Religious Studies* **18** (1982), 503–507.

Gellman, Jerome: 'God and Theoretical Entities', *International Journal for Philosophy of Religion* **13** (1982), 131–141.

Nathanson, Stephen L.: 'Nonevidential Reasons for Belief: A Jamesian View', *Philosophy and Phenomenological Research* **42** (June 1982), 572–580.

Grigg, Richard: 'Theism and Proper Basicality: A Response to Plantinga', *International Journal for Philosophy of Religion* **14** (1983), 123–127.

Kvanvig, Jonathan L.: 'The Evidentialist Objection', *American Philosophical Quarterly* **20** (1983), 47–56.

Martin, Michael: 'Pascal's Wager as an Argument for Not Believing in God', *Religious Studies* **19** (1983), 57–64.

CHAPTER 9.
GOD AND PERCEPTUAL SKEPTICISM

For sources on skepticism before 1979, see the bibliography prepared by Nancy Kelsik, in *Justification and Knowledge*, ed. George Pappas (Dordrecht: D. Reidel, 1979). For sources on Wittgenstein and the private language argument and rule-following, see the relevant entries in *Ludwig Wittgenstein: A Comprehensive Bibliography*, (Westport, Conn.: Greenwood Press, 1980), prepared by Francois H. Lapointe, and in 'Doctoral Dissertations on Wittgenstein', *Philosophy Research Archives* **6** (1980), no. 1407, prepared by Mostafa Faghoury.

I. Historical sources

Plato: *Phaedo.*
Plato: *Republic.*
Plato: *Theaetetus.*
Sextus Empiricus: *Against the Dogmatists* (*Adversus Mathematicos*).
Sextus Empiricus: *Outlines of Pyrrhonism* (*Hypotyposes*).
Hume, David: *Dialogues Concerning Natural Religion.*
Hume, David: 'Of Scepticism with Regard to the Senses', *Enquiry into the Human Understanding.*
Hume, David: 'Of Scepticism with Regard to the Senses', *Treatise of Human Nature.*

II. Contemporary sources
A. Books

Morawetz, Thomas: *Wittgenstein and Knowledge.* Amherst, Mass.: University of Massachusetts Press, 1978.
Vander Veer, Garrett L.: *Philosophical Skepticism and Ordinary-Language Analysis.* Lawrence, Kansas: Regents Press, 1978.
Ebersole, Frank B.: *Language and Perception: Essays in the Philosophy of Language.* Washington, D. C.: University Press of America, 1979.
Armstrong, D. M.: *The Nature of Mind and Other Essays.* Ithaca, N. Y.: Cornell University Press, 1980.
Cornman, James W.: *Skepticism, Justification, and Explanation.* Dordrecht: D. Reidel, 1980.
Dicker, George: *Perceptual Knowledge.* Dordrecht: D. Reidel, 1980.
Rescher, Nicholas: *Scepticism: A Critical Reappraisal.* Totowa, N. J.: Rowman and Littlefield 1980.
Carrier, Leonard S.: *Experience and the Objects of Perception.* Washington, D. C.: University Press of America, 1981.
Christopher, Leich M. and Steven H. Holtzman: *Wittgenstein: To Follow a Rule.* London: Routledge & Kegan Paul, 1981.

Klein, Peter D.: *Certainty: A Refutation of Scepticism.* Minneapolis, Minn.: University of Minnesota Press, 1981.

Mates, Beson: *Skeptical Essays.* Chicago: University of Chicago Press, 1981.

Nozick, Robert: *Philosophical Explanations.* Cambridge, Mass.: Harvard University Press, 1981.

Kripke, Saul A.: *Wittgenstein on Rules and Private Language.* Cambridge, Mass.: Harvard University Press, 1982.

Odegard, Douglas: *Knowledge and Scepticism.* Totowa, N. J.: Rowman and Littlefield, 1982.

B. Chapters of books, selections from collected essays

Armstrong, D. M.: 'Perception, Sense Data and Causality', *Perception and Identity*, ed., G. F. MacDonald. Ithaca, N. Y.: Cornell University Press, 1979.

Reed, T. M.: 'Dreams, Scepticism, and Waking Life', *Body, Mind and Method*, ed. D. F. Gustafson. Dordrecht: D. Reidel, 1979.

Taylor, Charles: 'Sense Data Rivisited', *Perception and Identity*, ed. G. F. MacDonald. Ithaca, N. Y.: Cornell University Press, 1979.

Taylor, C. C. W.: 'All Perceptions Are True', *Doubt and Dogmatism*, ed. Jonathan Barnes *et al.* New York: Oxford University Press, 1980.

Vesey, Godgrey: 'Of the Visible Appearances of Objects', *Perceiving Artworks*, ed. John Fisher. Philadelphia, Penn.: Temple University Press, 1980.

C. Journal articles

Hattiangadi, J. N.: 'The Crisis in Methodology: Feyerabend', *Philosophy of the Social Sciences* 7 (September 1977), 289–302.

Shirley, Edward S.: 'Sense Datum Terminology: The Argument from Illusion Versus a Private Language', *Journal of Critical Analysis* 6 (Summer-Fall 1977), 21–29.

Airksinen, Timo: 'Five Types of Knowledge', *American Philosophical Quarterly* 15 (1978), 263–274.

Caraway, Carol: 'Is Wittgenstein's View of the Relationship Between Certainty and Knowledge Consistent?', *Philosophical Investigations* 1 (Fall 1978), 16–22.

Cook, Monte: 'What One Sees Need Not Exist', *Journal of Critical Analysis* 7 (Summer-Fall 1978), 89–97.

Davis, Ralph: 'I May Be Dreaming Now: Another Dip into the Cartesian Well', *Philosophical Investigations* 1 (Spring 1978), 54–58.

Dunlop, Charles E. M.: 'Dreaming and Deception', *Philosophia* 8 (November 1978), 355–365.

Kreisel, Georg: 'The Motto of "Philosophical Investigations" and the Philosophy of Proofs and Rules', *Grazer Philosophische Studien* 6 (1978), 13–38.

Morreall, John: 'Size, Shape, Seeing, and Sense-Data', *Southwestern Journal of Philosophy* **9** (Fall 1978), 101–112.

Stove, D. C.: 'Part IX of Hume's *Dialogues*', *Philosophical Quarterly* **28** (October 1978), 300–309.

Tully, R. E.: 'Sense-Data and Common Knowledge', *Ratio* **20** (December 1978), 123–141.

Acock, Malcolm and Howard Jackson: 'Seeing and Acquiring Beliefs', *Mind* **88** (1979), 370–383.

Black, Max: 'Wittgenstein's Language-games', *Dialectica* **33** (1979), 337–353.

Carr, Brian: 'The Grounds of Uncertainty', *Philosophical Inquiry* **1** (Spring 1979), 205–214.

Charlesworth, Maurice: 'Sense-impressions: A New Model', *Mind* **88** (1979), 24–44.

Clark, Romane: 'Sensing, Perceiving, Thinking', *Grazer Philosophische Studien* **7/8** (1979), 273–295.

Grewendorf, Gunther: 'Is Wittgenstein's Private Language Argument Trivial?', *Ratio* **21** (December 1979), 149–161.

Harker, Jay E.: 'Odegard, Alston, and Self-Warrant', *Journal of Critical Analysis* **8** (Summer-Fall 1979), 19–22.

Oakes, Robert A.: 'Religious Experience, Self-Authentication, and Modality *De Re*: A Prolegomenon', *American Philosophical Quarterly* **16** (1979), 217–224.

Odegard, Douglas: 'Two Types of Scepticism', *Philosophy* **54** (1979), 459–472.

Pappas, George S.: 'Epistemic Theories of Perception', *Philosophical Inquiry* **1** (Spring 1979), 220–228.

Rescher, Nicholas: 'Appearance and Reality', *Grazer Philosophische Studien* **7/8** (1979), 123–144.

Richard, John and Ernst Von Glasersfeld: 'The Control of Perception and the Construction of Reality', *Dialectica* **33** (1979), 37–58.

Shiner, Roger A.: 'Sense-experience, Colours and Tastes', *Mind* **88** (1979), 161–178.

Sievert, Donald: 'Does Descartes Doubt Everything?' *New Scholasticism* **53** (1979), 107–117.

Unger, Peter: 'There Are No Ordinary Things', *Synthese* **41** (June 1979), 117–154.

Whittaker, John H.: 'Kierkegaard on Names, Concepts, and Proofs for God's Existence', *International Journal for Philosophy of Religion* **10** (1979), 117–129.

Candlish, Stewart: 'The Real Private Language Argument', *Philosophy* **55** (1980), 85–94.

Cheal, David: 'Rule-Governed Behaviour', *Philosophy of the Social Sciences* **10** (March 1980), 39–49.

Close, Daryl: 'More on Non-Epistemic Seeing', *Mind* **89** (1980), 99–105.

Dalrymple, Houghton: 'Can a Person Know That He Is in Pain?', *Southwest Philosophical Studies* **5** (April 1980), 55–63.

Forge, John: 'The Structure of Physical Explanation', *Philosophy of Science* **47** (June 1980), 203–226.

Hanfling, O.: 'Does Language Need Rules?', *Philosophical Quarterly* **30** (July 1980), 193–205.

Hinton, J. M.: 'Phenomenological Specimenism', *Analysis* **40** (1980), 37–41.

Kimball, Robert H.: 'Private Criteria and the Private Language Argument', *Southern Journal of Philosophy* **18** (Winter 1980), 411–416.

Lewis, David: 'Veridical Hallucination and Prosthetic Vision', *Australasian Journal of Philosophy* **58** (September 1980), 239–249.

Malcolm, Norman: 'Kripke on Heat and Sensations of Heat', *Philosophical Investigations* **3** (Winter 1980), 12–20.

Ruegsegger, Ronald: 'The Propositional Attitude in Perception', *Philosophy Research Archives* **6** (1980), no. 1408.

Shirley, Edward S.: 'A Flaw in Chisholm's Foundationalism', *Philosophical Studies* **38** (August 1980), 155–160.

Unger, Peter: 'Skepticism and Nihilism', *Nous* **14** (1980), 517–545.

Von Morstein, Peter: 'Kripke, Wittgenstein, and the Private Language Argument', *Grazer Philosophische Studien* **11** (1980), 61–74.

Badriyeh, Katherine: 'An Antiskeptical Theory of When and How We Know', *Dialectica* **35** (1981), 415–432.

Coyne, Margaret Urban: 'Beyond Rules: Mapping the Normative', *American Philosophical Quarterly* **18** (1981), 331–337.

Fogelin, Robert J.: 'When I Look at a Tomato There is Much I Cannot See', *Monist* **64** (1981), 109–123.

Fogelin, Robert J.: 'Wittgenstein and Classical Scepticism', *International Philosophical Quarterly* **21** (March 1981), 3–15.

Griffin, Nicholas and Merle Harton: 'Sceptical Arguments', *Philosophical Quarterly* **31** (January 1981), 17–30.

Hunter, J. F. M.: 'Wittgenstein on Seeing and Seeing As', *Philosophical Investigations* **4** (Spring 1981), 33–49.

Kalansuriya, A. D. P.: 'Sense-Data and J. L. Austin: A Re-examination', *Indian Philosophical Quarterly* **8** (April 1981), 357–371.

Kim, Jeagwon: 'The Role of Perception in *A Priori* Knowledge: Some Remarks', *Philosophical Studies* **40** (November 1981), 339–354.

Kunkel, Joseph: 'Dreams, Metaphors and Scepticism', *Philosophy Today* **25** (Winter 1981), 307–316.

Lingis, Alphonso: 'Sensations', *Philosophy and Phenomenological Research* **42** (December 1981), 160–170.

Maloney, Christopher: 'A New Way Up from Empirical Foundations', *Synthese* **49** (December 1981), 317–336.

Mosley, Jerald: 'Boardman's Dreams and Dramas', *Philosophical Quarterly* **31** (April 1981), 158–162.

Perrett, Roy W.: 'Solipsism and Religious Belief', *Sophia* **20** (October 1981), 17–26.

Plantinga, Alvin: 'Is Belief in God Properly Basic?', *Nous* **15** (1981), 41–52.

Rosenthal, Sandra B.: 'C. I. Lewis and the Structure of Perceptual Beliefs', *Tulane Studies in Philosophy* **30** (December 1981), 97–105.

Sanford, David H.: 'Illusions and Sense-Data', *Midwest Studies in Philosophy* **6** (1981), 371–385.

Smith, Michael P.: 'Unger's Neo-classical Scepticism', *Mind* **90** (1981), 270–273.

Teschner, George: 'The Undifferentiated Conjunction of Sensation and Judgment in Perception', *Philosophy and Phenomenological Research* **42** (September 1981), 119–122.

Wright, Edmond: 'Yet More on Non-Epistemic Seeming', *Mind* **90** (1981), 586–591.

Clark, Romane: 'Sensibility and Understanding: The Given of Wilfrid Sellars', *Monist* **65** (1982), 350–364.

Cook, John: 'The Illusion of Aberrant Speakers', *Philosophical Investigations* **5** (July 1982), 215–226.

Craig, Edward: 'Meaning, Use and Privacy' *Mind* **91** (1982), 541–564.

Crawford, Dan D.: 'Are There Mental Inferences in Direct Perceptions?', *American Philosophical Quarterly* **19** (1982), 83–92.

Givner, David: 'Direct Perception, Misperception and Perceptual Systems: J. J. Gibson and the Problem of Illusion', *Nature and System* **4** (September 1982), 131–142.

Heil, John: 'Seeing Is Believing', *American Philosophical Quarterly* **19** (1982), 229–240.

Horwich, Paul: 'On Refutations of Skepticism', *Nous* **16** (1982), 56–61.

Kraut, Robert: 'Sensory States and Sensory Objects', *Nous* **16** (1982), 277–293.

Le Catt, Bruce: 'Censored Vision', *Australasian Journal of Philosophy* **60** (June 1982), 158–162.

Pappas, George S.: 'Non-Inferential Knowledge', *Philosophia* **12** (December 1982), 81–98.

Pavkovic, A.: 'Hume's Argument for the Dependent Existence of Perceptions: An Alternative Reading', *Mind* **91** (1982), 585–592.

Ring, Merrill: 'Sensations and Kinaesthetic Knowledge', *Philosophy Research Archives* **8** (1982), no. 1485.

Robinson, William S.: 'Causation, Sensations and Knowledge', *Mind* **91** (1982), 524–540.

Ruegsegger, Ronald W.: 'Judging, Taking, and Believing: Three Candidates for the Propositional Attitude in Perception', *Philosophy Research Archives* **8** (1982), no. 1460.

Runzo, Joseph: 'The Radical Conceptualization of Perceptual Experience', *American Philosophical Quarterly* **19** (1982), 205–218.

Sadegh-Zadeh, Kazem: 'Perception, Illusion, and Hallucination', *Metamedicine* **3** (June 1982), 159–192.

Schachter, J. P.: 'The Private Language Passages', *Canadian Journal of Philosophy* **12** (September 1982), 479–494.

Standley, Gerald: 'The Limitations of Sense Experience', *Philosophy and Phenomenological Research* **42** (March 1982), 434–441.

Stevenson, Leslie: 'Wittgenstein's Transcendental Deduction and Kant's Private Language Argument', *Kantstudien* **73** (1982), 321–337.

Straughan, Roger: 'What's the Point of Rules?', *Journal of Philosophy of Education* **16** (July 1982), 63–68.

Tye, Michael: 'A Causal Analysis of Seeing', *Philosophy and Phenomenological Research* **42** (March 1982), 311–325.

Carrier, Leonard S.: 'Skepticism Disarmed', *Canadian Journal of Philosophy* **13** (1983), 107–114.

Goodman, L. E.: 'Skepticism', *Review of Metaphysics* **36** (June 1983), 819–848.

Grigg, Richard: 'Theism and Proper Basicality: A Response to Plantinga', *International Journal for Philosophy of Religion* **14** (1983), 123–127.

Hunter, J. F. M.: 'The Difference Between Dreaming and Being Awake', *Mind* **92** (1983), 80–93.

Hyslop, Alec: 'On "Seeing-As"', *Philosophy and Phenomenological Research* **43** (June 1983), 533–540.

Levine, Michael P.: 'Can There Be Self-Authenticating Experiences of God?', *Religious Studies* **19** (1983), 229–234.

Oakes, Robert; 'Reply to Michael Levine', *Religious Studies* **19** (1983), 235–239.

Saarinen, Esa: 'On the Logic of Perception Sentences', *Synthese* **54** (January 1983), 115–128.

Smith, David Woodruff: 'Is This a Dagger I See Before Me?', *Synthese* **54** (January 1983), 95–114.

Stuart, James D.: 'The Role of Dreaming in Descartes' Meditations', *Southern Journal of Philosophy* **21** (1983), 97–108.

Williams, Meredith: 'Wittgenstein on Representation, Privileged Objects, and Private Languages', *Canadian Journal of Philosophy* **13** (1983), 57–78.

Wright, Crispin: 'Keeping Track of Nozick', *Analysis* **43** (1983), 134–140.

Wright, Edmond: 'Inspecting Images', *Philosophy* **58** (1983), 57–72.

APPENDIX. TWO ARGUMENTS OF ST. ANSELM

I. Historical Sources

Anselm of Canterbury: *Proslogion*, Chapters 2–4.
Anselm of Canterbury: *Reply to Gaunilo*.
Gaunilo: *A Reply on Behalf of the Fool*.
Hume, David: *Dialogues Concerning Natural Religion*.

II. Contemporary sources
A. Books

Hopkins, Jasper: *Anselm of Canterbury*. Toronto: Mellen Press, 1976.
Evans, G. R.: *Anselm and Talking About God*. Oxford: Clarendon Press, 1978.
Herrera, R. A.: *Anselm's "Proslogion": An Introduction*. Washington, D. C.: University Press of America, 1979.
McInerny, Ralph: *St. Thomas Aquinas*. Notre Dame, Ind.: University of Notre Dame Press, 1982.

B. Chapters of books, selections from collected essays

Plantinga, Alvin: Chapter X, 'God and Necessity', *The Nature of Necessity*. Oxford: Clarendon Press, 1974.
Rowe, William L.: Chapter 3, 'The Ontological Argument', *Philosophy of Religion: An Introduction*. Belmont, Calif.: Wadsworth, 1978.
Parsons, Terrence: Chapter 8, Section 1, 'Traditional Issues from the Present Perspective', *Nonexistent Objects*. New Haven, Conn.: Yale University Press, 1980.
Mackie, J. L.: Chapter 3, 'The Ontological Arguments', *The Miracle of Theism: Arguments For and Against the Existence of God*. Oxford: Clarendon Press, 1982.
Sokolowski, Robert: Chapter 1, 'Beginning with St. Anselm', *God of Faith and Reason*. Notre Dame, Ind.: Notre Dame Press, 1982.

C. Journal articles

Hopkins, Jasper: 'On Understanding and Preunderstanding St. Anselm', *New Scholasticism* **52** (1978), 243–260.
Kielkopf, Charles F.: 'Dun Scotus's Rejection of "Necessarily Exists" as a Predicate', *Journal of the History of Philosophy* **16** (January 1978), 13–21.
Mason, Perry C.: 'The Devil and St. Anselm', *International Journal for Philosophy of Religion* **9** (1978), 1–15.
Rabinowicz, Wlodzimierz: 'An Alleged New Refutation of St. Anselm's Argument', *Ratio* **20** (December 1978), 149–150.
Stove, D. C.: 'Part IX of Hume's *Dialogues*', *Philosophical Quarterly* **28** (October 1978), 300–309.
Wainwright, William J.: 'On an Alleged Incoherence in Anselm's Argument: A Reply to Robert Richman', *Ratio* **20** (December 1978), 147–148.
Walton, Douglas: 'The Circle in the Ontological Argument', *International Journal for Philosophy of Religion* **9** (1978), 193–218.
Bedell, Gary: 'The Many Faces of Necessity in the Many-Faced Argument', *New Scholasticism* **53** (1979), 1–21.
Dazeley, Howard and Wolfgang L. Gombocz: 'Interpreting Anselm as Logician', *Synthese* **40** (January 1979), 71–96.

Doyle, John P.: 'Some Thoughts on Duns Scotus and the Ontological Argument', *New Scholasticism* **53** (1979), 234–241.

Friedman, Joel D.: 'The Mystic's Ontological Argument', *American Philosophical Quarterly* **16** (1979), 73–78.

Gellman, Jerome: 'On Arguing from God's Possibility to His Necessity', *Logique et Analyse* **22** (December 1979), 525–526.

Grim, Patrick: 'Plantinga's God and Other Monstrosities', *Religious Studies* **15** (1979), 91–97.

Joy, Glenn C.: 'The Perfection of Perfection: On How Not to Improve the Ontological Argument', *Journal of Thought* **14** (January 1979), 42–44.

Nasser, Alan G.: 'Divine Independence and the Ontological Argument: A Reply to James M. Humber', *Religious Studies* **15** (1979), 391–397.

Tichy, Pavel: 'Existence and God', *Journal of Philosophy* **76** (August 1979), 403–420.

Wald, Albert W.: '"Meaning", Experience and the Ontological Argument', *Religious Studies* **15** (1979), 31–39.

Baumer, Michale R.: 'Possible Worlds and Duns Scotus's Proof of the Existence of God', *New Scholasticism* **54** (1980), 182–188.

Beard, Robert: 'Is God's Non–Existence Conceivable?', *Southern Journal of Philosophy* **18** (Fall 1980), 251–258.

Campbell, Richard: 'On Preunderstanding St. Anselm', *New Scholasticism* **54** (1980), 189–193.

Clarke, Bowman L.: 'Beard on the Conceivability of God's Non-Existence', *Southern Journal of Philosophy* **18** (Winter 1980), 501–507.

Loptson, Peter J.: 'Anselm, Meinong, and the Ontological Argument', *International Journal for Philosophy of Religion* **11** (1980), 185–194.

Orenduff, J. M.: 'Existence Proofs and the Ontological Argument', *Southwest Philosophical Studies* **5** (April 1980), 50–54.

Preuss, Peter: 'Ontological Vertigo', *International Journal for Philosophy of Religion* **11** (1980), 93–110.

Read, Stephen: 'Reflections on Anselm and Gaunilo', *International Philosophical Quarterly* **21** (December 1981), 437–438.

Schufreider, Gregory: 'What Is It for God to Exist?', *New Scholasticism* **55** (1981), 77–94.

Tatarkiewicz, Wladyslaw: 'Ontological and Theological Perfection', *Dialectics and Humanism* **8** (Winter 1981), 187–192.

Tooley, Michael: 'Plantinga's Defence of the Ontological Argument', *Mind* **90** (1981), 422–427.

Davis, Stephen T.: 'Loptson on Anselm and Rowe', *International Journal for Philosophy of Religion* **13** (1982), 219–224.

Grim, Patrick: 'In Behalf of "In Behalf of the Fool"', *International Journal for Philosophy of Religion* **13** (1982), 33–42.

Gutting, Gary: 'Can Philosophical Beliefs Be Rationally Justified?', *American Philosophical Quarterly* **19** (1982), 315–330.

Hasker, William: 'Is There a Second Ontological Argument?', *International Journal for Philosophy of Religion* **13** (1982), 93–102.

King-Farlow, John: 'Nothing Greater Can Be Conceived: (Zeno, Anselm, and Tillich)', *Sophia* **21** (April 1982), 19–24.

Losoncy, Thomas A.: 'Anselm's Response to Gaunilo's Dilemma: An Insight into the Notion of "Being" Operative in the *Proslogion*', *New Scholasticism* **56** (1982), 207–216.

Menne, Albert: 'Concerning the Logical Analysis of "Existence"', *Monist* **65** (1982), 415–419.

Rohatyn, Dennis: 'Anselm's Inconceivability Argument', *Sophia* **21** (October 1982), 57–63.

Surin, Kenneth: 'The Self Existence of God: Hartshorne and Classical Theism', *Sophia* **21** (October 1982), 17–36.

Baker, John Robert: 'On the Conceivability of God's Non-Existence', *Southern Journal of Philosophy* **21** (1983), 313–320.

Lazerowitz, Morris: 'On a Property of a Perfect Being', *Mind* **92** (1983), 257–263.

Pottinger, Garrell: 'A Formal Analysis of the Ontological Argument', *American Philosophical Quarterly* **20**, (1983), 37–46.

Sen, Sushanta: 'The Ontological Argument Revisited', *Indian Philosophical Quarterly* **10** (January 1983), 219–242.

INDEX

PHILOSOPHICAL STUDIES SERIES
IN PHILOSOPHY

Editors:

WILFRID SELLARS, Univ. of Pittsburgh and KEITH LEHRER, Univ. of Arizona

Board of Consulting Editors:

Jonathan Bennett, Allan Gibbard, Robert Stalnaker, and Robert G. Turnbull

20. DONALD NUTE, *Topics in Conditional Logic*, 1980.
21. RISTO HILPINEN (ed.), *Rationality in Science*, 1980.
22. GEORGES DICKER, *Perceptual Knowledge*, 1980.
23. JAY F. ROSENBERG, *One World and Our Knowledge of It*, 1980.
24. KEITH LEHRER and CARL WAGNER, *Rational Consensus in Science and Society*, 1981.
25. DAVID O'CONNOR, *The Metaphysics of G. E. Moore*, 1982.
26. JOHN D. HODSON, *The Ethics of Legal Coercion*, 1983.
27. ROBERT J. RICHMAN, *God, Free Will, and Morality*, 1983.
28. TERENCE PENELHUM, *God and Skepticism*, 1983.
29. JAMES BOGEN and JAMES E. McGUIRE (eds.), *How Things Are, Studies in Predication and the History of Philosophy and Science*, forthcoming.